THE MEDIEVAL CHURCH

THE MEDIEVAL CHURCH

From the Dawn of the Middle Ages
to the
Eve of the Reformation

CARL A. VOLZ

ABINGDON PRESS
Nashville

THE MEDIEVAL CHURCH:
FROM THE DAWN OF THE MIDDLE AGES
TO THE EVE OF THE REFORMATION

Copyright © 1997 by Abingdon Press

All Rights Reserved.

This book is printed on acid-free, recycled paper.

Library of Congress Cataloging-in-Publication Data

Volz, Carl A.
    The Medieval church : from the dawn of the Middle Ages to the eve of the Reformation / Carl A. Volz
        p.   cm.
    Includes bibliographical references and index.
    ISBN 0–687–00604–X (alk. paper)
    1. Church history—Middle Ages, 600–1500.   I. Title.
BR161.V65   1997
270.3—dc 21
                                                                97–26621
                                                                CIP

99 00 01 02 03 04 05 06 — 10 9 8 7 6 5 4 3 2

MANUFACTURED IN THE UNITED STATES OF AMERICA

TO LYDIA

Loving Wife and Mother of

Carol, Martin, Stephen, Katherine, Michael

and

TO MY STUDENTS

Who have also been my mentors since 1964

CONTENTS

CHAPTER ONE

CHRISTIANITY AFTER THE FALL OF ROME

The Fall of Rome

The suggestion that the ancient Roman empire had "fallen" was a result of Renaissance thinking by those who sought to distance themselves from the "medieval" world and identify more closely with ancient Graeco-Roman culture. From the fourth to the thirteenth century more intellectual, theological, and institutional energy went into the concept of a continuity with ancient Rome than with its demise. Beginning with the monumental work of Edward Gibbon, *The Decline and Fall of the Roman Empire*, first published in 1787, historians have pondered this question and they have produced scores of studies offering reasons for Rome's decline and its meaning for posterity.[1]

If indeed such a fall occurred, it was limited to the Roman West, because the Eastern empire lived on for another thousand years until Constantinople was captured by the Turks in 1453 C.E. A modern commentator notes that "The fact is that 'the decline and fall of the Roman Empire' is a metaphorical usage in which the empire is compared with an edifice."[2] But the empire was not a building; it was a culture, a system of government, a heterogeneous group of peoples. Some have chosen to speak of disintegration and transformation rather than fall. There has been no agreement on when such a transformation began. Gibbon placed its beginning with the Severan emperors in the third century, but Henri Pirenne found an economic unity of the empire as late as the seventh century.[3] The fall of Rome is not a theme in Socrates, Sozomon, and Theodoret, church historians contemporary with the fifth century and the sack of Rome in 410, which they barely mention. The emperor Theodosius (d. 395) considered himself in succession with biblical he-

7

roes and saints. What was acknowledged was the victory of God through the foundation of a new Rome in continuity with the old. Suffice it to say that there was definitely a break between Roman civilization and the medieval world. Whether the change was gradual or swift, it remains a fact that however old Rome fell, there was a point at which it no longer stood.

Reasons proposed for Rome's demise are many: economic collapse, the impossibility of a city governing an empire, top-heavy bureaucracy, slavery, barbarization of the army, inner moral decay, decline of the family, barbarian invasions, the independence of the provinces, Christianity, and even Islam. Whatever reasons are selected, they usually have become part of a didactic program fostering lessons from history. Of greater interest is the use of the Roman empire as an apocalyptic paradigm, that is, the idea of a thousand year reign.

When the Holy Roman Empire was established by the German leader Otto I in 962 C.E., he intended to preside over a continuation of the ancient regime. Even earlier, when Charlemagne was crowned emperor in 800 C.E., it was with the understanding that he was standing in continuity with the old Roman emperors. Some claim that this apocalyptic dimension was also present in German National Socialism (the Third Reich) and in Communism.[4] There are some who find aspects of the Roman empire continuing within the structure, forms, and language of the Roman Catholic Church.

Beginning already in the late–third century the empire had been divided into East and West, with an emperor ruling each part, although there were periods of sole rulership. If a date for Rome's "fall" in the West need be given, 476 C.E. is usually suggested. It was in that year that the last legitimate emperor, Romulus Augustulus, a boy of fourteen, was overthrown by the barbarian Odoacer. The office of emperor in the West ended. The imperial insignia were sent off to the Eastern emperor, Zeno in Constantinople. The emperor in the East continued to rule over the entire empire, from Britain to Syria, at least in theory. It was in response to the sack of Rome by Alaric the Goth in 410 C.E., that Augustine wrote the *City of God* in which he proposes a philosophy of history, suggesting that in the place of the Roman empire, which he called "a gang of robbers," we now have the triumph of the Christian Church.

The Barbarian Invasions

By the time of Pope Gregory the Great (600 C.E.) the first wave of barbarian invaders had already settled down in the West following three centuries of enormous upheaval and confusion. It was among these inhabitants of Europe that Western Christian expansion took place during the time of the decline of the Western empire.

No entirely adequate or satisfactory reasons can be given for the *Voelkerwanderungen* or "wanderings of the people," which began already in 102 B.C.E. and before. Shortage of food, overpopulation, wars, the search for grazing lands, warmer climate, the lure of the stability of the Roman empire—all undoubtedly played a part. The barbarians, meaning basically non-Greek or Latin-speaking people, were Indo-Europeans whose earliest homelands were in southern Scandinavia, Denmark, the Baltic islands, and Germany east to the Oder River. They were not primarily intent on undermining or destroying the empire but rather on enjoying its benefits. Conflicts with the Romans are already recorded by Julius Caesar in his *Gallic Wars* (58–55 B.C.E.) and by Caesar Augustas's attempt to bring all German tribes under his rule (16 B.C.E.–9 C.E.). A German insurrection led by Arminius (Herman the German) defeated the Roman army in the Teutoberg Forest and for a time secured German liberty east of the Rhine and north of the Danube. The *Germania* of the Roman historian Tacitus (98 C.E.) is the only ancient work written exclusively about the Germans, and he praises their monogamy and chastity. The father was the autocratic head of the family, which was part of an organization of clans and tribes that together constituted a loosely defined nation. There was little unity among the tribes except for an occasional alliance. Kings were elected by all the males, and that only for war. Tacitus writes that "This election is by the folk in which the final decision on all matters rests with the people"[5] (i.e. the males) a practice which remained a strong medieval tradition, if sometimes only in memory, both in the church and secular governments (in the popular assembly of free men, the Germans would discuss issues while they were drinking in order to promote candor and honesty, but they would postpone decisions until they were sober.) In order to curb the violence of retribution for personal insults, the custom arose of paying a *wergild* or compensation for crimes, part of it going to the king. In this way punishment for crimes was removed from personal vendetta, giving rise to the modern fine, a sum of money to a government for the infraction of a law. In assessing guilt or innocence, the Germans developed a system of oath-sharers or compurgators, which eventually developed into the jury system. They had no concept of a state, but instead pledged loyalty to a strong leader, a practice that is later reflected in the personal bond of fealty as an aspect of feudalism.

The battle of Adrianople (376 C.E.) in which the Visigoths (West

Goths) from the Black Sea area defeated the Roman army and killed the emperor Valens marks the real beginning of the German invasions. Ammianus Marcellinus, a fourth century Roman historian, writes that "the forces of the emperor (Valens) maltreated the poor Goths and drove them to revolt."[6] It became the custom of the Romans to receive barbarian tribes into the empire as *foederati* or allies, and in this way many of the later Roman generals and armies were composed entirely of barbarians. From the late–fourth century, the empire that they invaded was nominally Christian, although the Nicene faith had not yet emerged as orthodoxy. It was under the emperor Valens and through the work of Ulfilas that the Visigoths embraced Arian Christianity. The Arians were followers of Arius, one of the central figures in the great trinitarian controversy of the fourth century. Arius denied the true deity of Jesus, insisting that he was a creature and hence not coeternal with God, whereas the Orthodox Church taught that Jesus was God in the flesh.

The Visigoths looked to Italy as a place to settle, and under Alaric they migrated westward. After the emperor Honorius reneged on his promise to give them land and food, they sacked Rome in 410 C.E. "They did not, however, set fire to the city . . . and would not permit that any of the holy places should be desecrated," wrote Jordanes somewhat later.[7] The sack of Rome caused an anguished outcry in all parts of the empire, and it was the occasion which prompted Augustine to write his monumental philosophy of history, *The City of God*. Eventually the Goths established a kingdom covering nearly all of southwest Gaul and Spain, with its capital at Toulouse. Ataulf, who followed Alaric as leader of the Goths, married the sister of Emperor Honoratus and was given the title of patrician (or governor) of Rome. In 507 C.E. the Franks under Clovis conquered the Visigoths, and in 589 C.E. at the Council of Toledo they accepted Nicene Christianity. It was on this occasion that the *filioque* (the clause that states that the Holy Spirit proceeds from the Father *and the Son*) was added to the Nicene Creed. In the eighth century the Goths were supplanted in Spain by the Muslims.

The Vandals came from the Roman province of Pannonia on the Danube, having been made allies of Rome and defenders of the frontier. They traveled across Gaul and into Spain, and in 429 C.E. under Gaiseric they crossed the Straits of Gibralter. Turning eastward, they besieged Hippo as Augustine lay dying, from where they took Carthage as their capital. In 455 C.E. they sacked Rome, and subjected the City to fourteen days of plunder and bloodshed. In North Africa they occupied a strategic position because they controlled Europe's lifeline of grain. Through piracy they controlled the Mediterranean for a time, but were defeated by the Roman general Belisarius in 534 C.E. They were the fiercest Arians, while the North Africans, never having recovered from the fatal blow inflicted by the Vandals, were the fiercest Catholics. Southern Spain is sometimes referred to as Andalusia, a reminder that this territory had once been settled by the Vandals.

The Burgundians received land in the Rhone Valley during the time of Honorius (395–423 C.E.). They were the first of the Arian barbarians to convert to Catholicism, but not in time to prevent Clovis, the Frank, from conquering them using their heresy as his excuse (534 C.E.). Clovis then married the daughter of the Burgundian king, giving him the right of inheritance. The Burgundians have been cited for "their humane laws, mild manners, tolerant disposition, and an appreciation of Catholicism acquired by friendly intercourse with Latin bishops."[8] They developed into a powerful principality in the late Middle Ages, challenging the emerging power of the French king.

The Huns came to Europe from central Asia, and it was their pressure on the Visigoths that caused the latter to seek entry into the Roman empire in 376 C.E. The height of their power came under Attila in the mid–fifth century, whose empire stretched along the Danube river. In 449 C.E. he invaded the West but was decisively repulsed by a combination of Roman and Visigothic forces at the battle of Chalons in 451 C.E., from which the Huns then turned south and ravaged northern Italy. It was at this time that the city of Venice was founded by refugees fleeing the Hunnish advance. When they threatened Rome, Pope Leo succeeded in turning them away from the City and Italy. Attila died in 453 C.E., and the Huns disappear from history. Modern Hungary has no relationship to the ancient Huns.

The Ostrogoths (East Goths) came from the area south of the Black Sea. When they threatened Constantinople in 489 C.E. the Emperor Zeno gave them permission to march westward to wrest Italy from the usurper, Odoacer, in which they succeeded after three years of warfare. The greatest ruler of the Ostrogoths was Theodoric (489–526 C.E.), who with his followers was a staunch Arian. Theodoric brought renewed prosperity and order to northern Italy, with Ravenna as his capital. He sought a peaceful amalgamation of his people with the resident Romans, acknowledging his loyalty to the Eastern emperor. Cassiodorus, his secretary, made Theodoric respectable by giving him a false genealogy. The philosopher Boethius was also on good terms with him until he was accused of treason and killed. Although he was an Arian, Theodoric acknowledged the primacy of the Roman bishop in spiritual affairs. In order to secure his position he entered into a series of dynastic marriages: one daughter married the king of the Visigoths, another the king of the Burgundians; his sister married a Vandal king; his niece, a king of the Thuringians. He himself married a sister of Clovis, the Frank. In 526 Theodoric died, and in 554 his kingdom, like that of the Vandals in North Africa, was reconquered by the Eastern emperor, Justinian.

The Franks, the real founders of Europe, came from two places. The Salien (salty) Franks lived near the North Sea. In the third century they became Roman *foederati* (clients and allies) in Belgium. In 486 C.E. Clovis became their leader at age fifteen, despite his youth. In that year his army defeated Syagrius, the last independent Roman ruler in Gaul. Other Franks were the Ripuarians (*ripa* = riverbank) who came from the area of the Rhine River near Cologne. In 496 C.E. the Frankish forces united under Clovis to defeat the Alemanni at Tolbiac, a battle famous for the conversion of Clovis to Catholic Christianity. He had vowed to do so if God would give him the victory in battle. Gregory of Tours (d. 594), the historian of the Franks, writing a century later states: "Then the king confessed the God omnipotent in the Trinity, and was baptized in the name of the Father, and of the Son, and of the Holy Ghost, and was anointed with the sacred chrism with the sign of the cross of Christ. Of his army there were baptized more than three thousand."[9] Saint Remy, after whom Rheims is named, presided at the baptisms. Alarmed at the power of the Franks, Theodoric married Clovis' sister, and Clovis in turn married the daughter of the Burgundian king. Clovis then defeated the Visigoths in 507 C.E., and the Eastern emperor, Anastasius, bestowed on him the honorary titles "consul and Augustus" as a counterbalance to Theodoric. At Clovis's death his territory was divided among his four sons (which indicates that the Franks had no concept of the state as a unity), who extended Frankish domination to all of France. Clovis and his descendants are known as the Merovingian Franks from Merowig, the shadowy founder of the tribe. In 638 C.E., Dagobert, the last of the good Merovingian kings died, and the territory was divided into an Eastern (Austrasian) and Western (Neustrian) half, a division which is one of the beginnings of modern Germany and France. The Merovingian rulers declined in significance—degenerate at 17, old at 18, dead at 19. The real leadership was in the hands of their chief executives or Mayors of the Palace, who succeeded them as rulers in 751 C.E. as the Carolingian Franks. It was during the time of the Merovingians, and frequently with their assistance if not direction, that the church expanded in Europe.

Throughout this period the church became a dominant force in society. By the end of the fourth century, Christianity was recognized as the preferred religion; indeed, after an edict by Theodosius in 392 C.E., as the only legitimate religion. In the West a vacuum of leadership resulted from the end of the imperial office in 476 C.E., and the bishop of Rome was a natural surrogate to fill the vacuum. "The ideal of the supremacy and independence of the spiritual power found its organ of expression above all in the Papacy."[10] The pope was still a loyal subject of the emperor in the East, but he also regarded imperial causes as inseparable from the Christian religion. In the fifth century Pope Leo made just such an explicit connection between Christianity and the welfare of Rome. In an address on the Feast of Saints Peter and Paul he said "These are they, who have brought you to such glory as a holy nation, a chosen people, a royal and priestly city that you might be made the head of the world by the Holy See of St. Peter, and might bear rule more widely by divine religion than by earthly dominion."[11] Leo is especially significant for clearly stating the primacy of the Roman See on the basis of the claim that its bishop is the "Vicar of Peter." In 451 C.E. it was Leo who met Attila the Hun and persuaded him not to invest Rome, although a similar effort four years later with the Vandals was less successful.

Christianity influenced western society in various ways. The civic and social centers were still the *civitates* or city-states, including the surrounding countryside. It was in these administrative centers that bishops settled and exercised their influence. In 550 C.E. there were 120 *civitates* in Gaul, each with its bishop. Roman territorial divisions were maintained (diocese and province) as well as Roman administration and the Latin language. Furthermore, bishops inherited the office of advocate for the poor (*defensor civitates*), which gave episcopal courts the right of litigation of all kinds. Christianity first spread in the cities of the empire; it was originally an urban phenomenon. In the countryside the peasants still clung to their former beliefs, the rites of seedtime and harvest, the veneration of sacred springs and trees. Because people dwelling in the country were known as *pagani*, and because they were slow to accept the new religion, the designation "pagan" has become associated with unbelievers or those outside the church.

The church was not independent or autonomous, especially under the Merovingians, but was rather controlled by the secular rulers who appointed priests, abbots, and bishops. On occasion a ruler would bestow an "immunity" on a church, which meant land was free and clear of all taxes or obligations to any secular lord. There was a flourishing of religious art, the liturgy, devotion to saints, popular piety, relics, and pilgrimages. Yet the harshness of life was little ameliorated. Champions of the faith such as Clovis did not hesitate to violate the canons of morality if it suited their purposes, and there is little reason to believe that his three thousand followers were any different following their baptism in the Rhine than they were before. Theodoric, an Arian, killed Odoacer with his own hands while serving as his host at a banquet. Organizationally the church was decentralized, and despite its claims, the Papacy was not strong.

Monasticism

Although the church found its earliest converts in the cities, and many who lived in the countryside were considered to be "pagans," the economic turmoil which caused and accompanied the fall of the empire in the West also witnessed the decline of urban life. Monasticism appeared providentially well suited to address the needs of the church for the centuries in which urban centers were in eclipse.

Monasticism first emerged in the East, where Christianity itself was born. According to Jerome, it was the visit of Athanasius to Trier and Rome during his years of exile (335–337 and 339–346) which introduced monasticism to the West. Apart from the theological factors that informed its origins, a societal factor now related directly to the times explained its success: the deliberate decision of women and men to cut themselves off from city culture in order to devote themselves to prayer and meditation under the simplest conditions in remote areas. Under Graeco-Roman values, urban life determined one's identity. Indeed, one of the worst possible punishments to be endured was that of ostracism —being cut off from one's city. Yet in the fourth century thousands of Christian ascetics gladly and willingly embraced the simple life of the desert, the forest, or the mountain in a conscious rejection of the city and its blandishments. By so doing, the monks served as the vanguard in the church's efforts to evangelize the scattered pagan and barbarian population of Europe. "In the rural districts of the West the monastery was the only center of Christian life and teaching, and it was upon the monks rather than upon the bishops and their clergy that the task of converting the heathen or semi-heathen peasant population ultimately fell."[12]

Martin of Tours (d. 397) was the earliest major representative of monasticism in Gaul. He followed the example of his father in joining the army, but when his obligatory twenty-year term expired, he became an anchorite near Milan. From there he moved to Poitiers in France, probably attracted by Hilary, the leading and most respected Latin theologian of the time. He entered a hermitage in Liguge, but despite his monastic profession he was also the Bishop of Tours for twenty-five years. As bishop, he established a monastery at Marmoutier near Tours. Many of his monks became bishops as well, thus bringing the monastic ideals into the mainstream of the church. Nothing that Martin may have written has survived, but the *Life of St. Martin*, written by his disciple Sulpicius Severus, spread his fame and the ideal of monasticism. Martin is the patron saint of military chaplains. By one count, nearly four thousand churches in France today bear his name.

Cassian (d. 435), another significant monastic figure in the Gallican church, spent some years in the East and at Rome before he settled in Marseilles, where he established two houses, one for men and another for women. His two most enduring works are the *Institutes* and *Conferences*, the fruit of his experiences with Eastern monasticism. In the first work he sets out rules for the monastic life and discusses the chief hindrances to a monk's profession; in the second he recounts the conversations he had with various prominent monks in the East. Both Martin of Tours and Cassian followed the rigorous ascetic ideals characteristic of monasticism in the East.

Vincent, younger contemporary of Cassian, became a monk on the island of Lerins just south of the mouth of the Rhone River. Both he and Cassian are often associated with the Semi-Pelagian "school" (see below) which developed in southern Gaul with Marseilles and Lerins as its centers. As with some disciples of Martin, monks from the school of Lerins often became bishops, thus spreading the monastic ideal among the faithful.

Caesarius of Arles (d. 542), one of the most prominent theologians to emerge from Lerins, was active in establishing the church in southern Gaul, and with the help of Theodoric succeeded in gaining for Arles the position of primatial see in Gaul. The school of Lerins was noted especially for its Semi-Pelagian leanings, and it is to Caesarius' credit that he brought an end to the controversy over grace by drafting a statement that was accepted by the church and ratified at the Council of Orange in 529 C.E. Semi-Pelagianism (the term itself is modern) sought a position midway between Augustine's strict predestinarianism, in which God unilaterally selected people to be saved by grace, and Pelagius's insistence on salvation through human effort. Vincent, Cassian, Faustus of Riez, and others suggested that the first steps toward the Christian life must be made by the human will, and grace will follow such human initiative. Caesarius, together with Prosper of Aquitane, proposed that human free will is incapable of moral goodness without grace, and that

God's help is needed even for the initial promptings of the human will. On the other hand, there was also agreement that if anyone is eternally lost, it is one's own fault, unlike Augustine's later extreme insistence that God has from eternity condemned those who are lost.

Western monasticism was shaped principally by Benedict of Nursia (480–550) who occupies a prominent place in the history of medieval Christianity, an influence that continues into our own day. What we know of his life has been preserved in the *Dialogues* of Gregory the Great, but he is known to us primarily from his *Rule* for monks, which became the premier Rule for all of Western monasticism. He wrote it in 529 especially for his own monastery at Monte Casino, just north of Naples, but in later years it was mandated by Emperor Louis "the Pious" (son of Charlemagne) to be the only legitimate Rule in the West. Benedict's work draws on the collective monastic experiences of the preceding five centuries, both East and West. What commends its use is its moderation and balance, its attention to human nature and to the average person, rather than extreme asceticism or religious virtuosity. It was easily adaptable to many situations, which accounts for the fact that up to modern times this rule has formed the basis for almost all Western monastic orders. His paternal gentleness is apparent already in the opening words of the *Rule*: "Listen carefully, my son, to the master's instructions, and attend to them with the ear of your heart. This is advice from a father who loves you; welcome it, and faithfully put it into practice."[13] Benedict intends to "establish a school for the Lord's service. In drawing up its regulations, we hope to set down nothing harsh, nothing burdensome."[14]

The *Rule* obliged the monks to three principal activities, the first being the work of God (*opus Dei*), which referred to worship, held seven times each day (Ps. 119:164). It was considered the primary obligation of the monk: "let nothing come before the work of God." He suggested that the entire book of Psalms should be recited or sung each week, and this became the main focus of the "offices" each day: Vigils, Lauds, Prime, Terce, Sext, None, Vespers, and Compline. It is from the monastic daily office that some of these services of worship have found their way into modern church practices, notably that of Matins, Vespers, and Compline.

A second daily obligation was that of spiritual reading (*lectio divina*), which was directed toward the spiritual growth of the monks. In time its meaning was expanded to include the copying of manuscripts and general intellectual activity. The third requirement of Benedict's monks was manual labor (*opus manuum*), which occupied from seven to eight hours daily. In the late–Roman empire such an activity was nothing short of a revolution in common attitudes, for it elevated the idea of honest labor as a virtue which in late–Roman times had been performed mainly by slaves. It is from these requirements that the Benedictine ideal—pray and work (*ora et labora*)—has been derived.

The Benedictine *Rule* does not mention the evangelical counsels of poverty, chastity, and obedience. These are assumed. But it does obligate the monks to a triple vow, beginning with conversion of life (*conversio morum*), which refers to the life in community and the monastic activities mentioned above. Second, stability (*stabilitas loci*), which means that the monk is pledged to remain a member of the same monastic house for life. It was the custom in Benedict's time for some monks to wander fitfully from house to house, changing loyalties at the slightest whim. Benedict permitted only one exception to the vow of stability, and that was if a monk desired to move to a house which observed more rigorous practices and discipline. Third was absolute obedience to the abbot, who was in the place of Christ. Although there were undoubtedly abbots who abused their position of trust, the *Rule* was much more demanding of the obligations and accountability of the abbot than of his privileges. Benedict's sister, Scholastica, formed a convent for women near that of her brother at Monte Casino and thus became the foundress of thousands of Benedictine houses for women during the medieval period and to modern times.

During the early Middle Ages, with the decline of urban centers and of commerce, society became decentralized and life was centered in a self-sufficient community. All that one required for sustenance was provided by the manor or the estate governed by a petty overlord. The monastery was an expression of this decentralization in the ecclesiastical sphere. Each unit contained everything necessary for the maintenance of life: fields, cattle, barns, craftsmen, winepress, dormitories, library, refectory, and an herb garden for the infirmary. Dominating the entire complex was the abbey church. Monastic isolation from society was never complete, since they established schools, received orphans, ministered to the poor and the sick, and engaged in limited commerce. In the course of time people sometimes came to live near a monastery, and towns grew up. In this way monasteries came to function as landlords and employers. Kings or noblemen would often endow a monastery with land or other gifts in return for which they were promised a place to live in their old age. It is not difficult to comprehend, under these circumstances, how some monasteries became very much involved in worldly affairs, which was often to the welfare of society but not to the primary goal of the worship of God through prayer and contemplation. For this reason one finds repeated attempts at reform in the history of monasticism.[15]

Learning and Letters

The cultural history of western Europe from the fall of Rome to the High Middle Ages is an attempt to recreate the splendor of the classical tradition. These writers usually attempted to imitate exactly the expressions, metres, and vocabulary of ancient Rome. The early church had been highly suspicious of classical learning, "fearing it like children fear goblins," said Clement of Alexandria. Tertullian is well known for his anti-classical diatribes—"what has Jerusalem to do with Athens?"[16] And yet the preservation of classical learning was due primarily to the church, specifically to the monks, who reshaped and transmitted it. The study of astronomy, rhetoric, preaching, grammar, and music was retained, and the church defended its right to use it by referring to Moses' command to the Israelites to "despoil the Egyptians."

Boethius (480–525) is the earliest of the "Latin transmitters" who served as an intellectual bridge between the Roman and medieval periods. A layman, as well as a friend and advisor to Theodoric the Ostrogoth, he was born into a distinguished Roman family at a time when the empire in the West was in eclipse. He was a member of the Roman senatorial aristocracy which had become thoroughly Christian. Rising rapidly in the ruling circles, he became a consul in 510, and entered the service of Theodoric as his Master of Offices, which placed him in charge of domestic administration and foreign policy. After only one year in office, he was charged with treason and other crimes and, following a year in prison, was executed. It was while in prison that he wrote the work for which he is best known, *The Consolation of Philosophy*, which is a remarkable work in itself, but even more so because of its failure to mention any of the accepted Christian themes or even Jesus Christ.

Boethius translated Aristotle's *Categories* and *De Interpretatione*, with commentaries. He also translated the *Introductions to the Categories* by Porphyry, third-century Neoplatonist philosopher. It was primarily through these works that knowledge of Aristotle was retained in the Middle Ages. He also wrote books that became standard texts in subsequent years: *De arithmetica*, *De musica*, and *De geometria*. These latter books formed the basis of the educational structure called the *quadrivium*, a term which Boethius coined. In the last century of the

Roman Republic, Varro had described nine "liberal arts" as the content for a solid education of a free (*libera*) person. In the fifth century, Varro's classification was commented on by Martianus Capella, who reduced the number of liberal arts to seven. These seven were subsequently subdivided into two groups—the four basic studies of geometry, astronomy, arithmetic, and music (*quadrivium*), and the higher studies of grammar, rhetoric, and logic—(*trivium*). The first four evolved into a study of the physical sciences and mathematics, while the latter three included history, philosophy, and the arts. Boethius's translations of Aristotle and Porphyry were essential ingredients of studies in the *trivium* throughout the medieval period. The study of the seven liberal arts was considered basic and preliminary to the study of theology.

The influence of Boethius on eleventh- and twelfth-century thought, including that of Thomas Aquinas, has been called second only to that of Augustine. "The schools of the eleventh and early twelfth centuries owed to him almost all they had, not only of the authentic works of Aristotle but also of their knowledge of his doctrines."[17] Boethius, more than any other individual, was the direct ancestor of the scholastic method.[18]

Cassiodorus (v. 485–580), a contemporary of Boethius in the employ of Theodoric, also came from a noble Roman family. He was consul of Rome in 514 and chief of the civil service by 526. Unlike Boethius, he remained in the good graces of Theodoric, serving as his secretary and as a primary intermediary between the Arian ruler and the Catholic population. He founded two monasteries at Vivarium where he encouraged secular as well as religious learning and the copying of manuscripts, thereby establishing the monastic tradition of scholarship that preserved the classical culture of Europe. The Roman aristocrats saw that they were heirs to a precious legacy in the classical tradition, a legacy which they included as part of the Christian heritage. Among the numerous works of Cassiodorus were the *Variae*, twelve books of imperial edicts and decrees; *De anima* in which he supports the spirituality of the soul; and the *Historia Ecclesiastica Tripartita*, a compilation of church history from three previous historians—Socrates, Sozomen, and Theodoret. The most influential of his works was the *Institutiones Divinarum et Saecularium Litterarum*, which supported the use of sacred and secular studies in Christian education. The work discusses bibliography, the method of study, how to collect and copy manuscripts, and the necessity of studying history. Cassiodorus is a primary example of the manner in which the classical tradition of the Greeks and Romans became assimilated into Christian culture. In his preface to the *Institutes*, Cassiodorus expresses regret that while there were many scholars who were familiar with secular letters, very few were conversant with the Bible, and it was to rectify this situation that he produced his book.[19]

Isidore, Bishop of Seville (c. 560–636), was another writer who flourished during the late empire and whose influence continued to be felt throughout the medieval period. Before he entered a monastery, he was brought up by his older brother, Leander of Seville, whom he succeeded as bishop. He devoted his energies to fighting Arianism, spreading the Catholic faith, and working for the conversion of the Jews. To this end he founded schools and convents, and he presided over several Spanish councils. The work for which he is especially well known is the *Etymologies*, an encyclopedia of the general knowledge of his time containing information on grammar, rhetoric, mathematics, medicine, and history. The book was arranged according to the unifying principle of the origin and meaning of words which resulted in some fanciful explanations. For instance, *amicus* (friend) is derived from *animi custos* (guardian of the soul); or a person cries more easily while kneeling in prayer because the knees and eyes of an unborn infant are close together in the womb. The shortcomings of his method should not obscure the significance of his work, however, in which the whole breadth of human knowledge available at his time was organized. He also wrote important books on theology, history, and cosmology which were known throughout Europe in the Middle Ages.

Dionysius the Areopagite (c. 500) was a contemporary of Boethius and a profound mystical theologian. He assumed the name of Paul's Athenian convert (Acts 17:34) but in fact he was a fifth-century Syrian mystic who issued his writings in the name of Dionysius, and is therefore more accurately referred to as Pseudo-Dionysius. Very little is known of his life, but his influence on theology, East and West, was considerable.

Dionysius, together with many Greek patristic writers, as well as Augustine, held to many of the characteristic doctrines of Neoplatonism. These include the uniqueness of God, the superiority of Being to attributes, and the idea of Being itself. In order to gain access to knowledge of God one must follow a path of negation. Reality is also conceived in terms of a vast hierarchy of beings, both on earth and in heaven. "The principal parts of the Dionysian legacy to the West were the negative and superlative theology, the strongly hierarchic conception of Being, an elaborate angelology, and the doctrine of mediate illumination and spiritual knowledge conferred by the sacraments and by angelic ministration."[20] The Dionysian writings aim at achieving a synthesis between

Christian dogma and Neoplatonic thought. These are arranged under four titles.

The *Celestial Hierarchy* speaks of the nine orders of angels who mediate God to humans; the *Ecclesiastical Hierarchy* speaks of the sacraments and the three-fold path of mystical union with God, namely purgation, illumination, and union. The goal of the faithful is to experience deification or union with God. The *Divine Names*, which speaks of the attributes and being of God; and the *Mystical Theology*, which returns to the central theme, the mysticism of the divine darkness which is also the ineffable light. It describes the ascent of the soul to union with God (*apotheosis*). Dionysius became known in the West through the translations of John Scotus Erigena (d. 877). He was read and commented on by many of the later medieval theologians, including Thomas Aquinas and Bonaventure. The medieval mystics were deeply in his debt. He has been referred to as "the most highly influential mystic of the entire medieval world."[21]

Two poets and hymn writers from the Merovingian period are especially remembered in the church today. Aurelius Clemens Fortunatus (d. ca. 413) was a lawyer and then a Roman governor. In later life he became a monk and wrote twenty-eight hymns which have come to us, the most popular being "Of the Father's Love Begotten," a Christmas hymn, and "O Chief of Cities, Bethlehem," commonly sung during Epiphany. Venantius Fortunatus (d. 609) was Bishop of Poitiers, who wrote eleven books of poems, a metrical life of Martin of Tours, and whose fame today is associated with his Good Friday hymn, "The Royal Banners Forward Go."

East and West

The division between the two halves of the Roman empire had its origins centuries before a formal separation took place. Emperor Diocletian recognized the need for a co-emperor at the turn of the fourth century, and he divided the empire into two jurisdictions, the one being ruled from Nicomedia in the East and the other from Rome in the West. This was primarily because of the empire's size and the need for defense. Two emperors could more effectively repulse or negotiate with the barbarians who threatened its frontiers from both East and West. After Constantine's sole rule, the empire was again governed by co-rulers (with the exception of Julian, who ruled alone for eighteen months). This shared governance came to an end in 476, when the barbarian Odoacer expelled Romulus Augustulus, the last emperor in the West. The empire, however, was still considered a single unit, from Britain to Syria, under the rulership of the one emperor in the East, whose capital was at Constantinople. Indeed, until 751 even the bishops of Rome, some of whom came from the East, sought to have their elections validated by the Eastern emperor. In the West, strong barbarian kings vied for domination, sometimes being recognized by the Roman emperor in the East as his consuls or representatives. It was during this political instability in the West after 476 that the Bishop of Rome gained in prestige and authority as the *de facto* successor of the imperial office and a sign of unity.

The division in the empire was not caused only or primarily by politics, but more significantly by a difference in culture. The East was predominantly Greek in language and outlook, whereas the West was Latin. The East was a cohesive economic and political entity, with thriving cities and commerce, strong armies under the command of an all-powerful court, which in turn set a high standard for refinements in art and aesthetics. Since 392 C.E. Christianity had been the only legitimate religion, and its hierarchy was well organized under the patriarch in Constantinople. Under the Byzantine system (by which name the Eastern empire came to be known) the church was dominated by the emperor, and in time it practically became a department of state with the patriarch answerable to the emperor. It may be that in his panegyric *The Life of Constantine* Eusebius set the stage for this development by referring to the emperor as the thirteenth apostle and vicegerent of God.

The West, on the other hand, was in political disarray, with various barbarian tribes competing for domination. Commerce and urban life were in decline; there was a coarsening of manners, and life was often brutal. Although the church was used by the various political rulers, there was in Western theology both the theory and the practice of the church's independence from, and indeed domination of, the state. Augustine had clearly articulated this view in his *City of God*, and Pope Gelasius (d. 496) with no less vigor had written of "two powers by which the world is chiefly ruled, the sacred authority of the priests and the royal power. Of these, that of the priests, is more weighty."[22] Although the Papacy was not yet strong enough to put theory into practice, centuries later these assertions of independence would come to play a crucial role in the relationships between church and governments.

For several centuries following the decline of Rome in the West most Christians lived in the East. It was here that church organization and theology took shape, and the first ecumenical councils were held. The fourth such council, that at Chalcedon (451 C.E.), condemned Monophysitism (the belief in "one nature") which held that in the person of the incarnate Christ there was but a single, and that divine, nature. Not all the churches accepted this decree, notably the Copts in Egypt, the Ethiopians, and the Jacobite Church in Syria. The Nestorians were accused of holding an opposite position, that there were two separate persons in the incarnate Christ, one divine and the other human, an accusation they denied.

After the council of Chalcedon, Nestorians continued to prosper in Syria and Persia. (Persians, being in constant rivalry with the empire, preferred a form of Christianity which had been condemned by the Eastern church.) Nestorian missionaries evangelized parts of India, creating the Mar Thoma Church which still flourishes there today. Other Nestorians traveled as far as China, where they enjoyed the favor of the Mongol empire, establishing churches and monasteries. They left a memorial stele about 781 which can still be seen today in the Shengsi museum in Xian.

While the Nestorians ignored Chalcedon and went their own way outside the empire, within the Roman East there was a sharp reaction against the Chalcedonian decree. While not extreme Monophysites, many believed that the church had conceded too much to the Nestorians. In 482, Emperor Zeno (d. 491), with the acquiescence of Patriarch Acacius, issued his *Henotikon* or Edict of Union. In it he declared that the faith as defined by Nicea (325) and Ephesus (431) was sufficient, and he denied ecumenical legitimacy to Chalcedon, stating that the "two nature" question should be left open. The Bishop of Rome rejected the idea, because it ignored the work of Pope Leo at Chalcedon and it sought to do by diplomacy what ought to be done by a council. The pope thereupon excommunicated Acacius, causing a schism that lasted for thirty-seven years, ending in 519. Although the parties were then reconciled, the ferment continued. Emperor Justinian (527–565) proposed that the faith and writings of three theologians with Nestorian leanings (all deceased) be condemned. This anathema of Theodore of Mopsuestia, Ibas of Edessa, and Theodoret of Cyrrhus was known as the "Three Chapters." Vigilius, the Bishop of Rome, was brought to Constantinople where he was intimidated by the emperor into agreeing to the condemnation of the three, although many bishops in the West had supported them. A council was held in Constantinople in 553 which condemned the Three Chapters, with Vigilius assenting to the decree. This synod is recognized as the Fifth Ecumenical Council. Throughout the controversy, the Empress Theodora played a leading role in favor of the Monophysites, and after her death Justinian the emperor was increasingly cool to their cause. It is also fair to say that political considerations, power struggles, and the attempt to control the church (Caesaropapism) played a greater role than the interests of orthodox theology. "The second council at Constantinople with its partial reaction to Chalcedon and its trend toward monophysitism tells us more concerning the growing consolidation of the Church of the East and the emperor's authority over it than it does about the inner life of the church and its teaching."[23]

Meanwhile the Monophysite cause was championed in Syria by Jacob Baradaeus (d. 578), who organized an independent church with its own hierarchy and clergy not in communion with the Greek imperial church. Remembering their founder, these believers came to be called "Jacobite" Christians, and they still exist today in Syria. In Egypt and Ethiopia a similar movement was in progress which rejected Chalcedon and revered the memory of Cyril of Alexandria (d. 444), who had been a leading proponent of Monophysitism. These churches severed their ties with the great church in Constantinople and became independent. They successfully survived the Arab conquests of the seventh century and remain the dominant form of Christianity there today, acknowledging the Coptic patriarch of Alexandria.

In 681 the Sixth Ecumenical Council was held in Constantinople to deal with the issue of Monothelitism. This was related to Monophysitism in that its advocates proposed that there was only one will in Jesus Christ. This idea went back to a document drawn up by Emperor Heraclius (d. 641) in 638 called the *Ekthesis*, in which he utilized a letter from Pope Honorius (d. 638) to support his one-will proposal. The council declared against the Monothelites and condemned the pope (posthumously) for his acquiescence to the heresy, declaring instead that Christ was possessed of two wills, human and divine.

We have already seen that the Roman imperial presence came to an end in the West when the Teuton Odoacer replaced Romulus Augustulus in 476 C.E. Seven years later, Theodoric, the Ostrogoth, killed Odoacer and was recognized as the vicegerent of the Eastern emperor. The Ostrogoths settled in the Po valley in northern Italy, but Theodoric was, in fact, the ruler of the entire peninsula. He attempted to maintain a stability of power through marriage alliances with the Franks, Vandals, and Visigoths, which succeeded for a time. Although he was both a barbarian and an Arian, and the greater population was Roman and Nicene Christian, he made a deliberate effort to rule impartially and justly, taking into his employ two of the most influential Christian writers of his time, Boethius and Cassiodorus. In 523 the Eastern emperor, Justin (518–527), issued a law which excluded pagans, Jews, and heretics (meaning Arians) from public employment. At the same time religious harmony was re-established between the East and the West, and Theodoric feared that this was a two-fold attack on his power. The Arians reacted with a persecution of the Catholics, and Boethius fell victim to this purge. Theodoric imprisoned Pope John I at Ravenna, where he died. "Arianism was the foe that brought papacy and aristocracy together and made of both the loyal subjects of Byzantium."[24] Theodoric died in 526 without an heir.

At this time, Justinian I (527–565), succeeded to the imperial throne, whose activities would leave an indelible mark on Byzantium and the church. We have a contemporary account of his governance by the historian Procopius, who actually accompanied the troops on their expeditions. His works are: *A History of the Wars*, *On the Buildings*, an account of Justinian's building activity, and *Secret History*. Allied with Justinian in his governance was his wife, Theodora, a woman of strong will, intelligence, and learning. As we have seen, her sympathies were with the Monophysites in the religious struggles. Critics of Justinian claim that the queen often was the real power in the empire.

Justinian was determined to reconquer the West from its barbarian overlords. His first attack was against the Vandals in northern Africa and the Visigoths in southern Spain. Under the leadership of his general, Belisarius, he succeeded in restoring Roman hegemony in these areas and in restoring property to the Romans and especially to the Catholic churches. Indeed, his motivation in the Reconquest was primarily religious, to reconquer the West for Catholic Christianity. Procopius writes that "finding that the belief in God was, before his time, straying into errors and being forced to go into many directions, he completely destroyed all paths leading to such errors and brought it about that it stood on the firm foundation of a single faith."[25] Under the leadership of General Narses and General Belisarius, the Ostrogoths in Italy were defeated. As a result of the Reconquest, government in the West was entrusted to a new official, the *Exarch*, who served as the emperor's representative. Narses was the first to hold this office, which was centered in Ravenna. The landed territory which supported the new official was known as the exarchate. Although the exarch was expected to support the Romans in the West against further exploitation by the barbarians, they were either powerless to do so or they joined in the exploitation. Unfortunately for Italy, the reconquest was short lived. In 568 the Lombards coming from the north invaded and subdued northern Italy, leaving the exarch untouched but irrelevant behind his walls in Ravenna. In 751 the Lombards expelled the last exarch from Ravenna.

Of far more lasting significance was Justinian's contribution to jurisprudence, an area in which he placed the jurist, Tribonius in charge. He codified all Roman laws since 450 B.C.E. (earlier the Theodosian Code of 438 had codified only those since Constantine c. 325 C.E.) This work was divided into the Digests (decisions of jurists), Constitutions (edicts, rescripts, decrees, and letters), Institutiones (a manual based on Gaius from 200 C.E.), and the Novellae or laws of Justinian himself. All of this was systematized and indexed to make it readily accessible. The Code of Justinian became the primary code of law for the Middle Ages, leading to the *Corpus Juris Civilis* after the twelfth century. The Code was not only a Christian document, beginning with a statement of faith and the condemnation of heretics, but it also legitimized the control of the ruler over ecclesiastical affairs. As such it placed Caesaropapism—*regis voluntas suprema lex* (what the ruler wills is the supreme law)—into law, a reality which characterized the subsequent history of the Byzantine church. The Code states in part that "The priesthood and the empire are the two greatest gifts which God, in His infinite clemency, has bestowed upon mortals; the former has reference to Divine matters, the latter presides over and directs human affairs, and both proceeding from the same principle, adorn the life of mankind. . . . Therefore we have the greatest solicitude for the observance of the divine rules."[26] It was left to the emperor to determine what the rules were. The Code also influenced the development of canon law in the West.

Justinian's crowning achievement was the construction of the Church of Holy Wisdsom in Constantinople (*Hagia Sophia*) referring to Christ. The ground plan is in the form of a Greek cross, with a dome above each of the four transepts and a much larger dome over the central area. Expanse rather than height was the ideal. Procopius gives a full description of the church. The altar was of precious stones, covered with gold. The platform from which the gospel was read and emperors were crowned was of precious metals, silver and ivory. The walls were covered with fine marble. "So the church has become a spectacle of marvelous beauty, overwhelming to those who see it, but to those who know by hearsay altogether incredible. For it soars to a height to match the sky. . . . It exults in indescribable beauty."[27] On Christmas Day 537 when it was dedicated, Justinian said, "I have vanquished thee, O Solomon."

Justinian also built the Church of the Holy Apostles, on the site at which emperors were buried from the time of Constantine to the eleventh century, and which was also the cathedral of the patriarch. He had the monastery of St. Catherine constructed at Mount Sinai and the church of San Vitale in Ravenna. Throughout his reign, Justinian was solicitous of orthodox teaching, the unity of the church, and imperial oversight. In 529 he closed the pagan Academy in Rome, the last bastion of classical letters, thus giving expression to the belief that the church had triumphed in its struggle with classical culture.

CHAPTER TWO

THE EXPANSION OF CHRISTIANITY

By 600 C.E. Christianity had largely superseded former religious
loyalties in the lands dominated by the Franks west of the Rhine and
south beyond the Pyrenees including much of Spain. But this "social
triumph of the church" following the fall of Rome was precarious at best,
and there was considerable syncretism with the pagan gods as to what
was to be discarded, what retained, and what assimilated.[1] Monasticism
played a decisive role in the spread of Christianity in these years, and
as it expanded throughout Gaul so did the Christian faith. Up to the
time of Gregory I, no single missionary had been sent by a church or
bishop to do evangelism (excepting possibly the Arian, Ulfilas, who had
been commissioned by the Council of Antioch [341] to go to the Goths).
With Gregory we find the first company of evangelists sent with the
specific purpose of bringing the gospel to the pagans.

Gregory I, "the Great"

Gregory is one of the polar figures in church history whose activities
left an indelible impression upon the course of subsequent events. He
has been called the founder of the medieval papacy, the bridge between
antiquity and the Middle Ages, and the greatest statesman of the early
medieval church. He was born c. 540, the son of a senator, and he rose
rapidly in the civil service. At one time he was the prefect (governor) of
the city of Rome, but thereafter he renounced worldly position, founded
seven monasteries, and entered one himself. Pope Pelagius II (579–590)
appointed him as ambassador (*apocrisiarius*) to the court at Constantinople, where Gregory experienced firsthand the life of the capital. His
experiences there created lasting impressions about the Eastern empire
which would inform his later decisions as pope. When he returned to

Rome he became the abbot of one of the monasteries he had established, and was subsequently elected pope in 590 A.D.

Gregory was the consummate Roman administrator in his attention to duty, sense of responsibility, and ability to govern. By this time the Roman church owned considerable properties in Italy, Sicily, and Provence which had been neglected, usurped, ravaged, or lost to predators, the Lombards, or the Eastern emperor. Gregory immediately set to reclaim these lands and placed them under his own representatives, to whom he gave detailed instructions on the planting of crops and the use of land. This "Patrimony of Peter" he said, was to be used to alleviate poverty, and he set about to restore these revenues for this purpose.

As we have seen, shortly after Justinian's reconquest of Italy the Lombards nullified his efforts by capturing northern Italy and settling there. They had ravaged the land, leaving it utterly desolate. Gregory offered this account of what he saw: "Everywhere we see mourning, from all sides we hear lamentation. Cities are destroyed, military camps are overturned, fields are laid waste. . . . We see some led captive, some mutilated, others murdered, and she herself (Rome) who once seemed to be mistress of the world, what has remained of her is abundantly afflicted with tremendous misfortunes."[2] He concluded by saying that he was attacked daily by the sword and by woes. He was convinced that he was living near the end of time, and that soon Christ would return as judge.

The Lombards were threatening Rome, and Gregory's experience in the East convinced him that no help would come from that quarter. Therefore he concluded a peace treaty with the Lombards on his own authority, without reference either to the exarch at Ravenna or the emperor, thereby establishing a precedent for papal independence of action in temporal affairs. Owing to the failure of Byzantium to defend Rome, Gregory also acted independently to stave off famine by seeing to the needs of the sick and starving, using his own private resources. In a letter to the empress he reflected his frustration: "If your piety were to remain unaware of what is being done in these provinces, I should be punished by the severe Judge for my own sin of silence."[3]

In 590, even before his papal election was ratified by the emperor (who still controlled all papal appointments) the bubonic plague was raging in Rome. As a corporate expression of repentance before God, he directed the populace to march in procession chanting the *Kyrie eleison*. Years later the story was told that as the procession passed by Hadrian's tomb (emperor, 117–138) they saw the archangel Michael replacing in its sheath the sword of vengeance, as a sign that the plague would soon be over. A statue of Michael still stands atop the tomb commemorating this event, and the mausoleum has since been known as the castle of Sant' Angelo (Holy Angel). Gregory's concern for the poor was one of the most distinguishing marks of his fourteen years as pope. He established *xenodochia* or shelters for the infirm, sick, and strangers, and arranged for monthly distributions to the needy.

Gregory found the competence of his clergy at an appallingly low level, which prompted him to write *Pastoral Care*, probably his most popular work. In later years every bishop, upon his consecration, was given a copy of this work, together with ring, staff, and mitre. The book begins by saying, "The governance of souls is the art of arts," which requires wisdom and humility. Pastors should "find their joy not in ruling over men but in helping them," and flattery leads to one's downfall "when he believes himself to be such as he hears himself professed to be." The work contains thirty-six case studies of likely counseling situations. In addition to counseling, Gregory devotes over half of his work to the need for good preaching.[4]

As an administrator Gregory insisted on regular reports from the bishops under his jurisdiction, he demanded that vacant parishes be provided for, and that clergy be educated in the bishop's household. It was the custom at that time that all church revenues be equally divided four ways: for the bishop, the clergy, the physical maintenance of the church, and for the poor. Gregory saw to it that money for the poor went to the establishment of *xenodochia* and that the bishops allotted the clergy their full portion. All of this was within Gregory's immediate jurisdiction as Bishop of Rome, amounting to 1,800 square miles and known as the Papal States or Patrimony of St. Peter. But he also had a keen sense of papal responsibilities beyond his immediate episcopal jurisdiction. He sent letters of advice and of reproof to church leaders far removed from Rome. "Gregory's letters crackle with commands and reprimands."[5] When he heard that King Reccared of Spain had left Arianism for the Catholic church (589), he sent Leander of Seville the pallium (a garment of white wool draped over the shoulders) as a sign of approval and advancement in the hierarchy. Gregory was clear about the prerogatives of the Holy See. When the patriarch of Constantinople, John the Faster, assumed the title of "ecumenical," implying that he was the principal bishop of the church, Gregory sent him a letter of remonstrance, insisting that Rome was the truly ecumenical church by virtue of the fact that it had been founded by Peter. At the same time he sent a letter of reproof to Maurice, the emperor, demanding that he correct the patriarch. As against the inflated title assumed by John, the pope henceforth referred to himself as "servant of the servants of God." Altogether 852 letters of Gregory are extant.

In addition to *Pastoral Care*, Gregory wrote the *Moralia*, a commentary on Job which is a repository of casuistry and asceticism. The book utilizes a three-fold method of interpretation—literal, mystical, and allegorical, with an emphasis on the latter. It is highly moralistic, written especially for monks, and is the longest of his works. The *Dialogues*, reflecting the piety of the time, is full of miracles and extraordinary events. It contains the first biography of Benedict, the founder of Western monasticism, and was used as a model for medieval hagiography. In this work he also laid the foundation for the doctrine of purgatory and the beneficent effect of masses for the repose of the dead. In terms of popular piety, Gregory promoted the use of the sign of the cross, the collection of relics (only if authentic), emphasized the realism of Christ's body and blood in the Eucharist, and promoted the work of Dionysius the Areopagite and angelology. Although he has been credited with innovations in the liturgy—i.e. Gregorian chant—this type of music was simply the Graeco-Roman music of the day, and the Gregorian Sacramentary was not introduced until two centuries later. He took an active part in training boys' choirs to lead in the liturgy, establishing the *schola cantorum* (school for singers) for this purpose. Gregory was also active in the promotion of monasticism, himself being the first monk to serve as pope.

The work of Gregory as administrator, as an independent churchman who successfully resisted the emperor, the Eastern patriarch, and the military presence of the Lombard, and his solicitude for the whole church sufficiently indicates his interest in the expansion of Christianity. He attempted the conversion of the Arian Lombards, but in this he was disappointed. His most celebrated initiative in evangelism was the mission of forty monks he sent to Britain, under the leadership of Augustine, in 597 A.D. Although by this time Christianity had already been established in large parts of Britain, it was this mission that put into motion the process by which the church in Europe and England would come under the Roman See. Years later the Venerable Bede offered an explanation for Gregory's interest in England. He reported that one day some merchants who had recently arrived in Rome displayed their wares in the market. Included for sale were some boys "who had fair complexions, fine-cut features, and fair hair. Looking at them with interest, he inquired what country and race they had come from." He was told they had come from Britain, and that they were pagans. After further inquiry about their race, he was told they were Angles. "That is appropriate," he said, "for they have angelic faces, and it is right that they should become fellow-heirs with the angels in heaven."[6]

Britain and Ireland

We do not know when Christianity first appeared in Britain. Already at the turn of the second century, Tertullian (d. 240) and Origen (d. 254), in describing the spread of Christianity, refer to believers among the Celts and Britons.[7] Five British bishops were present at the council of Arles (314 A.D.) and another was at the council of Sardica (343 A.D), so it is apparent that Christianity existed there long before Constantine. Britain had never been thoroughly Romanized, and in the mid–fifth century while Rome was defending itself against numerous invaders, its forces were recalled. This left Britain open to attacks from the Saxons, Angles, and Jutes in the east and north. (It was at this time that the legend of King Arthur developed.) From the fifth century onward we gain more certain knowledge of events in Britain.

Pelagius, the author of the heresy that came to be known by his name, came to Rome from Britain some time before the sack of 410, "stuffed with the porridge of the Scots," says Jerome (Scots were Gaelic people of northern Ireland who settled in Scotland in the fifth century and gave it their name.) Pope Celestine (422–434), the most ardent papal contender against Pelagianism, sent Germanus of Auxerre to Britain in 429 to oppose the Pelagian heresy. We do not know how successful he was, but in 447 he revisited Britain, and the legend is that he led his troops to a victory over the Picts and Saxons, leading them with the war cry of "Alleluiah!" This military success notwithstanding, Germanus's work in England apparently bore little fruit. A contemporary of Germanus was Ninian (d. 432), who was consecrated in Rome to serve as a bishop and evangelize in Britain. Upon his return to England after his consecration he met Saint Martin of Tours in Gaul. Ninian established a monastery at Whithorn which became a center for missionary activity. Faustus of Riez (fl. 400–450), a leader of the Semi-Pelagian school of Lerins, also came from Britain, which leads us to the conclusion that the British church in the first half of the fifth century was growing in numbers and influence.

The earliest name associated with missions to Ireland is Palladius (fifth century). It was at his suggestion that Pope Celestine sent Germanus to Britain, and the same pontiff sent Palladius to Ireland. Little is known of his success, although the sites of three churches founded by him have been identified. The best-known missionary to Ireland was

Patrick of Armagh (d. 461), although little that is certain is known of his life. He was born in England, the son of a deacon, Calpurnios, and the grandson of a presbyter. Despite the titles of his forebears, Patrick writes that his home was not religious, and that he grew up ignorant of the faith.[8] When he was sixteen he was kidnapped by pirates who sold him to some Druid worshipers in Ireland. After six years of herding pigs he escaped, and through various adventures found his way back to England. He wrote that it was during his captivity that he was converted. From this point the story of his life is shrouded in mystery until the point some years later at which he returned to Ireland as a missionary, having been consecrated a bishop in England. His area of activity was largely confined to northern Ireland. Although his writings make no mention of Armagh, it is probable that he made his headquarters there, which subsequently became the primatial see of Ireland in part because of its traditional association with Patrick.

Christianity was already present in Ireland upon Patrick's arrival. Part of his strategy was to foster the growth of religious communities as centers for evangelism, and he may have been a monk himself.[9] There were no towns in fifth-century Ireland, and therefore no bishoprics or dioceses as on the continent. Society was organized along tribal lines with the tribal patriarch as leader and final arbiter. This dictated a mission strategy which was directed at the heads of clans, because as the leader believed, so did the followers. Such a decentralized society, organized along tribal communities, made monasticism a natural and powerful institution for evangelism. Although legends about Patrick abounded after his death, we have only two genuine writings of his— *Confessions* and *Letter to Coroticus*—two short works written in Latin. Patrick's supposed use of the shamrock to illustrate the Holy Trinity is an edifying story, and the cleansing of Ireland of snakes is first suggested in the ninth century. We know that Patrick founded monasteries, organized scattered Christian communities, converted pagans, and encouraged the study of Latin. He died in 461.

The Christianization of Ireland was accomplished entirely through the influence and spread of monasticism. Abbots rather than bishops became the spiritual and administrative leaders of the church. The episcopal office remained, but it was either assumed by an abbot, or by someone who was under the direction of an abbot. The sixth century witnessed the flowering of monasticism in Ireland and among the people known as Celts, who inhabited an area which included Wales, Brittany, and western Scotland. Wales produced three monastic leaders who are closely associated with the establishment of Christianity there.

The first of these was David (d. 600), who became the patron saint of
Wales, and was known for the severity of his discipline and as a promoter
of austere monasticism. According to tradition he founded twelve monasteries, one of them at Menevia, which is now St. David's. Little is
known of his life, but his memory was invoked in the eleventh century
with a view toward establishing the independence of Welsh bishops
from the See of Canterbury. The second, Cadoc, was a disciple of Finnian
of Clonard, while the third, Gildas (d. 570) wrote *De Excidio (The Ruin
and Conquest of Britain)*, the first history of Britain and also the earliest
history of the Celts. He also wrote two sets of disciplinary canons.

The Irish church in the sixth century displayed three general characteristics: monasticism, individuality, and learning. As already indicated, the church was guided by abbots, not bishops. The monasteries
were characterized by a severity which rivaled that of the Egyptian
desert. One of the most significant institutions to arise from Irish monasticism, later to be adopted by the entire church, was the private
penitential system, i.e. making private confession to a priest who im-
posed a penance. In order to assist the priest in assessing spiritual tariffs
there emerged penitentials or handbooks of penances. Up until this time
the church in its original homeland—the Mediterranean basin—recognized only public confession for serious public sins, to be followed by a
public penance, one that was allowed possibly only once in a lifetime.
Under the influence of the Irish, confession and penance became private
for minor and for mortal sins, and confession was to be made frequently.

Ireland was administered along clan and tribal lines. Because Roman influences had been slight, there were no provinces and few cities.
With its system of self-sufficiency it was well suited to tribal organization. At times the abbot may literally have been the *paterfamilias* of his
family. Each of the monasteries with its daughter houses kept a Rule laid
down by its Father Founder. Celtic monastic organization in place of
continental dioceses caused tensions later when Irish missionaries
clashed with Roman usages on the continent.

Irish Christianity was also marked by individuality. It had very loose
ties with Rome, and the monks observed a date for Easter and a tonsure
different from Rome (the tonsure was the shaving of the head as a rite
of admission to the clerical office). In the West the entire head was
shaved except for a circle of hair, representing Christ's crown of thorns.
In Ireland the hair was shaved in front of a line extending over the head
from ear to ear. In general the Irish were much less organized than was
the Roman church, with priests wandering at will, performing rites with
little regard to jurisdiction or order. One distinguishing feature of Irish

monasticism was *peregrinatio pro Christo* or wandering for Christ. This involved undertaking dangerous journeys or placing oneself in jeopardy for the sake of Christ. One such celebrated voyager was St. Brendan of Clonfert (d. 578) who reached Iceland and some say may have touched North America. Another facet of Irish individuality was the large number of anchorites who populated remote and barren places, such as the Dingle peninsula, Dunmore Head, the westernmost point of Ireland, or small islands off the western coast, such as Skelig Michael. Today one can still see many of the beehive huts of hermits from these early days, including the best preserved of all the corbelled stone churches, the Gallerus oratory.

From the early days of the Druids the Irish placed high value on intellectual work and study, and the church inherited this tradition of scholarship. When the barbarian invaders on the continent made learning and letters difficult, indeed, destroyed much of the valuable legacy of Graeco/Roman literature, Greek and Latin classics found a refuge among the Celts. A contemporary historian discusses the knowledge of Greek among the Franks as "an Irish monopoly."[10] In 536, we are told, fifty continental scholars were studying in Ireland, and a few years later seven shiploads of foreign scholars were attracted to these schools. During a plague in England in 664 many left for Ireland either to study or to join stricter monasteries. Bede writes that "the Scots most willingly received them and provided them with food and books free of charge."[11] Together with learning went the multiplication of scriptoria and the reproduction of books, from which they developed skills in manuscript illumination. The most famous of these priceless treasures are the *Book of Durrow* (675), the *Lindisfarne Gospels* (696), and the *Book of Kells* (800). Among the artistic remains from this period are more than thirty standing stone crosses (known as high crosses) from ten to twenty-two feet high, usually with a circle at the junction of the beams and decorated in various panels with scenes from the life of Christ. Although there are some affinities between Irish and Egyptian monasticism, for which some claim direct influence through contacts via the straits of Gibralter, in one respect they differ. Whereas Egyptian monks came primarily from among the poor and uneducated classes, the Irish were recruited from the middle class and the aristocracy. This was a factor in Ireland's deserved reputation as being the home not only of saints but of scholars as well.

Columba of Iona was one of the earliest of the *peregrinatia*, the pilgrims for Christ. He was a disciple of Finnian of Clonard and a member of the royal family who, in 563, landed at Iona, a small (six square miles) island off the western coast of Scotland. With twelve followers he established a monastery which became a center of Celtic Christianity from which missionaries were sent to Scotland; the hymn *Altus Prosater* (The Great Creator) has been attributed to Columba. It speaks of creation, sin, and judgement, and is arranged so that each line begins with the succeeding letter of the alphabet.[12] Columba died in 597. The Iona mission extended to the Anglo-Saxons in eastern England when King Oswald of Northumbria, who had been exposed to Christianity in his youth, gained the throne in 633 and requested a missionary to revive the work of an earlier Roman mission led by Paulinus (see below). Aiden (d. 651) was sent from Iona and established himself on the island of Lindisfarne (the Holy Isle) off the eastern coast of Scotland. It became a second center, with Iona, for the evangelization of northern England and Scotland. Aiden trained a group of missionaries who were active among the East Saxons, and whose work laid the foundation for Christian Britain.

The year of Columba's death (597) was the same year that Pope Gregory's mission, led by Augustine, landed in England, setting the stage for the interplay between the Celtic missions which were already present and the new arrivals from Rome.

When Augustine landed in Kent, he found an England which was loosely subdivided into seven kingdoms (the Heptarchy) each governed by its own king. Ethelbert was the king of Kent, and Bertha, his wife, was a daughter of the king of the Franks and a Christian. Ethelbert met the missionary in the open (for fear of magic in a closed place), and Augustine arrived with his followers, bearing a silver cross, an icon of Christ, and chanting a litany. The king not only received him graciously, but allowed him to work at Canterbury and was himself baptized at Easter in 601, becoming the first Christian king in England.[13] It was Pope Gregory's plan that Augustine establish himself in London, win the Celtic Christians to Roman obedience, and establish a second bishopric at York. When he died in 604, Canterbury had been established as the primatial Roman See in England, but the other plans awaited development. After his death and that of King Ethelbert there was a pagan reaction which undid much of Augustine's work. In 601 Pope Gregory sent Paulinus to assist Augustine. In 625 Edwin, King of Northumbria (after whom Edinburgh is named), married Ethelburga of Kent. Paulinus, who had been consecrated as bishop to introduce Christianity in the north, accompanied the new queen. He made York his center and cathedral. Edwin and his followers converted, but when he was killed in 633 the mission collapsed. Christianity in Northumbria was revived again by Aiden and his associates from Lindisfarne in the late–seventh century. By 650 most of England, except Sussex, was nominally Christian, belonging to one of two forms of Christianity. The Celts, who had already been active since the fifth century, were unorganized, individualistic and autonomous. Abbots were the most influential leaders as monasticism was the center of church life. The Roman mission, on the other hand, was recent, well organized, administered by bishops from cathedral centers, and who were, most significantly, obedient to the pope. King Oswald of Northumbria, one of the earliest of the devout medieval kings, saw that the church was in crisis, and took decisive action: he called for a council at Whitby in 664 to bring an end to the confusion.

Whitby was in northern England along the coast of the North Sea, a double monastery for both men and women. The chief proponent of obedience to Rome was Rilfrid of Ripon, who despite his education at Lindisfarne (a Celtic center which was traditionally suspicious of Rome) appealed to the authority of St. Peter. Colman, Abbot of Lindisfarne, defended the Celtic tradition and appealed to St. John. King Oswy was the judge, and he ruled in favor of the Roman tradition when he learned that Peter was the keeper of the keys of heaven (Matt. 16:18) and that the Bishop of Rome was his successor. Although the Celtic churches did not immediately acquiesce in the decision, the council's decree eventually united the English church.

Perhaps of more significance than the council itself was the new Archbishop of Canterbury who arrived four years later (668), Theodore of Tarsus, whose authority was acknowledged throughout the English church. That Theodore was a Greek monk testifies to the fact that the church still considered itself one indivisible body from Britain to Persia). After conducting a tour of all the churches, he divided them into seven jurisdictions corresponding to the Heptarchy, each with its own bishop. He then made further subdivisions corresponding to the old tribal divisions, with the result that there were fifteen dioceses, all acknowledging the Archbishop of Canterbury as their superior. All monasteries were henceforth to be under the jurisdiction of the local bishop, no small concession on the part of the Celts. In 673 Theodore called a council of all the bishops at Hertford which ratified this arrangement and adopted rules and procedures to govern the English church. Benedict's *Rule* was also introduced to English monasticism, but it was not required to be followed. Thus it was that although England was still politically divided, it was ecclesiastically united. "Theodore's organizational and pastoral abilities were revealed above all in the fact that he favored neither Saxon nor Celt, but reconciled all in a single body in which the two traditions complemented and fed each other."[14] However, the church in Ireland did not participate in these councils, nor did it acknowledge the jurisdiction of Canterbury. A very young contemporary of these events was Bede the Venerable (672–735), who at age seven was sent to the monastery at Wearmouth from where he transferred to Jarrow. Throughout his lifetime Bede wrote some fifty-five works, including *The Ecclesiastical History of the English People*, for which he is best known and for which he richly deserves the title "The Father of English History." Among the other attributes of this remarkable man was his ability to write on science, cosmography, and patristics, as well as sensitive and balanced works in history, in spite of the fact that he never traveled more than fifty miles from his home.

Missions to the Continent

By the fifth century Christianity in Gaul was well over three hundred years old, but the church there had fallen on evil days. Following the baptism of Clovis and three thousand of his men in the Rhine in 496, most of the barbarian tribes between Paris and the Pyrenees eventually turned to Christianity. As the new faith expanded under the Merovingian Franks (as the descendants of Clovis were known), the secular princes thoroughly dominated the church. Christianity was often a thin veneer covering a still vibrant Teutonic paganism. Gregory of Tours, the most important historian of this period and author of the *History of the Franks*, said this of the church in France during the late–sixth century: "In these times when the practice of letters declines, nay, rather perishes in the cities of Gaul, there has been found no scholar trained in the art of ordered composition to present a picture of the things which have befallen." He continued by deploring the many evils, the savagery of people, the fury of kings, the new heresies, and the lukewarm faith of the people. He pointed out how avaricious laymen with the help of the king established themselves as abbots and bishops and how the gross manners of the nobility undermined Christian morality throughout the land.[15] Therefore toward the end of the sixth century not only were there large areas of Europe—such as east of the Rhine—which had not yet received the gospel, but those areas that had been converted were in need of reform. It was in this situation that we witness one of the more interesting phenomena of the early medieval church, that of countless numbers of Anglo-Saxon missionaries flocking to the continent intent on reviving a flagging church or converting the pagans.

The first of these was Columban (d. 615), a physical giant and a moral rigorist who was determined to revive the Gallican church by preaching, moral example, disputation, and occasionally through feats of strength.[16] At some point in 590 he arrived in Gaul near Mont Saint Michel with a shipload of fellow monks from Ireland, the vanguard of many English and Irish monks who would continue to cross the channel all the way down to the twelfth century, giving expression to their ideal of voluntary exile, *peregrinatio*, for Christ. In his lifetime Columban established some forty monastic houses as mission centers. His center in Gaul was at Luxeuil, where he enjoyed some success in reforming the Gallican church and converting pagans. His fiercely independent ways alienated him from both Frankish rulers and bishops. His Irish settlements were autonomous, exempt from episcopal or secular oversight, following the Celtic belief that an abbot was superior to a bishop (Christ Himself was addressed as the divine abbot.) The Irish also observed a date for Easter different from the Gallican church. Indeed, Columban took it upon himself to write to Gregory the Great in imperious terms. "Do you bid us, Holy Father, to keep a Victorian Easter on the twenty-second day of the moon? . . . Why do you keep a dark Easter, you the diffuser of light throughout the world? . . . Please spare us the scandal of seeing you at variance with St. Jerome, for who disagrees with him must be banned as a heretic."[17] Columban's rigorism can be seen reflected especially in the Rule he laid down for his monks. Whoever failed to make the sign of the cross over his spoon at dinner was punished with six strokes of the lash, and whoever did not kneel to receive a blessing when entering or leaving the monastery received twelve strokes. There were also punishments for failure to say grace at table, and remarks which detracted from the abbot were classified with homicide. In 603 the Gallican bishops convened a council to discipline Columban, but when he appeared he lectured the assembled prelates on their vices. He went too far, however, when he threatened the king with excommunication and denounced the vicious life of Queen Brunhilde, calling her a new Jezebel. She expelled him from Gaul, but he succeeded in jumping ship, traversing the length of Gaul, and founding a new monastery on Lake Geneva which became known as St. Gall after one of his followers. This monastery was famous during the medieval period for its excellent scriptorium. After three years Columban left and established another monastery at Bobbio in Lombardy, where he died in 615.

The labors of Columban could not reverse a deteriorating situation, and the late–Merovingian period witnessed the decay of central authority with the church becoming territorial, controlled by self-serving princes. Ecclesiastical organization broke down with the fragmentation of the kingdom, fostering a spirit of independence which was detrimental to the church's work. A three-fold task awaited the missionaries from Britain: the reconversion of Gaul, the reorganization of the church, and the evangelization of the territories outside the old Roman empire in the West.

The Anglo-Saxons brought with them the organizational experience of the Roman church as it had been introduced to Kent by Augustine of Canterbury and subsequently to all of England by Theodore of Canterbury and Wilfrid of York. The missionaries who arrived after Columban brought with them a combination of Irish zeal and Roman discipline. The first territory to be evangelized outside the old Roman boundaries on the continent was Belgium, Holland, and the coasts of the North Sea inhabited by the Frisians. On one of his five trips to Rome, Bishop Wilfrid of York (d. 709), was shipwrecked on the coast of Holland where he remained for the winter and baptized many. But the missionary who was the true "Apostle to Frisia" was Willibrord (d. 739), who came from Saxon Northumbria and had spent some time with Wilfrid at the monastic house at Ripon, from whose previous exploits in Frisia he undoubtedly received inspiration to go. In 690, after spending twelve years in Irish monasteries, Willibrord arrived on the shores of Frisia with eleven companions. Three years later he traveled to Rome to secure papal authorization and support for his work, and shortly after this he was consecrated archbishop by Pope Sergius, with Utrecht as his center of operations. The Frankish king, Pepin II, supported him in his work. Thus Willibrord inaugurated an alliance between both the papacy and the secular ruler which would closely tie the continental church to the Roman See under the patronage of the princes. Alcuin, his biographer, describes the success of his activity. "He traversed every part of the country, exhorting the people in cities, villages, and forts where he had previously preached the Gospel to remain loyal to the faith and their good resolutions." As the number of the faithful increased daily and a "multitude" came to the faith, many made over their properties to the missionary, which he accepted. He built churches, and appointed priests and deacons to serve them. "Thus the man of God, favored by divine grace, made increasing progress from day to day."[18] Although he spent nearly fifty years in Frisia, little is known of Willibrord's activities. An expedition to the Danes had little success. His work in Frisia was under continuous harassment by Radbod, Prince of the Frisians, who associated Christianity with a political threat by Pepin the Frank. Willibrord and his companions succeeded in bringing most of Belgium, Holland, and the German shores of the North Sea to the church.

Winfrid of Nursling—later known as Boniface, and a younger contemporary of Willibrord—was the best-known and most successful Anglo-Saxon missionary. For thirty years he consolidated the existing churches and pushed the frontiers of Christianity north to Scandinavia. He was born in Wessex about 680, and from age five was reared in English monasteries. In 716 he went to Rome where he received authorization for mission work from Pope Gregory II. In 722 he left Frisia for Hesse and Thuringia, where he realized some success in converting tribal chieftains to the faith. In the same year the pope consecrated him bishop and commissioned him to convert "the races in the parts of Germany and on the east side of the Rhine."[19] It was on this occasion that he received the name of Boniface. The pope outlined Boniface's mission in a letter which read in part: "You are to teach them (the pagans) the service of the kingdom of God by persuading them to accept the truth in the name of Christ . . . instill into their minds the teaching of the Old and New Testaments, doing this in a spirit of love and moderation." He was also advised to use the sacramental discipline prescribed in the official ritual formulary of the Holy Apostolic See.[20] The pope also wrote letters of commendation on behalf of Boniface to Charles Martel, the *de facto* Frankish ruler, and to those bishops whose assistance would be helpful in his evangelistic work, which embraced both the reform of the Gallican church and the conversion of pagan Germany.

He also received advice from England. The Bishop of Winchester sent a letter advising him on the proper approach to the pagans, "to show how you may overcome with the least possible resistance this barbarous people." The bishop warned against arguing with the pagans about their gods, as this would merely antagonize them. The missionary should rather remind them of the works of Christ, the universality of the faith, and the omnipotence of the Creator. "From time to time their superstitions should be compared with our Christian dogmas and touched upon indirectly," but this should not be done "in an offensive and irritating way."[21]

About 743 Boniface founded the monastery of Fulda as an outpost for the evangelization of Bavaria, a house exempt from episcopal supervision and subject only to the pope. Under its abbot, Sturm, this monastery grew to be the motherhouse for all of Germany and an influential center of Christianity. Sturm was sent to Rome and Monte Casino in order to learn the Benedictine *Rule*, which was then followed at Fulda.[22]

In his work of reforming the Gallican church, Boniface called a series of councils under his authority as papal legate, which he had received from Gregory III, at which time he made Mainz his archepiscopal residence (Mainz has enjoyed primal status among the churches of Germany ever since). In 754 he returned to Frisia and, while in the act of baptizing new converts, died at the hands of roving bandits. He was buried at Fulda, where his tomb remains to this day.

In addition to monks, Boniface was assisted in his work by numerous women, for whom he founded convents. Two abbesses whose lives have come down to us are Leoba and Walpurga. The biographer of the first tells us that Boniface sent a messenger asking that Leoba "be sent to accompany him (Sturm) on his journey to Monte Casino and to take part in this embassy: for Leoba's reputation for learning and holiness had spread far and wide and her praise was on everyone's lips."[23]

Boniface and his Anglo-Saxon followers brought organization, discipline, and reform to the continent, and they assured future ecclesiastical stability through the foundation of numerous monasteries inhabited by local converts. They introduced a system of ecclesiastical provinces, insisting that all bishops be subject to the pope, and they attached clergy to specific responsibilities (unlike the Irish). These missionaries also introduced that relationship between secular power and ecclesiastical institution which characterized the medieval period. As to the Irish characteristics of Boniface's work, one writer says that "Boniface had no direct and personal debt to Irish teachers," and he resisted those who labored outside the Roman obedience. "His general policy toward the Celtic *peregrini* . . . was one of suspicion or even hostility . . . a serious menace to unity and order."[24] Another, in a statement critical of Boniface, suggests that "he reaped the fruit of their (Celts) labors and destroyed their further usefulness, which he might have secured by a liberal Christian policy."[25] But in a real sense, Boniface was both the successor as well as the censor of his Celtic pioneers. Irish missionaries, following the example of Columban, continued to flock to the Continent. By the twelfth century a number of Irish foundations were flourishing in Germany, intended primarily for the Scots and Irish. These houses became known as *Schottenkloster*, with the monastery of St. James in Ratisbon as the motherhouse.

The conversion of the Saxons was associated with Frankish imperialism more than any other missionary enterprise on the continent. In 772 Charlemagne undertook a campaign against the Saxons in order to "win them for Christ" by force of arms if need be and through the destruction of their gods. Missionaries were sent into Westphalia to begin the work of evangelism, and hostages were taken from the Saxons to insure their safety. Two of the monks sent to preach were Willehad and Sturm. At a great gathering of Saxon chieftains at Paderborn in 777, most submitted to Charlemagne, with the usual sign of submission being the reception of Christian baptism. One leader, Widukind, was absent, and he became the center of Saxon resistance to Charlemagne and Christianity. For the next eight years Widukind and his men raided Frankish territory, penetrating as far as the left bank of the Rhine while Charlemagne was engaged elsewhere in defense of his kingdom. In 782 the Frankisk ruler lost all restraint when he beheaded 4,500 Saxons for being traitors and murderers. Finally, in 785 Widukind's resistance was broken, and the recalcitrant Saxons received baptism. It was about this time that Charlemagne took his revenge by promulgating the brutal Capitulary (ordinance) on Saxony, which said in part: "If anyone out of contempt for Christianity shall have despised the holy Lenten fast and shall have eaten flesh, let him be punished by death. . . . If anyone of the Saxons shall have wished to hide himself unbaptized and shall have scorned to come to baptism, let him be punished by death."[26] We do not know whether this savage edict was ever enforced, because Alcuin, Charlemagne's principal advisor, wrote to him immediately: "According to St. Augustine faith is an act of the will and cannot be enforced. A man can be forced into accepting baptism but not faith. . . . Little benefit will accrue the truth of the Catholic faith."[27] He suggested that if the "sweet Gospel" were preached with as much vigor as laws were enforced, perhaps the Saxons would willingly and wholeheartedly embrace the faith. Alcuin's admonition was effective, as the Saxon Capitulary was shortly repealed or softened. The last great apostle to Saxony, Liudger (Ludger, d. 809), was a pupil of Alcuin who became Bishop of Münster. Two of his followers, Adalhard and Wala, founded the monastery of New Corbie which served as a missionary center for Saxons as Fulda had for northern Germany.

The conversion of the Saxons paved the way for the evangelization of Scandinavia, which was inaugurated through a fortuitous diplomatic negotiation. King Harald of Denmark sought the aid of Louis, "the Pious," son of Charlemagne, in his contest for the Danish throne. Louis suggested that aid would be assured if Harald would espouse the Christian faith, and in May 826 Bishop Ebbo of Rheims baptized Harald, his family, and four hundred warriors. The way was thus open for Ansgar, a monk of New Corbie, to begin preaching in Denmark and Sweden. In 831 the pope created Hamburg as an archepiscopal see to serve as a center for Scandinavian missions, and Ansgar became its first bishop. Several years later this center was destroyed by pirates, and Hamburg-Bremen was established as a united archdiocese. Ansgar, who continued his work until his death in 865, is known as the "Apostle to the North." But the eradication of paganism in Sweden took much longer than in the rest of Scandinavia. In the twelfth century the Cistercian monks continued the work, and it was not until 1164 that Sweden received its first metropolitan see when the pope conferred this dignity upon Uppsala.

Despite the royal baptism of Harald in 826, Denmark remained unconverted. The German emperor, Otto I (936–973) defeated Harald Bluetooth (a successor to the earlier Harald) in the mid–tenth century, facilitating the conversion of the Danes. A chronicler of the event recorded that "A meeting between Otto and the king of the Danes was arranged at Morso. There the holy bishop, Poppo, explained the Catholic faith to King Harald. He carried a red hot iron in his hand and showed the king that it did not burn him."[28] Thereupon the king and the Danish army were baptized, and orders were given that all Danes should likewise accept the true faith.

The conversion of Norway came about primarily from its close ties with England rather than the continent. King Olaf Tryggveston (995–1000), who was baptized in England, and King Olaf Haroldsson (St. Olaf, 1014–1030), did much to spread the faith in Norway. Tryggvesson first elicited a promise from his army to follow him in whatever he did, and he followed that up when "he asked all men to become Christians." He punished those who refused, "and so it happened that in the whole kingdom all people accepted Christianity."[29] Christianity was solidified in the north when Canute was sole ruler in Norway, Denmark, and England (1016–1030). Lund, the center of Christian missions to Norway, became an independent archbishopric in 1104. Iceland received Christianity from Norway while Tryggvesson was king. Dankbrand of Bremen is given credit for this work, as he succeeded in winning over many to baptism; but his most important convert was the King of Iceland, who, "one thousand years after the birth of Christ made Christianity a law in Iceland."[30]

From the homelands of Christianity, especially Asia Minor, missionaries were active in spreading the gospel north and west. Of great interest to missiologists is the conversion of Moravia and Bohemia by two celebrated brothers, Cyril (d. 869) and Methodius (d. 885). In 863 King Ratislav of Moravia petitioned the Eastern emperor for missionaries, and he was sent Cyril and Methodius. They had grown up in Thessalonica and were familiar with Slavic culture and language. In order to support his work, Cyril invented an alphabet (Cyrillic, the ancestor of modern Russian) and translated the Bible and liturgy into Slavonic. After four years of fruitful activity they were summoned to Rome by the pope, who sanctioned their liturgy and ordained them as bishops. Cyril died shortly after this, but Methodius returned to become the first Archbishop of Moravia, from where Christianity spread into Bohemia. In their method we see a sharp contrast with that pursued in the West. They developed a new language as teaching devices. The faith was presented not as a foreign element but rather as something indigenous to their culture, and they spent time explaining their dogma to their hearers. About the same time Bulgaria was evangelized and came under the jurisdiction of the East. It became the center of missions to the Slavs.

Russia derived its faith from Constantinople and the Greeks. About the year 988 King Vladimir, in order to derive the benefits of what he believed to be a superior Greek culture, married the sister of the Eastern emperor and allowed himself to be baptized. This event is usually accepted as the beginning of Russian Christianity. He and his men forcibly rooted out the worship of idols, and they introduced the Slavonic Bible and liturgy which had come to them from Cyril via Moravia and Bulgaria. The Russian church was therefore closely allied with Byzantine Christianity, but retained its own language, custom, and rites.

Mission Methods

In all of these efforts at spreading the faith, the primary goal of Christian missionaries was winning the consent of the pagans to receive baptism.[31] The activity was almost invariably inaugurated by the establishment of permanent missionary centers in pagan areas, which were self-sufficient monastic communities. They first cleared the land, planted crops, constructed buildings, including a chapel, and in every way established themselves as permanent residents. This symbol of permanence by itself made a strong impression both on the pagans and on the missionaries themselves. Using the monastery as their home base, they traveled wide stretches of territory, contacting pagans wherever they could be found. Boniface established a monastery at Amoneberg in Hesse which served as his center for a time, and then moved on to found one in Thuringia. Alcuin writes that Willibrord traveled throughout the towns and villages of Frisia, and churches there retained his memory for centuries.[32] Other missionaries, including Willibald, Liudger, Wynnebald, and Willehad all followed the same pattern. Unlike previous Irish missionaries, however, the Anglo-Saxons were closely and directly supervised from the home monastery. They did not wander too far distant, and provisions were made for a periodic return to the home base. Despite monastic initiatives in this work, supervision came from the bishop who, like Permin in the early eighth century, may often have been a bishop-abbot. "Each of Boniface's successive steps up the hierarchical ladder was intended at least partially as a means to allow him to retain the direction of missionary activity over a constantly enlarging missionary field."[33] Supervision assumed accountability, and each returning missionary was expected to give a report of his activities.

The nature of the pagan religions that the missionaries confronted can only be described in general terms. It was polytheistic, with a hierarchy of gods including elves, spirits, departed souls, witches, and demons as lower intermediaries. It was a religion of fear, aimed at placating the anger of the gods, who determined the entire course of human affairs. It was this-worldly, looking for tangible material rewards in this life. As with many religions in antiquity, it had little to do with personal morality, but with success in personal undertakings and with the welfare of the tribe. In this sense all ancient religions were communal, including that of the Roman empire. Religion was more for the welfare of the *polis* (the state) than for the individual, and that is why large groups of people would convert en masse. Divine punishment awaited traitors and betrayers of the state, but religion was often indifferent to one's private ethics.

This being the case, Christian missionaries almost always addressed crowds rather than individuals. Personal instruction, when evidence of it can be found, was always confined to kings or princes, who in turn would be able to move their people. Preaching, in village after village, was the primary means of reaching the people with basic Christian teachings. It was clearly imperative, therefore, to find preachers who could communicate with the pagans in their native tongue. Then, as today, missionary work in linguistics often led to the formation of an alphabet and to the first written form of a particular tribe's language, usually portions of the Bible.

The contents of missionary preaching attempted to inform the pagans about the origins of the universe and of humankind, the fall into sin, the deluge, and the coming of Christ as Redeemer. The Bible played an important role in their work. At different times Boniface wrote to England for more copies of the Bible, and Pope Gregory II advised him to use both testaments to convert the pagans.[34] Missionaries also pointed to the superiority of their god over all others, to his omnipotence, justice, and mercy. To the audience which looked for material rewards, the pagans were reminded that the Christians were usually better off in worldly goods than they were. They constructed new buildings with stone, cleared land, planted vineyards, diverted streams, built mills, worked in metal, established schools, and grew wealthy. It was clear that some god was favoring them. Another favorite theme was to attack forms of pagan worship and to point out the futility of worshiping inanimate things. Lebuin's sermon to the Saxons included these words: "The statues which you believe to be gods and which you, deceived by the devil, worship, are only gold or brass or stone or wood. They do not live; they do not move; they do not think. They are the work of men. Not one of them could be of help to itself or to anyone else."[35]

In general, the missionaries did not instruct their converts in the basic rudiments of the faith, i.e. the doctrine of the Trinity, the sacraments, the creed, or personal belief. Instead, they took more dramatic action by destroying the objects of pagan worship. The best known of these incidents was when Boniface felled the sacred oak of Thor at Geismar, an act that gave him instant credibility. But others, such as Willibrord, Sturm, Liudger, and Willehad resorted to similar measures. Charlemagne personally supervised the destruction of the Irminsul, a temple in Saxony. Their intention was not simply to demolish, but to convince the pagans of their gods' powerlessness to avenge this insult, and to demonstrate the superiority of the Christian god.

Since pagans sought material gain, Christian rulers often obliged. Bede writes that Pepin "rewarded with many benefits those (Frisians) who wished to receive the faith."[36] While it was the rulers, notably Charlemagne, who offered gifts and positions to the pagans in return for their submission to baptism, it was often the missionaries who benefited. There can also be little doubt that there was often, if not usually, cooperation between missionaries and secular rulers in their attempts to convince the pagans to be baptized.

Despite the material support of secular authorities, missionaries could not realistically rely upon such help, especially where the Franks had no jurisdiction or presence. There remains ample evidence that the examples of the missionaries themselves and their way of life added credibility to their message. Admittedly, hagiography is not a reliable reflection of reality, but the hagiographical sources of this period refer too often to the virtues of the missionaries—virtues such as mercy, charity, patience, courage, industry, and devotion to their God—to be dismissed out of hand. Willibrord provided for beggars, Boniface stood firm rather than flee in the face of war, Liudger invited paupers as well as the wealthy to eat with him, others aided the aged, treated the sick,

and helped the oppressed. That the missionaries often enjoyed a personal bond of friendship with their converts is beyond question.

Yet the missions were not always successful. Some pagans brought
counter arguments against the new faith. In one exchange of letters
Boniface is chagrined to admit that the English people and especially
the king "were scorning lawful marriage and living in wanton adultery
like the people of Sodom."[37] He concedes that pagan sexual practices
were superior to that of the Christians. Boniface also wrote to the pope
complaining that some Christians were undermining the effectiveness
of his preaching by leading sinful lives.[38] But more than merely rejecting
the message, some pagans resorted to violence. Boniface himself died
as a martyr, as did Willehad's companions in the great Saxon rebellion
of 782. Yet eventually Christianity supplanted paganism, and by 1050
most Europeans were baptized, even though vestiges of pagan belief
and practices often remained beneath a thin veneer of orthodoxy.[39]

Islam and Spain

Early in the seventh century a new religious and military force was
gathering strength in the Arabian peninsula. The rise of Islam dates from
622 A.D, Mohammad's flight with his followers from Mecca to Medina,
an event known as the Hegira. Mohammad succeeded in bringing
together the Bedouin and nomads of the vast stretches of the Arabian
desert under one religion, which taught an uncompromising monotheism in the worship of Allah. The sacred book of Islam (which means
submission to the will of God), was the Koran, which Mohammad
claimed had been revealed to him as God's word through the mediation
of the archangel Gabriel. Before he died in 636 Mohammad returned in
triumph to Mecca, which became the most sacred city of Islam and the
Ka'ba (black cube) its most sacred shrine. Islam teaches that there is no
God but Allah, and that Mohammad is his prophet. In addition to this,
each believer must pray five times daily, kneeling and facing toward
Mecca; give charity to the poor of the Muslim community; observe the
holy month of Ramadan by fasting between sunrise and sunset; and, if
possible, make at least one pilgrimage to the Ka'ba at Mecca during his
or her lifetime. Mohammad tried to elevate the ethical standards of his
time by preaching forgiveness, abolishing infanticide, imposing dietary
restrictions including prohibitions against the consumption of pork and
alcohol, and limiting the number of wives each man could have to four
at one time. By insisting on a strict monotheism and total submission to

Allah, the new faith brought with it a heightened morality and a challenging discipline which appealed to Mohammad's followers.

After the prophet's death he was succeeded by Abu Bakr as caliph (which means representative) followed by the prophet's son-in-law, Omar (634–644). It was the latter who organized a military force which quickly subdued Arabia, Syria (including Damascus), and Egypt, and in 638 captured Jerusalem following a four-month siege. Jerusalem became (with Mecca and Medina) the third holy city of the Muslims. Omar agreed to generous terms for the inhabitants, permitting both Jews and Christians the freedom to continue practicing their religions in return for payment of taxes. This policy of freedom of religion was continued by the Muslims throughout their conquests. A brief civil war (651–656) over the succession to the caliphate resulted in the founding of the Ummayad dynasty, which moved the capital from Mecca to Damascus, where they ruled until they were successfully challenged in 750. Their successors were the Abbasids, who moved the capital of Islam to Baghdad, inaugurating a golden age of Arabic culture in the Middle East. Islam also divided into two branches of observance, the Sunni (meaning way or path) who were faithful to the Ummayads, and today constitute the large majority of Muslims; and the Shia, or Shiites, who comprise about ten percent of Islam, largely centered in Persia (Iran). The Sunni accept the authority of the first three caliphs and the developed traditions handed down by legal experts. The Shiites reject the first three caliphs and hold that authority resides in the Imams, the messengers of God in every age.

The Ummayads continued Islam's expansion, first by dominating the eastern Mediterranean Sea and then by resuming the march westward across North Africa. Carthage fell in 698 followed by Algeria and Morocco where the fierce Berber resistance was finally broken. In fact, the Berbers embraced the new religion with near fanaticism. It was a Berber general, Tarik, who in 711 led the Muslim advance into Visigothic Spain across the straits between Africa and Spain—which have since become known as Gibralter (gib-al-Tarik or rock of Tarik). Meanwhile the Islamic advance in the East continued, with Constantinople being its primary target. Gradually the Byzantine empire was reduced to what is modern Turkey, with all of Persia and Syria under Islamic control. For five years they attempted to take Constantinople (673–678), but they were driven back by the newly invented "Greek Fire." Failing in this, they turned to the west coast of Asia Minor and took the area around the seven churches founded by St. Paul. In about fifty years the once mighty Byzantine empire was reduced to being a mere shadow of its former greatness.

In Spain the Berbers were joined by the Arabs, and together they conquered most of the Iberian peninsula with ease, due in part to the factionalism among the defending Visigoths. Toledo, the capital city, fell, and soon the invading forces had crossed the Pyrenees into Septimania, the area in southeast France between Barcelona and the mouth of the Rhone River, making Narbonne the capital. From this base the Muslims sent a force north to Tours, the famous shrine of St. Martin and magnet for pilgrims. Charles Martel, leader of the Franks, defeated the Muslims in 732 at the battle of Tours, and sent the invaders into retreat back to Narbonne. This battle has been celebrated in the West as decisive for European history, because it marked the limits of Muslim expansion and the beginning of a reaction which ultimately (seven centuries later) expelled the Muslims from Spain. Some recent historians, however, suggest that the battle of Tours was more significant for its symbolism than for its military success.[40]

As stated before, wherever Muslims subdued a people they permitted religious freedom, insisting only that the conquered people pay taxes. In Spain, therefore, Christians and Jews were allowed to continue their religious practices. The conquerors, however, attracted many converts to their faith. Arabic became the official language, and a new coinage was instituted. Arab-speaking Spanish Christians were known as Mozarabs, and a distinctive Mozarabic Rite developed that was used until the eleventh century, and survives in parts of Spain to this day. In the mid–ninth century the Bishop of Seville had the Bible translated into Arabic. Christians remained dominant in the northwest corner of Spain (Asturia) and in the northeast (Barcelona). By the end of the tenth century Asturia had become enlarged into Leon and the county of Castille; Barcelona had expanded to become the kingdom of Aragon, and the Basques sandwiched between these two northern kingdoms became the kingdom of Navarre. By 1100, therefore, most of northern Spain (between a fifth and a quarter of the whole country) was predominantly Christian. In 1085 Castille and Aragon joined forces to reconquer Toledo from the Moors (Spanish Muslims).

Within Islam a major crisis was brewing in the eighth century which finally erupted in 750 when the Ummayads were overthrown by the Abbasids, who moved their capital to Baghdad. In Spain, however, the Moors continued their loyalty to Ummayad rulers. The fall of Toledo in 1085 prompted the Muslims to invite the Almoravides, Berbers from North Africa, to come to their aid. Not only did they succeed in halting the Christian advance, but they successfully made war against the Moors as well. It was during these confusing times that a number of opportunists arose who sought their fortunes through strategies of shifting loyalties and calculated self-interest. The most famous of these was El Cid (Lord Champion; 1040–1099), from Castille, who is often associated with the Reconquest (Reconquista) of Spain, but whose actual history calls into question the heroic legend.

Medieval Spain produced thinkers whose contributions played a significant role in relation to Christian theology. Averroes (1126–1198) was a Muslim who came from Cordova and Seville; he wrote commentaries on Aristotle which helped to introduce Aristotelian philosophy to Christian theologians. His thought was also tinged with Neoplatonism as well as the use of allegory, for which reason he came under suspicion by the church. Averroism exerted a strong influence on scholasticism in thirteenth-century Europe. Maimonides (1135–1204) was a Jewish philosopher who also came from Cordova and was revered as the greatest Talmudic scholar of his day. Among other things he wrote a commentary on the Mishna, but his work entitled *The Guide for the Perplexed* exerted the greatest influence on Christian thought. In it he sought to harmonize faith and reason, science and revelation, using Aristotelian categories in his construction. He is also credited with playing a leading role in defending the immortality of the soul as a principle of Judaism. Both Albert, "the Great," and Thomas Aquinas were influenced by Maimonides.

Travelers to southern Spain today can still see much architectural evidence of the Arabic presence there in medieval times. The best known of these treasures is the Alhambra in Granada, built in the twelfth century as a fortified citadel which connected the Sultan's palace and his court.

The effect of the Muslim expansion on Christianity can be clearly seen in the fact that, of the five traditional patriarchates, the chief sees of Christendom (Jerusalem, Rome, Alexandria, Antioch, Constantinople), all but Rome were by the end of the medieval period under Muslim rule. This fact undoubtedly enhanced the claims of Rome to be honored as the primatial see of the church, together with its tradition of Petrine foundation.

CHAPTER THREE

THE CHURCH IN THE NINTH AND TENTH CENTURIES

The Church under the Carolingians

We have already discussed the rise of the Merovingian Franks under Clovis and his descendents. During the period of their dominanace, the sixth through the early eighth centuries, the church was the only cohesive and moral force in a turbulent society. It was primarily the church that provided for a system of justice, alleviated the distress of the needy, provided a rudimentary system of education, and held before the people the ideals and challenges of the faith. From 600 on the Mayors of the Palace (*major domo magistri palatii*), the king's chief assistants, assumed more power at the expense of the royalty, especially in East Francia (Germany or Austrasia). In 687 Pepin of Heristal defeated Neustria (West Francia or much of France), and he united the Franks under one rule. His son was Charles Martel, who defeated the Muslims at the battle of Tours in 732; Martel's son, also a Mayor of the Palace, was Pepin, "the Short" (741–768). It was during the time of these strong governors that the Anglo-Saxon missions to the continent were undertaken, and the rulers did not hesitate to use the church's mission to foster their own programs of expansion. Willibrord, Wilfred, Boniface, and their many associates were often perceived as agents of Frankish aggression as well as representatives of the new religion. "The monks were the driving force behind the whole colonizing movement."[1] The secular powers also used the church as a source of revenue, often selling spiritual offices to the highest bidder, who usually lacked any religious qualifications. When Charles Martel was preparing to do battle with the Muslims he expropriated large tracts of church land with which to reimburse his troops. A church that was controlled by a lay lord, in which appointments to ecclesiastical offices were often made without regard to church procedures or spiritual qualifications, was known as a proprietary church. Under these circumstances it is not surprising that the church itself was in need of reform.

In 751 Pepin, "the Short," sent two messengers to Pope Zacharias to inquire whether it was right that a ruler with no power should continue to enjoy the title of king. The pope replied that the ruler who actually wielded the power should be the legitimate ruler, and he authorized Pepin to assume the title. Boniface, representing the pope, annointed Pepin with holy oil and crowned him king of the Franks. Thereupon the last remaining Merovingians were displaced, and the new dynasty of Carolingians emerged, named after its most illustrious representative, Charles, "the Great" (Charlemagne or Carolus Magnus). The crowning of Pepin and later the coronation of Charlemagne, both at papal initiative, constitute one of the most momentous turning points in medieval history. Meanwhile, the Lombards conquered Ravenna and expelled the exarch, the representative of the emperor in Constantinople. The pope appealed to Pepin for help, and he responded by marching into Italy and defeating the Lombards under their king, Aistulf, taking from him the lands of the exarchate of Ravenna and giving them to the pope. This gift is known as the "Donation of Pepin," (754) and it was the foundation of the territory in central Italy which became known as the Papal States. This marked the beginning of a Papal-Frankish alliance, an arrangement which was the result of papal need for protection against the Lombards and interference by the Eastern emperor, and it gave the Franks legitimacy as successors of Clovis.[2] It also marked the end of the exarchate in Ravenna, the Eastern emperor's representative and his "eyes and ears," as well as any menace the Lombards might pose to the Papacy.

Pepin's sons, Charlemagne and Carloman, succeeded him in 768, and from 771 until his death in 814, Charlemagne was sole ruler of what today is France, Saxony, Switzerland, Bavaria, and Italy north of Rome. His impact on the development of medieval institutions was profound. He sought supremacy over the Western church and the direction of its internal affairs by appointing and dismissing bishops, calling and controlling synods, and deciding questions of dogma and liturgy. He placed into civil law the requirement that the liturgy must be sung, the mass celebrated according to the Roman Latin rite, and baptismal immersions cease. He established twenty-one archbishoprics in the empire and made tithing compulsory. In 794 at the council of Frankfort he issued the *Libri Carolini* which rejected the Byzantine church's use of images in worship. The decrees that were most far-reaching had to do with education, in which he insisted that every parish was to provide a school for all children of the church regardless of class; "not only children of servile condition but also of free men."[3] This declaration comes from his best known capitulary, the *admonitio generalis* of 789, where in eighty-two articles he legislated matters of theology, discipline, liturgy, and education. He insisted that clergy wear distinctive garb that would identify them as priests in order to inhibit some from frequenting brothels and taverns under the anonymity of lay dress. He further declared that "We consider it useful that bishops and monasteries . . . ought to be zealous in teaching those who by the gift of God are able to learn."[4] This legislation was primarily for the education of the clergy. He standardized the text of the Apostles' Creed, made the Vulgate (Jerome's fifth-century Latin translation) the official text of the Bible and promoted the use of the Benedictine *Rule* in all monasteries. Most church leaders acquiesced in the strong initiatives taken by their ruler, agreeing with Agobard of Lyons, who wrote "would to God that all men were governed by one law administered by one very holy king."[5]

There is clearly no doubt that Charlemagne continued, indeed, intensified, the proprietary church system of the Merovingians. It is also evident that much of his legislation was to the church's benefit. In a celebrated letter to Pope Leo III in 796 Charlemagne stated his views on the relationship between pope and ruler. "It is our task with divine help to shield everywhere with our arms the Holy Church of Christ from all enemies abroad, from the incursion of the heathen and the devastations of the infidel, and to fortify her from within by the profession of the catholic faith." It was the pope's task "to assist the success of our arms with your hands raised in prayer to God like Moses."[6]

Relations between the pope and the emperor led to an event whose meaning was disputed even by eyewitnesses, and subsequently by historians up to the present. A contemporary chronicler describes the action on Christmas Day in 800 at St. Peter's Cathedral in Rome: "On that very holy day of the nativity of the Lord when Charlemagne at Mass before the tomb of the blessed apostle Peter arose from prayer, Pope Leo placed on his head a crown and all the Roman people cried out, 'To Charles Augustas, crowned by God, great and peace-giving emperor of the Romans, life and victory.'" He was then "adored" by the pope in the same manner, and he was called "emperor and Augustas."[7] In the conflicts between popes and kings during the rest of the Middle Ages the symbolism of this event was interpreted by adherents of both sides to support their claims of primacy. The following conclusions, however, can be agreed upon.

1. The coronation continued and strengthened the concept of the Roman empire. No one yet had suggested that it had "fallen," but rather it was identified with the fourth kingdom in the vision of Daniel (Dan. 2:40–45).

2. The coronation strengthened the concept of unity in Western Christianity. There was now an office superior to any king, and its authority was derived from God. At the same time anti-papal political forces saw in the emperor a powerful ally equal in status to the pope whose authority was also by divine right.

3. The coronation in effect repudiated the authority of the Eastern emperors, which intensified the tensions between East and West.

4. The fact that it was the pope who crowned the emperor was used to prove the superiority of popes over kings. Charlemagne's biographer notes that the emperor was not pleased with this aspect of his coronation. "He was so much opposed to this at first that he said he would not have entered the church that day had he been able to foresee the pope's intention, although it was a great feast day."[8] Some years later Charlemagne had his son and successor, Louis the Pious, crown himself by taking the crown from the altar. By this he intended to indicate his conviction that imperial right owed nothing to a mediary (pope) but it was the direct gift of God. Charlemagne never called himself emperor, which implies that he did not seek the title but reserved it for the ruler in Constantinople.

It is probable that the document known as the "Donation of Constantine" was created in the papal chancery at Rome during the struggle over the temporal power of the Papacy in the eighth century. It is a spurious text based on a romantic version of Constantine's conversion, in which he confers on the Roman church the privilege to govern all the priests within the Roman world. The emperor's motive was his gratitude to Pope Sylvester for curing him of leprosy. The legend also reports that as a sign of his contrition, Constantine prostrated himself and laid aside his royal insignia. The document adds to this legend by describing the emperor as giving to the pope all the insignia of the imperial office. The pope refused to wear them and returned them to the emperor, an act which was interpreted to mean that the bestowal of the imperial dignity was a papal right. The emperor also conveyed to the pope his palace in Rome in addition to "all the provinces, palaces, and districts of the city of Rome and Italy and the regions of the West." The emperor then moved his capital to the East, "for it is not right that an earthly emperor should have authority there, where the rule of priests and the head of the Christian religion have been established by the emperor of heaven." In addition to receiving the temporal jurisdiction throughout the West, Constantine also conferred on the pope primacy over the patriarchs of Antioch, Constantinople, Jerusalem, and Alexandria.[9] The genuineness of the document was not challenged until the fifteenth century when Lorenzo Valla and others demonstrated its spuriousness. Although it was written two hundred years earlier, it was not used to support papal claims until 1054, and that against the Eastern patriarch.

The cultural decline of the late Roman empire continued into the eighth century in the West, due in large part to the conditions created by the barbarian invasions and the lack of central government and stability.[10] Charlemagne is credited with reversing this trend through legislation which established schools and fostered reforms in morals and church life. This was the first of the two great renaissance movements in the Middle Ages, the other coming in the twelfth century. The Carolingian renaissance was nourished by the best minds available whom Charlemagne invited to his court. He began by establishing the palace school at Aachen under the direction of Alcuin of York (d. 804). A Saxon and later the abbot of St. Martin's abbey in Tours, Alcuin served as Charlemagne's personal advisor and was responsible for many of his ecclesiastical policies. During the fifteen years that he was in Aachen he established a library, wrote educational manuals, and revised the liturgy, but he is credited primarily with retrieving the legacy of the past.[11] The basic instruction was in the liberal arts. Alcuin was responsible for the education of the royal family, and it was not beneath the dignity of Charlemagne himself on occasion to sit in school with the children. His biographer, Einhard, is eloquent about his native intelligence and gift of speech. "He also tried to write and kept tablets and little books in bed under his pillows so that when he had time he might accustom his hand to forming letters. However, the labor was begun late in life and did not achieve much success."[12]

Rabanus Maurus (d. 856), a student of Alcuin, was one of the most significant theologians of the age. He was the Abbot of Fulda for two decades and after that served as the Archbishop of Mainz, thus guiding both the monastic and ecclesiastical centers of Germany. He was active in fostering missions and composed a manual for the education of monks and priests. He engaged in several theological controversies (see below). Theodulf of Orleans (d. 821) was the bishop of the city whose name he bears, where he introduced reforms, built schools, elevated worship practices, and devoted himself to art and architecture. He was also a poet of note, composing works describing the court life of Charlemagne, but he is best known to later ages as the author of the processional hymn for Palm Sunday, "All Glory, Laud, and Honor."

Einhard (d. 840), is best known for his *Life of Charlemagne*, which is modelled after the lives of the Caesars written by the Roman historian, Suetonius. As such it is remarkably perceptive of Charlemagne's character and motivations, and offers us a clear picture of the age.[13] Another historian of merit was Paul the Deacon (d. 800), a Lombard, who was from Monte Casino. He wrote a *History of the Lombards* which is our primary source for Lombard history of this time, as well as a commentary on the Rule of Benedict. Walafrid Strabo (d. 849), a monk of Reichenau, representing the second generation in the Carolingian awakening, is credited with composing the *Glossa Ordinaria*, a compilation of patristic commentaries on the Bible which became a standard text in later years. He is also the principal author of liturgical writings for this period. Anticipating later controversies over authority, he squarely based all churchly offices upon the Petrine commission of the pope, just as all imperial offices ultimately derived from Caesar, but the pope alone held plenary authority. Notker of St. Gall (d. 912), a much later writer, is noted for his collection of stories about Charlemagne, and Peter of Pisa was a teacher of grammar in the school at Aachen. Agobard of Lyons (d. 840), archbishop of that city, opposed the proprietary system of church control by lay rulers, insisting that secular rulers should be protectors of church rights and not administrators of churches. He attacked lay owners of churches, both diocesan and monastic, anticipating the investiture controversy by two centuries. He also opposed excessive veneration of images, witchcraft, the idea that hail and thunder were magic, and trial by ordeal. Amalarius of Metz (d. 850), a student of Alcuin, was a liturgical scholar whose primary work was *On Church Offices*, an allegorical explanation of Gallican and Roman rituals.

These thinkers and writers, as well as many more unknown to us, flourished under the aegis of Charlemagne, bringing about a rebirth of culture, learning, letters, and Christian faith. They were not original thinkers but custodians of the legacies they inherited from the early church and late Roman civilization. They were known for their breadth of learning and for preserving their religious and cultural heritage for future generations. As to Charlemagne, "there developed an idea of the pervasive religious and moral responsibility of the ruler. Christianity enormously expanded the perspectives in which rulers could think of themselves . . . [as] an engine of expanded royal government."[14] The single greatest agent in this transformation was Charlemagne.

Decline and Revival

Charlemagne was succeeded by his son, Louis I, "the Pious" (814–840). As indicated above, Louis had crowned himself under his father's supervision in 813. But three years later, following his father's death, he was crowned again by the pope in Rheims Cathedral. This time he was also annointed with oil, the first time this was done in an imperial coronation. The meaning of this act was that now the ceremony was a churchly liturgical rite which imitated the annointing of kings by prophets in the Old Testament, making the one annointed a defender of the Roman church and responsible to the pope. Although the full ramifications of this act were not pressed at the time, a precedent had been established for papal prerogatives which would be revived in future struggles over the governance of Christendom.

Benedict of Aniane (d. 821) was a monk who became an advisor of Louis, but his primary importance to history was as the "second founder of Benedictinism." He was a reformer who lived the life of an ascetic, and, inspired with this ideal, he advocated not only a more disciplined regimen for monks, but he also opposed the proprietary system. He succeeded in convincing Charlemagne to grant his monastery freedom from all control, either by a bishop or lay lord, reserving his sole loyalty to the pope. This freedom from external influences is known as exemption. Benedict also promoted the idea that monasteries should join in filiations or federations rather than each one being an independent house under episcopal or lay supervision. This was the beginning of the concept of monasteries becoming an order (although Pachomius in Egypt may have had this in mind in the fourth century). A meeting of monastic leaders was called by the emporer, held in Aachen in 817, which enacted legislation that had a significant impact on the future of medieval monasticism. The Benedictine *Rule* was established as the only acceptable Rule for monks; agricultural labor was regarded as unsuitable for monks, who should be engaged in prayer; monks were forbidden to teach any except the monastery oblates (young monks in formation); and considerable additions were made to the daily prayer life of the monastery. In addition to this, Benedict of Aniane produced two significant works: the *Codex Regularum*, a collection of monastic rules written prior to the Benedictine, and the *Concordia Regularum*, which was a concordance of parallel passages from various rules to compare with those of Benedict. Each succeeding reform movement in monasticism looked to the Capitulary of 817 as its ideal.

Charlemagne's empire disintegrated following his death. Among reasons cited for this are its over-extension and the impossibility of governing a territory that exceeded modern Germany and France in extent. The empire contained numerous ethnic and tribal loyalties—Avars, Lombards, Saxons, Bavarians—that were constantly agitating to be independent. Another factor undermining unity was the invasions of Europe which marked the ninth and tenth centuries. There was also a dearth of strong personalities. Men with such characteristic names as Louis, "the Pious," Charles, "the Simple," Charles, "the Fat," Louis, "the Child," and Louis, "the Stammerer," made futile attempts to regain imperial stability. But the more immediate problem of Louis was civil war among his sons for title to the throne. After he died (840) a settlement was reached at Verdun in 843 whereby Louis, "the German," received East Francia (Germany), Charles, "the Bald," received West Francia (France), and Lothair received the title of emperor as well as northern Italy and a strip of land running to the North Sea (Lotharingia; this strip, or corridor, contained Alsace and Lorraine, territories which remained in contention between France and Germany up until World War II). The empire in reality was never restored, and the vicissitudes of its various territories must henceforth be addressed separately, but first we must consider the new invasions of Europe from the south, north, and east between 800–1000.

As early as the 820s Muslim pirates began to ravage the northern coast of the Mediterranean from northern Spain to Italy. These pirates were known as the Saracens and included Arabs, Berbers, and Moors. They conquered Sicily, Corsica, and Sardinia, and invaded southern Italy, sacking Rome itself in 846. Although these pirates did not settle and establish governments, they nevertheless inflicted serious economic and physical hardships on their victims, and made travel dangerous. The leader of the Frankish resistance was Louis II, son of Lothair, who spent most of his life fighting the Saracens; in spite of his efforts, Islamic hegemony over the Mediterranean lasted until the eleventh century.

Far more threatening to the stability of Europe were attacks by tribes from Scandinavia to the north, known collectively as Vikings. These attacks began as early as 787 with the Danes invading England. In 878 Alfred the Great (d. 899), at the Treaty of Wedmore, brought some peace by permitting the Danes to settle in eastern England, a territory known as the Danelaw, in return for which they also accepted Christianity. (Today Danish placenames can still be detected in the suffixes "by" and "thorpe," and the Anglo-Saxon by "ton" or "ham"). From about 840 on the Vikings attacked West Francia, aiming primarily at the population centers—Cologne, Rouen, Nantes, Orleans, and Bordeaux. Paris was sacked repeatedly in 845, 851, and 861. In 882 Charles, "the Fat," gave up Frisia as a Danelaw. In 885 Paris was again the victim of attack by forty thousand men in seven hundred vessels, but the following year they were diverted with a bribe. Favorite targets for looting were the monasteries, as a century of peace had brought them gold, precious gems, and priceless manuscripts, and the monks offered little effective resistance. In many places ecclesiastical centers were destroyed, along with their libraries, and the residents were killed or dispersed. "Christianity was deprived of its intellectual centers: it was virtually beheaded."[15] The church saw the Norse ravages as God's punishment and sometimes preached resignation and surrender. In 911 Charles, "the Simple," gave a large territory of western France to the Normans and their leader, Rollo. In time they settled on the land, became stabilized, and cultivated what today is called Normandy.

While the western Franks were suffering the depradations of the Saracens and especially the Vikings, eastern Francia was inundated by the Magyars, the founders of Hungary. Already during Charlemagne's lifetime his oldest son, Charles, spent most of his life campaigning against them in central Germany. In 919 the Saxonian dynasty replaced the Carolingians in East Francia, and it was they who successfully defended the West against the Magyars. It was a great victory at Lechfeld by Otto I in 955 which is usually associated with the final defeat of these invaders. "One of the most serious features of these three waves of invasion . . . was that they were simultaneous, so that in the second half of the ninth century Carolingian Europe was threatened on all sides at once."[16] The general results of these invasions was depopulation, decline of agriculture, impoverishment, disruption of life, the end of unitary rule with the fragmentation of political power, and the destruction of property, primarily that of the church.

With the decline of the Carolingians and the dismemberment of Charlemagne's empire new rulers emerged to fill the vacuum. In France the Capetian dynasty began in 987 and continued for over three centuries until 1328. This is not to imply that kings enjoyed authority or power, for tenth-century France was made up of hundreds of centers of power with a few larger and more influential fiefs controlled by lords who were virtually kings in their own right. Feudalism, which followed upon the collapse of the Carolingians, was a politically decentralized society. Hugh Capet (987–996), the first of the new dynasty, was crowned by the Archbishop of Rheims who said that "the throne is not by hereditary right," thus declaring Hugh's election by the nobles legitimate. This "election" (which simply meant the assent of the most powerful princes) was primarily brought about by the efforts of Gerbert of Aurillac, one of the ablest churchmen of his time, who later became Pope Sylvester II. Hugh's son, Robert I (996–1031) followed, and distinguished himself by plotting against the nobles to extend the royal domain. Henry I (1031-1060) was succeeded by Philip I (1060-1108) whose policy of extending the king's authority by annexing the lands of nobles succeeded in strengthening royal authority. He is sometimes called the father of French bureaucracy. It was during his time that the Duke of Normandy, William, invaded England in 1066, thus ending Anglo-Saxon rule there.

The Carolingian line came to an end in Germany in 911. At the time, and throughout medieval history to early modern times, Germany was dominated by five powerful families known as the stem duchies; Saxony, Bavaria, Franconia, Swabia, and Lorraine. Henry I (919–936), the first of the Saxon dynasty, made kingship strong. His attitude toward the church was cordial, using bishops as allies in his struggle against the nobility, but he refused to receive royal coronation. He renewed the fight against the Magyars when they came to collect tribute money which had been promised by his predecessor by giving them a dead dog instead. In the ensuing battles he defeated the Magyars. Otto I (936–973) received the royal annointing from the Archbishop of Rheims and adopted a policy of supporting the bishops. As with most rulers of the time, he personally appointed bishops to their office, and he retained the right of approving decrees of church councils. Otto was the first of several German rulers for whom Italy held a fatal fascination. The pope, the notorious John XII, invited Otto to free Italy from another ruler, Berengar. In this Otto succeeded, and as a reward the pope conferred on him the imperial crown in 962, thus reviving once again the Roman imperial image, only this time it was the Holy Roman Empire, a political entity that lasted, at least in name, until Napolean declared it dead in 1806. Otto, who was accustomed to obedience from his bishops, expected the same from the Bishop of Rome. When John XII was found to be intriguing against him, Otto deposed him and set up his own pope. In his policy of expansion of German influence, Otto also created the metropolitan see of Magdeburg for the Slavs, the bishopric of Posen for the Poles, and that of Prague for the Bohemians. He was also active in promoting the conversion of the Hungarians. Otto is known to history as "the Great" with good reason. His empire extended as wide as Charlemagne's, he supported Christian missions, the petty nobility were brought under one strong ruler, and the Hungarians were finally defeated.

Otto II (973–983) lacked much of his father's foresight and wisdom. He became embroiled in dynastic quarrels, including a formidable coalition which formed against him. He went to war with the king of France, and then he turned south to Italy, where he deposed a pope accused of murder and replaced him. He unsuccessfully attempted to conquer southern Italy, and he died enroute home to Germany where several revolts had broken out during his absence.

Otto III (983–1002) spent much of his time in Italy. He had his cousin elected pope as Gregory V, and when he died Otto raised Gerbert of Aurillac to the Papacy as Sylvester II (the first French pope), whom we have already met as influential in securing the French throne for the Capetians. Otto III died in Italy, not quite twenty-two years old, "the youthful dreamer of universal empire who never got beyond the realm of theory."[17] He died without heirs, and Henry II (1002–1024), in the Saxon dynastic line, became emperor. His rule was effective and just. Following the policies of his predecessors, he favored the church and controlled it, freely making ecclesiastical appointments with the understanding that his office combined both temporal and spiritual obligations. He was canonized a saint in 1146.

With the death of Henry II the Saxonian line came to an end; Conrad II (1024–1039), great-great-grandson of Otto I, began the Franconian line of rulers. He succeeded in pacifying the frontiers and in bringing order to northern Italy, but he alienated the clergy through unwise episcopal appointments and his control of the church. Although Henry III (1039–1056) was religious and in favor of church reforms, he also inherited the prevailing imperial theory of absolute control over ecclesiastical affairs. In 1046 he journeyed to Rome to be crowned emperor, but upon his arrival he discovered that three rival candidates claimed to be pope. At the council of Sutri, Henry dismissed all three and selected his own candidate, who died shortly thereafter, as did Henry's next appointee, both poisoned by anti-imperial factions. Henry's third appointee, Leo IX (1049–1054), lived only five more years, but in this time he appointed dedicated reform-minded cardinals from north of the Alps (i.e. non-Italians), "which was a radical innovation that changed the whole institutional structure of the Roman church."[18] Leo traveled throughout France and Germany, holding councils which promulgated sweeping reforms, and in so doing he set into motion the great controversy over investitures, which we shall consider later. It is ironic that high on the list of such reforms was freedom from imperial control of the church; but in the mid–eleventh century such control was often to the benefit of the church, and it was the emperor's appointment of a reform minded pope which brought about the challenge of his right to do so.

The first great medieval pope after Gregory, "the Great," was Nicholas I (858–867) who aimed to free the Papacy from the control of rulers. In a letter to Michael III, the Eastern emperor, Nicholas wrote: "It is plainly proved that the secular power can neither bind or loose the Roman pontiff, whom, as is well known, Constantine called God, and God cannot be judged by man."[19] When King Lothair II (855–869) wanted to divorce his wife, the pope forbade him to do so despite the fact that the king had secured the approval of his own bishops. Archbishop Hincmar of Rheims was forced to restore a bishop whom he had deposed. The Archbishop of Ravenna despoiled some papal properties and declared himself autonomous. Nicholas excommunicated him despite the protests of Louis II. He intervened directly in the affairs of the Eastern church during the Photian schism by declaring against the patriarch's legitimacy. It was during this time that the Pseudo-Isidorian decretals came to light, a collection of genuine and forged materials probably from Germany whose primary purpose was to free bishops from temporal rulers and from the authority of archbishops, reserve ecclesiastical cases for church courts, and to a lesser extent support papal primacy. Altogether this collection includes over one hundred spurious papal letters as well as the Donation of Constantine. It was not until the investiture controversy that the decrees were used to support the papal position. Their veracity was questioned during the fifteenth century, and they were proved to be forgeries in the seventeenth century. The importance of the ninth century in the history of the Papacy lay in the precedents of primacy which were established for the future.

Hincmar of Rheims (806–882) was another strong ninth-century prelate who supported the integrity and autonomy of the metropolitan against secular rulers and the pope. He strongly opposed Lothair I, King of Lorraine; he deposed one bishop for attacking his privileges, but he was restored by Pope Nicholas I, and he deposed his own nephew as bishop for refusing to acknowledge his authority, insisting on the rights of a metropolitan over his bishops. He also crowned Charles, "the Bald," as king despite the pope's objections, and he was actively involved in several of the theological disputes of his time, as we shall see. He was probably the first exponent of Gallicanism, the assertion by the French church of complete freedom from the authority of the papacy.

Early in the ninth century (910) a monastic reform movement began with the establishment of the monastery of Cluny by Berno of Baume, whose founders sought to return to a literal understanding of the Rule, to simplicity of life, and to prayer. They were influenced by the reforms enacted earlier by Benedict of Aniane and the council of Aaachen in 817, but which had never been attempted. One of the most significant aspects of the new foundation was its charter, given by Duke William of Aquitane, in which he gave the monks the right of free election of their abbot and protection from all infringements from outside, placing them directly under the protection of the pope. It was an exempt house, which privilege would be extended to all houses derived from or affiliated with Cluny. Under the succession of a long line of able abbots, Cluny grew to be the a formidable order with its reforms spreading throughout Europe. By 1100 the total number of houses which adhered directly to Cluny or followed its regimen was more than 1,150. These affiliations were of various kinds:

1. Daughter houses under the direct jurisdiction of Cluny's abbot.
2. Monasteries incorporated into the Cluniac system but retaining their own abbot.
3. Associates of Cluny with freedom greater than those listed above.
4. Those who followed Cluniac usages but had only ties of friendship.

The Abbot of Cluny was like a feudal lord at the apex of a pyramid.

The chief duty of these monks was one of prayer, in which they departed from the Rule, for they observed little *lectio divina* and no manual labor, which was done by servants. Silence was heavily emphasized, from which there developed an elaborate sign language. What Cluny offered to Europe was "the spectacle of true monks, detached, humble, chaste and obedient, occupied in the continual service of God by means of a highly developed type of liturgical worship."[20] The Cluniac monk spent almost the entire day at worship. In 1132 the church at Cluny was the largest in Europe (555 feet long).

The influence of Cluny was immense. Numerous houses in Europe followed its customs and were leaders of local reform movements. Also in England we find a tenth-century revival reflecting Cluny's ideals, led by a triumvirate of strong abbots: Dunstan, Abbot of Glastonbury; Ethelwold, Abbot of Abingdon; Oswald, Abbot of Westbury. From these centers various other monasteries soon sprang up. In order to bring uniformity into the English practices, a document was drawn up in 970, the *Regularis Concordia*, which set out the customs to be followed. The solemn liturgy is considered the chief work of monks with daily Communion, and they enjoy a special relationship with royalty who are the protectors of the monasteries with all abbatial elections subject to their approval. Thus, after the disintegration of the Carolingian empire and the anarchy accompanying the barbarian invasions, European Christianity was poised at the threshold of the twelfth century, with confidence born of a sense of Christendom but with serious unresolved issues, primarily in the right relationship between sacred and secular, church and society, pope and emperor.

Theological Controversies

Theology in the early Middle Ages was largely derived from and an interpretation of the Augustinian tradition. The *Sentences* of Isidore of Seville and the work of the Venerable Bede leaned heavily on Augustine, and for centuries this traditionalism went unchallenged. There were, however, several theological controversies, some of which were precipitated by unresolved tensions within the Augustinian tradition itself. Adoptionism, a revival of the heresy of Paul of Samosata, was more reflective of the continued vitality of Arinaism in Spain, brought earlier by the Visigoths and Vandals. Its leaders, Elipandus of Toledo and Felix of Urgel (d. 818) claimed that Christ's deity was a result of his adoption into the godhead. Their teachings were condemned by three synods under Charlemagne, and Alcuin as well as Agobard of Lyons wrote books against Felix.

One area in which Augustine remained unclear was the Lord's Supper. His writings, as well as those of others, could be used to support various interpretations of Christ's presence in the Eucharist. Paschasius Radbertus (d. 865) taught that by the consecration the elements were truly changed into the body and blood of Christ, although this occurred inwardly; externally the elements retained their original characteristics. His work, *On the Body and Blood of the Lord*, is the first monograph on the Lord's Supper in Christian history.[21] He also denied that unbelievers truly received Christ in the sacrament. Ratramnus, supported by Rabanus Maurus, insisted that Christ's presence was real but spiritual. At the time Ratramnus prevailed, but popular piety sided with Radbertus's emphatic realism, which won the day at the Fourth Lateran Council in 1215, which declared transubstantiation a dogma (see chapter 7). Radbertus also taught that the Virgin Mary, in order to preserve her perpetual virginity, gave birth to Christ *clauso utero* (the womb was not opened in giving birth). This notion, however, had no future in the church.

Another unfinished item from Augustine's legacy had to do with anthropology and the ultimate destiny of humans.[22] Augustine taught that God had preordained some people to salvation and others to condemnation. At the Council of Orange (529) the idea of a predetermined condemnation was rejected without naming Augustine or impugning his memory, making possible a more optimistic view of human nature. Gottschalk (d. 869), friend of Walafrid Strabo, monk of Rabanus Maurus, and student of Ratramnus, taught a rigid form of double predestination in which he said that from the beginning of time God had determined who would be condemned. His critics, principally Rabanus Maurus (d. 856) and Hincmar of Rheims (d. 882), pointed out that his views restricted the universal availability of God's grace and of redemption, made God the author of evil, and called into question the role of free will. They suggested that a distinction must be made between foreknowledge and predestination. Gottschalk was condemned, died unreconciled, and he was buried in unhallowed ground. The controversy had in reality to do with reconciling Augustine with Augustine. Gottschalk also became involved in a Trinitarian controversy in which he defended the idea of using the term "triune deity" for God, a concept which was found unacceptable.

These controversies involved only the church in the West. The church in the East, meanwhile, was engaged in its own theological turmoils, all of them relating in some fashion to European Christianity as well. The first of these was the Filioque controversy. The Nicene Creed as completed in 381 declared that the Holy Spirit "proceeds from the Father." At the Synod of Toledo in 529 the creed was expanded to include a double source of deity for the Spirit, "who proceeds from the Father *and the Son*" (*filioque* = and the Son). This was done as an anti-Arian polemic; by declaring a dual source of life for the Holy Spirit the status of the Son as equal to the Father was reinforced. Although Toledo was only a local synod, the custom of reciting the clause gradually grew in the West, and by 800 when the creed entered the liturgy the Filioque was commonly accepted. In 809 at a Synod of Aachen, Charlemagne declared it orthodox, but it was not until after 1000 that it was accepted in Rome. The addition was vigorously opposed in the East, and it has been a point of contention in all the efforts at reunion between the churches ever since, down to our own time. At least two issues are at stake: one is whether the Bible and tradition support naming the Son as a source of the divine nature, and a second is the propriety of changing creeds to suit a political agenda, and whether a local council or bishop (pope) has such authority. In other words, to whom does the creed belong?

The most serious and volatile theological controversy of the eighth and ninth centuries was basically internal to the Byzantine church, but it also affected relations with the West. This was the iconoclastic controversy, which lasted from 726 to 843. The icon (image) was to the Eastern Christians more than a mere picture or mosaic. It was the "window" through which one could apprehend the divine, and as such an icon could be said to possess the divine presence itself. One's attitude toward an icon could express one's attitude toward the person represented (perhaps like the picture of a loved one), and the faithful were accustomed to bringing flowers, candles, and incense to their icons, carrying them in procession and kissing them as part of the liturgical rites.

In 726 Emperor Leo III declared that all such images were idols, and he ordered their destruction. His reason for this has remained a puzzle, but suggestions have been made that it was due to Monophysite influence, which minimized the human side of Christ. Also, some who came from eastern Syria, the home of Leo III, looked with suspicion on things physical, and they believed that a likeness of God or Christ painted on a board, or any emphasis on the humanity of Jesus, was Judaistic and blasphemous. Another motive may have been political, as Leo tried by this means to gain greater control over the church and especially over the multitude of monks, most of whom were strongly attached to their icons. A persecution of "iconodules" ("idol worshipers," as their opponents derisively called them) was unleashed, but strong support for the use of icons in worship came from John of Damascus, the leading Byzantine theologian of the time and possibly of the century. "It is disastrous to suppose that the Church does not know God as He is, that she degenerates into idolatry. . . . The one thing to be aimed at is not to adore a created thing more than the Creator, nor to give worship except to Him alone."[23] Pope Gregory III held two synods at Rome condemning Leo's action (731), but many monks in the East became martyrs in the cause of icons. In 787, under the regent Irene, the Seventh Ecumenical Council at Nicea reversed Leo's policy and permitted icons to receive *doulia* (veneration). Unfortunately, Charlemagne received a faulty translation (or interpretation) of these proceedings, and in the Caroline Books of 794 (probably written by Theodulf of Orleans), he condemned the council, though later popes and theologians accepted it as ecumenical.

Shortly after Irene's regency the controversy again broke out, but in 843 another woman, the regent Theodora, reaffirmed the decisions of 787, thus bringing the issue to a close. The first Sunday in Lent has since been observed by churches in the East in honor of icons and in recognition of the end of the controversy as the "Great Feast of Orthodoxy."

Shortly after the end of this controversy another arose, the Photian schism, which seems more overtly a matter of power than theology. In 858 Emperor Michael III deposed the patriarch, Ignatius, replacing him with a respected theologian, Photius. Both sides appealed to Pope Nicholas I, whose legates favored the change, but the pope reversed their actions and said that Ignatius was still the lawful patriarch. Photius responded with a strong condemnation of the West in general and of the pope in particular, the first Eastern theologian to accuse Rome of innovation in the Filioque. "They are preaching a novel doctrine, that the Holy Spirit proceeds not from the Father alone, but from the Son as well . . . This is enough to bring ten thousand anathemas upon them."[24] Pope Nicholas answered in kind with a letter to all the bishops in the West in which he claimed the primacy of the Roman See. Meanwhile there was a dispute about whether Rome or Constantinople should evangelize Bulgaria. Ignatius, having been restored to the patriarchate, began to consecrate bishops in Bulgaria, which Nicholas denounced. After Ignatius' death Photius was again appointed patriarch, this time with Nicholas' approval.

The final melancholy scene between East and West took place in 1054 when the patriarch, Michael Cerularius, published a manifesto accusing the Latins of four errors: (1) the use of unleavened bread in the Eucharist, (2) the custom of fasting on Saturdays, (3) the eating of meat of strangled animals, (4) forbidding the Alleluia in Lent. Two further complaints were the use of the *filioque* and the papal enforcement of celibacy on priests. Cerularius closed the Latin churches in Constantinople and ordered Latin monasteries to conform to Greek usages. Pope Leo IX (1049–1054) protested by contending that Rome was superior to all the churches, and the Greeks were being permitted their aberrations only by suffrance. The pope sent three legates to Constantinople to discuss their differences, but they were received with insolence. The patriarch ordered the pope's name removed from the diptychs (list of authorized names for whom prayers are said), and in retaliation the papal legates laid on the altar of Hagia Sophia a sentence of anathema against Cerularius and his followers. The patriarch in turn excommunicated the pope, and the schism thus begun has continued to the present.[25]

The Byzantine Ethos

The church in the East developed a life and style different from that in the West, the beginning of which we have already considered.[26] One of the legacies of old Rome to Byzantium was the supremacy of the emperor in matters of religion as well as state. Constantine himself had called the first ecumenical council; each of the six subsequent councils, all held in the East, was likewise convened by emperors who promulgated their decrees as imperial law. The concentration of civil as well as religious power in the hands of the secular ruler has been called caesaropapism, although the term was unknown in medieval times. The obverse situation, when a religious leader also wields secular power, has been called a theocracy. In the West there were times when society appeared to veer from one to the other, but basically there was an attempt made to distinguish the two. The differences between East and West are sometimes traced back to Augustine and Eusebius. Where Augustine saw the relationship between church and state as one of tension between the "city of God" and the "city of the world," with the former possessing a moral superiority, Eusebius saw the state as the protector of the church and the emperor as God's vicar on earth, His image, to whom the church owed support and gratitude. Emperor and patriarch were to work in harmony for the welfare of society, as Emperor Leo VI wrote in the ninth century: "The peace and felicity of subjects in body and soul depends on the agreement and concord of the kingship and priesthood in all things."[27] But the ideal was rarely realized. Emperor Leo III claimed authority from St. Peter to feed the flock of God, privileged to preach and to call councils, and to administer the church.[28]

In church structure the patriarch was at the apex of the hierarchy, assisted by metropolitans who were set over ecclesiastical provinces, each of which was subdivided into bishoprics. Although most parish priests were married, bishops were required to be celibate, which accounts for the fact that many of them came from monasteries. During the fourth century the patriarch of Constantinople claimed precedence over all other Eastern churches because he resided in the capital. The three other eastern patriarchs at Jerusalem, Antioch, and Alexandria resisted his pretensions, as did the pope at Rome, primarily because Constantinople was not of apostolic foundation. But the Muslim conquests of the older churches during the seventh century left the patriarch of Constantinople as the sole leader of the Eastern churches. His authority never became as centralized as that of the Papacy in the West, but he governed the churches as "first among equals," leaving each of the metropolitans and bishops largely in control of their own jurisdictions.

Monasticism was a strong factor in the life of the Eastern church, and by the eighth century tens of thousands of men and women lived in religious communities or alone. The eremitical examples of early Egyptian hermits appealed to many and, unlike Western monastics, Eastern monks usually did not become involved in the life of the church in the world, excepting those who became bishops. Mount Athos in Greece, isolated on a narrow peninsula in the Aegean, was well populated with hermits, and to this day it remains a magnet for the eremitical life. Byzantine monks never organized themselves into orders, but the Rule of Saint Basil remains foundational for the cloistered life.

Byzantine worship was surrounded with rich ceremonial and conducted in churches decorated with mosaics and frescoes representing Christ and the saints. The Liturgy of the Eucharist, usually that of St. John Chrysostom or Saint Basil, was celebrated as a timeless event, an appearance of Christ in which the worshipers experienced the actual event of the Supper, not as it was or will be but as it is forever. The service began with the "Little Entrance" and the singing of the Trisagion ("Holy, Holy, Holy") followed by the Lessons and sermon. Then came the "Great Entrance" in which the celebrant carried around the church the bread and wine which were to be consecrated while the choir sang and the people responded to the exalted entry of Christ Himself. The Nicene Creed and the commemoration of the living and dead followed (diptychs), and then came the consecration of the elements themselves, in which the *epiklesis* or prayer for the Holy Spirit was central. (In the West the words of Christ, "Take, eat, etc." came to be considered the heart of the liturgy.) Most of the liturgical action took place at the altar which was closed off from the worshipers by the *iconastasis*, the icon screen. All communicants received both wine and leavened bread with a spoon from a single chalice. Although the Eastern church was never much concerned with fixing a definite number of sacraments, it observed the same rites as the West except confirmation. In the East baptism of infants by immersion was immediately followed by chrismation; infants as well as adults therefore communed at the Eucharist.

Byzantine Christianity emphasized the incarnation of Christ and the mysteries attending the relationship between Christ's human and divine natures. The saving nature of the incarnation is most clearly expressed in the words of Athanasius, "God became human that humans might become divine." (In the West the tendency was to hold Christ's crucifixion as being of central importance.) Christ's divine nature was the primary focus of devotion, as can be seen in the iconographic figure of the *Christus Pantokrator*, the All-Ruler who presides in most Orthodox churches from the height of the apse. As in the West, the Virgin Mary as well as the saints were included in devotional piety. The rites, sacraments, liturgy, and art assisted to transport the believer out of the material world into the presence of the divine, and the Easter festival was celebrated with special solemnity as the event which liberated Christ from his human form.

Scripture and the decisions of the first seven ecumenical councils together were considered the basis of the Orthodox faith. ("Orthodox" in its restricted sense has from earliest times applied to those churches in communion with that of Constantinople.) The Nicene Creed of 381 was accepted as the only authoritative creedal statement and as such is the one creed that almost all Christians confess. In addition to Scripture and the councils, theological tradition is also authoritative, including the writings of theologians. Perhaps the most authoritative of these is John of Damascus (d. 749), whose contributions were more in the nature of method than in originality. His major work, *The Fount of Knowledge*, is in three parts: an appreciation of the philosophy of Aristotle in the elucidation of Christian dogma, a description of one hundred heresies, and an exposition of the Orthodox faith (*De Orthodoxa Fide*) with special reference to the two natures of Christ. "When we speak of the divinity we do not attribute the properties of the humanity to it. Thus we never speak of a passible or created divinity. Neither do we predicate the divine properties of the flesh, for we never speak of uncreated flesh or humanity. In the case of the person, however, whether we name it from both of the parts or from one of them, we attribute the properties of both natures to it."[29] John taught the divine maternity of Mary, her exemption from original sin, and her bodily assumption into heaven. He also emphasized a real presence of the body and blood of Christ in the Eucharist. Two of his Easter hymns are still favorites today: "Come, Ye Faithful, Raise the Strain" and "The Day of Resurrection." Thomas Aquinas was greatly in debt to John of Damascus for his methodology.

Theodore of Studios (d. 826) was another influential theologian, a vigorous opponent of iconoclasm who supported churchly independence from lay control. His energy and organizing genius made his monastery at Studios the center of reform in the East. His writings include a short and long *Catechesis*, an *Exposition of the Liturgy of the Presanctified*, spiritual orations, a list of canonical penances, several works against the iconoclasts, poetry, and correspondence.

While Western Christianity was in its deepest humiliation, the Eastern church was enjoying its greatest strength. Byzantine culture, the creation of the church, was in full flower, and Constantinople combined the intellectual glory of ancient Athens with the military might of Rome. The Western crusaders, coming from their feudal, rustic, provincial enclaves, stood in amazement at the glory of the East. "So long as Constantinople endured as a free Christian city, its Church remained the most civilized religious organization that the world had so far known."[30]

CHAPTER FOUR

RECOVERY IN THE WEST

Reform of the Papacy

The period from 1050 to 1130 has been called "one of the great turning points in European history," a period of enormous commercial expansion, the rise of urban communities, and the first expression of a truly middle class.[1] The Gregorian reforms of the Papacy led directly to the investiture controversy and to relative freedom of the church from state control, which led in turn to papal domination of secular rulers. That papal reform was urgently needed there is no doubt. After Nicholas I (d. 867) until 964 the Papacy suffered a series of incompetent and dissolute incumbents, due in large part to the fact that it was the prize of warring aristocratic families in Rome. By the year 1000 there was an awakening perception of the need for greater discipline and higher standards for all clergy, but especially for the papacy. Two evils in particular which needed to be addressed were simony (buying and selling church offices) and clerical marriage. The Ottonian rulers in Germany intervened in papal affairs by appointing such exemplary men as Sylvester II (999–1003), but they were not successful in bringing stability. Reform was initiated from outside the Papacy in the Cluniac movement which was sweeping over Europe, and found in King Henry III (1039–1056) of Germany a staunch supporter. It was he who convened a synod at Sutri in 1046 which deposed one pope and elevated another, to be followed in quick succession by four more German appointees. "Whether his reasons were political or religious hardly matters. Henry's purpose was to lift the Papacy out of the field of Roman party politics, and this was desirable for political as for moral reasons."[2] It was with one of these German appointees, Leo IX (1049–1054) that real reform began.

One of Leo's goals was to rescue the Papacy from the Roman factions that had held it captive. He first appointed new cardinals to assist him, all except one from across the Alps. Humbert, a French monk and scholar, was strongly opposed to simony; Hugh Candidus was the pope's foreign ambassador; Hildebrand, the future Gregory VII, was administrator of the papal estates; and Peter Damian, a Camaldolese monk and ascetic who was zealously opposed to simony and clerical marriage, acted as court theologian. With these appoinments Leo declared his independence from Roman factionalism, and during his short five-year pontificate he spent less than six months in Rome. No reigning pope had been north of the Alps in two hundred fifty years. Leo's vision of the Papacy was that the pope was the head of all of Christendom, and this understanding prompted immense and unprecedented activity during his rule. Although such claims to universal jurisdiction had been made by others, most popes had little notion of themselves as leaders of Christendom. "The idea of the Papacy as a moral force, or as the directing head of a Church community, took shape north of the Alps, first in the hands of the Anglo-Saxon missionaries in the days of St. Boniface, and then in the hands of the eleventh century reformers."[3]

Leo took his program of moral reform to France and Germany, and there he convened a number of councils at which priests and bishops were interrogated about their lives. Not everyone agreed with the pope or supported his agenda. Lay patronage of church offices had been customary for centuries, often to the mutual benefit of both parties, and there was resistance to changing the *status quo*. Rulers often relied upon the loyalty of their clerical appointees as a counterbalance to the nobility. As to clerical marriage, it was obvious that monks living in a community should be celibate, but it was not so clear why priests who were living in a committed and exemplary monogamous relationship were endangering the moral standards of society. But with married clergy there was also the danger that church lands would become the hereditary possessions of sons, reducing the right of appointment by bishops or lay lords. Clerical marriage, therefore, had as much to do with hereditary rights as with theological rationale. Although Leo's attempt to reform the Papacy was welcome and successful, his initiatives to rid the church of simony and clerical marriage met with resistance. The Archbishop of Rouen was stoned and barely escaped with his life in 1072 when he attempted to punish married priests.[4] It was clear that moral example and moderate persuasion would not be sufficient to bring about a change, so the next step in the reform program was to reinforce papal authority.

Two events signal the expansion of papal claims. The first was in the controversy with the Eastern patriarch Cerularius which was in reality a confrontation between two forces, each of which claimed to possess authority which the other denied, resulting in mutual excommunication. The second was in the promulgation of a new collection of canon law. An earlier collection, the *Decretum*, compiled by Burchard of Worms in 1012, barely mentioned the pope, being concerned primarily about priestly lives. The new canon law, called "Collection in 74 Titles," appearing about 1050, was primarily concerned with papal prerogatives. In this the pope was also assisted by appealing to the Pseudo-Isidorian decretals which supported papal primacy. In light of later events, it should be emphasized that Leo was primarily interested in the moral reform of the clergy; he did not oppose the practice of lay investiture of clergy by lay rulers. He and Henry III remained on good terms throughout his pontificate. In 1054 the pope led an army against Norman invaders of southern Italy who were threatening papal territories; the army was defeated, and Leo was captured and died.

Leo was followed by two popes of short duration in office, during whose time a treatise by Humbert appeared, *Three Books Against Simoniacs*, proposing that all sacraments performed by simoniacal priests were invalid and attacking lay investiture, the first time this was included in the reforming agenda. It was undoubtedly with the advice of Humbert that in 1059 Pope Nicholas II (1059–1061) issued a decree that radically changed the way in which popes were elected. Henceforth they were to be selected by the cardinal bishops, agreed to by the other cardinals, and approved by the clergy and people of Rome. (Since the sixth century, cardinals had been the principal advisors of the pope, ranked in order as cardinal-bishops, cardinal-priests, and cardinal-deacons.) This effectively excluded all lay rights in the process, particularly those of the emperor. Predictably the German bishops refused to acquiesce in the decree, but to no avail. The decree reads in part: "To be sure that the disease of venality will have no opportunity to creep in, the churchmen shall have the leading part in effecting the election of the pope, and the others shall only be followers."[5] It is not without significance that Henry III had died prematurely in 1056 at age thirty-seven, in the pope's arms, leaving his six-year-old son, Henry IV, as heir. While these momentous decisions were being made in Rome, the empire was ruled by Henry's widow, Empress Agnes, serving as regent for their son. During the minority of Henry IV, two more popes were elected by the college of cardinals, thus establishing a precedent for the new system. The papal reform party also allied itself with anti-imperial forces in Germany which sought to take advantage of the boy-king. Pope Nicholas II signed a peace treaty with the Normans in southern Italy, thus freeing the Papacy from that threat for a time. As part of this treaty the Norman ruler, Robert Guiscard, agreed to defend any pope elected by the cardinals, thus backing up the new electoral decree with military might. The Germans reacted by declaring all of Nicholas' actions null and void.

Alexander II (1061–1073) continued his predecessor's policies as pope by declaring all sacred acts performed by married clergy as invalid, and by opposing simony. Peter Damian attempted a reconciliation with the German king by suggesting that there should be friendship and understanding between them, but in these efforts he was strenuously resisted by Hildebrand, the future Gregory VII, who by this time had become the most powerful figure in the papal curia, to whom Peter Danian referred as my "holy Satan." It was "less through deliberate antagonism than through the development of events after 1056, that a head-on collision was in preparation."[6] Henry IV began to rule in his own right in 1065 when he turned sixteen, and Hildebrand, though not a priest, was seized by the Roman mob and forcibly installed into office following the death of Alexander II in 1073. It was only later, after he had received ordination, that the cardinals duly elected him, and he assumed the name Gregory VII. The stage was set for an unprecedented struggle between papacy and empire, because the problem at hand was primarily with the German king and not with the other rulers of Europe.

The issue was the ambiguity inherent in the fact that clergy were to be obedient to ecclesiastical authority by virtue of their vows and to secular authority by virtue of being their subjects through land holdings. Both pope and emperor claimed to rule by divine right, and each side appealed to biblical precedent and the Western tradition. The question of lay investiture was also filled with ambiguities. In the Middle Ages, wealth lay in the land, and there was no question about the rights of lay lords to be in possesion of land, to defend it against attack, and to parcel it out among vassals. Churchmen, especially bishops, also required land for their support. Sometimes the land was the direct possession of a lay lord, who therefore had the right to appoint a vassal of his own choice to cultivate it. Even when it was church land the lay lord retained his rights of defending the domain, especially if it was a duchy along his borders, in which case a strong military presence was mandatory. Lay lords understandably were inclined to appoint good administrators or skilled soldiers to the position, with the qualifications associated with the office of bishop being secondary. This is why lay lords viewed with alarm the church's claim to the sole right of making ecclesiastical appointments. The proprietary church system was everywhere. By the eleventh century few important church officials were selected by church leaders; most bishops were lay appointees who owed their position to a lay ruler's favor. In 1050 there were seventy-seven dioceses in France, of which the king controlled twenty-five; the rest were in the hands of dukes, counts, or viscounts.[7] Under these circumstances it was often impossible for ecclesiastics to discharge their responsibilities conscientiously. Sometimes leading prelates took their secular duties as royal administrators or counts more seriously than they did their spiritual functions. When a lord bequeathed land upon a vassal, he followed a ceremony in which a clod of earth or some token symbolizing the land was given to the kneeling vassal, who in turn pledged his loyalty to the lord. The vassal did not own the land but was responsible for its good management. It reverted to the lord by the terms of the agreement. At issue in the investiture controversy was whether kings and princes, when they conferred temporal duties and responsibilities (lands and buildings) on bishops, could also give them the rights of spiritual office by means of the ring and pastoral staff. The pope questioned the right of lay rulers to influence clerical appointments. Because these issues were symbolized in the ceremony of investiture, the struggle between pope and emperor has become known as the Investiture Controversy.[8]

The Investiture Controversy

During the minority of Henry IV there were rebellions of nobles throughout Germany, most seriously in Saxony. Upon reaching his majority Henry's first task was to regain imperial control over these fractious rebels. During this time Henry followed a conciliatory attitude toward the Papacy since he could ill afford to fight both the pope and the rebels simultaneously. As a result, Gregory VII did not hesitate to put his program into action. Less than a year after his elevation, at a Lenten Synod of 1074, he declared that simoniacal priests were forbidden to celebrate the sacraments, were to be expelled from office, and married priests likewise were barred from celebrating mass. The decrees met with stiff resistance, including that of the majority of the clergy of France, Germany, England, and Scandinavia. In France "the leaders of the church, at a Synod held in Paris (1074), openly proclaimed the papal commands absurd and frankly said nobody could conform to them even if they wanted to."[9] The next year at a Roman Synod the pope declared his opposition to lay investiture in clear and unequivocal terms. "We decree that no one of the clergy shall receive the investiture with a bishopric or abbey or church from the hand of an emperor or king or of any lay person, male or female. If he shall presume to do so he shall clearly know that such investiture is bereft of apostolic authority, and that he himself shall lie under excommunication until fitting satisfaction shall have been rendered."[10] At about the same time the papal office produced the *dictatus papae* (meaning "dictated by the pope"), a list of twenty-seven private opinions held by the pope which gained wide circulation. The document consisted of extravagent claims for papal primacy: "The Roman Church was founded by God alone," "The Roman pontiff alone can with right be called universal," "That he alone can depose or reinstate bishops," "That it may be permitted him to depose emperors," "That he himself may be judged by no one."[11] Although most of these ideas had surfaced before, what made this document significant was that it "outlines a doctrinal program, terse and comprehensive, which if put into execution would show a command of power and a degree of centralization never exercised or contemplated hitherto."[12]

Henry IV meanwhile had finally subdued the rebellious Saxons, although they continued to be a threat to imperial stability, and he was free to turn his attentions to the south. In defiance of the pope's decrees on lay investiture, he appointed an Archbishop of Milan as well as bishops to the Italian Sees of Fermo and Spoleto. The pope sent him a letter of rebuke: "How little you care for our warnings or for doing right was shown by your later action. . . . We warn you with a father's love that you accept the rule of Christ."[13] The king (not yet crowned emperor) summoned a council of German bishops that met at Worms in January 1076 to denounce the pope and refuse to recognize him as legitimate. The letter to the pope began "Henry, King not by usurpation, but by pious ordination of God, to Hildebrand, now not pope but false monk."[14] In it the king defends his divine right to the throne and the claim to be judged by no one but God. The letter ends with the admonition, "Descend! Descend!" Henry also sent a letter to the German bishops defending his action. Gregory responded at the Lenten Synod of 1076 by deposing the king and excommunicating him. This act released all of Henry's subjects from their oath of allegiance. The turbulent princes of Germany, who were never happy under a strong king, used this occasion as a legitimate excuse for revolt, and Henry was forced to agree that a council be held in Augsburg in February of 1077 with the pope presiding and Henry present to determine whether a new king should be elected. It was a foregone conclusion that Henry's deposition would stand, so he was determined that the council should not meet.

In January 1077 the pope, en route to the Augsburg council, was resting at the castle of Canossa in northern Italy when the most dramatic episode of the controversy occurred. King Henry appeared outside the castle as a penitent, begging the pope's pardon. This act placed the pope on the defensive. As chief pastor of Christendom he could not refuse absolution to a penitent sinner, even though the king's display of sorrow was no doubt motivated by shrewd politics. The pope had no choice but to absolve him; the deposition remained in force, although the council was not held. The image of a monarch, clothed in penitential garb, humbly beseeching pardon from the pope, has been used in art and literature to demonstrate the power of the Papacy in the Middle Ages. The truth appears to be more complex, for it was by his act at Canossa that Henry divided his enemies, forced the papal absolution, and ultimately regained his throne.

After Canossa many of Henry's vassals acknowledged him once again as their legitimate ruler, but others elected Rudolph of Swabia as his successor. Germany was ravaged by civil war while the pope took three years to decide between the claimants to the throne. In 1080 he declared in favor of Rudolph and repeated the excommunication against Henry, together with a prophecy of disaster, but this time it had little effect in Germany. The German bishops in support of Henry elected to consider Gregory deposed and chose Guibert, Archbishop of Ravenna, as an anti-pope. Meanwhile, Rudolph was defeated and killed in battle. The armies of Henry now marched to Rome and besieged it for three years. Finally in 1084 the king's troops succeeded in breaking through to St. Peter's where they consecrated Guibert as pope. In their truce with the Papacy the Normans had pledged to defend the pope, and Gregory summoned them now to make good on their promise. Under the leadership of Robert Guiscard they marched on Rome, but the German troops had already left, so the Norman "defenders" looted the city, razed it by fire, and withdrew to the south with Gregory as their captive. When he died a few months later (May 1085), his last words are said to have been, "I have loved justice and hated iniquity, therefore I die an exile," a parody on Psalm 44.

The conflict between pope and emperor should not be understood as one between church and state, because in the eleventh century there was no institution corresponding to the modern state. More important, all the participants in the controversy were within the church. The conflict was more one of the right ordering of a unitary society where all members adhered to the same religion with considerable overlap between the sacred and secular. To dramatize the difficulty of understanding the issue in terms of "sides," a large number of bishops (not only the Germans) also resisted what they perceived as papal encroachments upon their autonomy. By 1083 about one-third of the cardinals had also abandoned Gregory. The significance of Gregory VII lies not so much in his actions as in the program itself, the precedents he set, and the ideals he articulated. By 1200 much of his program had been realized.

The conflict between king and pope stimulated a war of propaganda between theorists on both sides. "For the first time in medieval Europe we may speak of such a thing as public opinion."[15] Brian Tierney points out that "hardly any of the major participants propounded really extreme doctrines of papal or royal power. . . . There was a great need for intellectuals to reconsider the theoretical issues that lay behind the open strife of pope and king."[16] One of Henry's staunchest supporters was a lawyer from Ravenna, Peter Crassus, who defended royal prerogatives in terms of Roman law. Another called "The Anonymous of York" (1100) also supported a royal theocracy and insisted that kings should rule the church, offering the novel argument that "in Christ the royal power is greater and higher than the priestly in proportion as his divinity is greater and higher than his humanity."[17] As to priests, "God makes the sacrament efficacious; they (merely) administer it." Manegold of Lautenbach was a papal theorist who formulated a contract theory of government. He believed that since it is the people who elevate a king, the same people can depose him. "If he (the king) breaks the compact by which he was elected and ruins and confounds what he was established to order correctly, the people are absolved from their duty of submission."[18] A tract titled *De Unitate Ecclesiae Conservanda* supported a dualistic theory, as did Ivo of Chartres, who wrote that kings have a right to invest bishops with their temporalities (lands and buildings), but clergy should be free to occupy themselves with spiritualities. Hugh of Fleury was a moderate royalist who made a distinction between investing with ring and staff (spiritualities) and earth (temporalities). The introduction of Roman legal precedent into political thought was certainly one of the most significant results of the controversy, generally serving the interests of the secular rulers. Up until the eleventh century medieval princes relied heavily on clergy as advisors and administrators, as they were the only educated persons available. (Our word "clerk" is derived from this practice.) After the Investiture Controversy and the revival of Roman law they tended to look to the emerging class of lay lawyers for counsel. This change tended to secularize princely bureacracies and would accelerate the growth of nationalism.

Gregory VII was followed briefly by Victor III (1084–1088) and then by Urban II (1088–1099). Urban, who had studied at Cluny, began skillfully to build up support for the Papacy among the new dynasty of

Norman rulers in England, and since Guibert the anti-pope was still in Rome, he found refuge and support with the Capetian rulers of France. But he is best known to posterity for calling the First Crusade at a council at Clermont in southern France in 1095. By taking this initiative he was placing the Papacy at the head of a major undertaking involving all of Europe, thus restoring much of the prestige the office had lost. His invitation to join the crusade included these telling words: "Let those who have formerly been accustomed to contend wickedly in private warfare against the faithful, fight against the infidel and bring to a victorious end the war which ought long since to have begun."[19] He is referring to the civil strife and internecine warfare in Europe occasioned in part by the investiture conflicts. He suggested that instead of fighting one another, it is better to join forces against the infidel (i.e. Muslims who controlled the Holy Land).

King Henry V (1106–1125) continued the struggle with the papacy, but the First Crusade saw the realization of Urban's intention, in that it diverted Europe's attention to a new and more exciting field of endeavor. The Gregorian epoch came to a close with the Concordat of Worms between Calistus II and Henry V (September 1122), in which the emperor agreed to the canonical election of bishops and to the investiture of spiritual authority (ring and staff) by the archbishop. The king was permitted to be present at the election and to invest the bishop with the temporalities of the office. In effect, lay lords retained a decisive influence in the selection of bishops, for without income from land which was the king's prerogative to give, bishops would be unable to maintain themselves. One commentator on the settlement at Worms has said that "Though much ink had flowed, and pamphlets had fluttered abroad like leaves in a gale, on the question of the supremacy of pope or emperor, it remained undecided."[20] In many respects the right relationship between secular governments and religious institutions on matters of mutual interest remains a source of contention today.

The Crusades

The Abbasid caliphate of Islam, with its capital at Baghdad on the Tigris, lasted from 750–1055. During that time the Islamic world enjoyed an economic and cultural superiority far exceeding that in the West. Industry and trade flourished throughout the East—China, India, Asia—extending into Russia, Scandinavia, and Spain. "The cultural achievements of the Abbasid period were more impressive and more enduring than anything attained in the West before the twelfth century."[21] They were especially adept in the sciences, mathematics, and medicine, and from them the West inherited Arabic numerals. But Islam was politically decentralized, consisting of many autonomous countries from Spain (which remained Ummayad) to Baghdad. It was undoubtedly this situation of disunity which attracted an Asiatic tribe, the Seljuk Turks, new converts to Islam, to westward expansion. In 1055 they occupied Baghdad and captured the caliph, in whose name they ruled as sultans, pursuing their program of further conquests. In 1071 they routed the Byzantines at the battle of Manzikert and by 1079 they occupied Jerusalem. The Eastern emperor Michael VII appealed to Pope Gregory VII for help, but he was too deeply embroiled in the controversy with Henry IV to provide assistance. During the next twenty-five years the Turks pushed on to Nicea, which lay at the very gates of Constantinople itself, and again a plea went out for help, this time from Emperor Alexius I (1081-1118), who believed that disunity among the Turks made it an opportune time to strike back.[22] Pope Urban II responded with his call for a crusade at the Council of Clermont in 1095. As we have seen, this offered an opportunity to channel the more restive and militant energies of westerners away from intramural conflict into a united campaign which offered rewards. The pope promised that a crusader's family and personal property would be under a special papal protection, and whoever fell in battle was guaranteed a plenary indulgence for all sins. In the Clermont speech the pope shrewdly reminded his listeners that the land "flows with milk and honey like another paradise of delights," and that France, suffering from famine that year, was "too narrow for your population."

Although this economic incentive was no doubt attractive, the pope also touched a strong religious sensitivity in his appeal. The twelfth century was a time of heightened spiritual zeal, of which the several hundred Cluniac monasteries throughout Europe were both a cause and an effect. For the average Christian who had no opportunity for deeds of heroism for the faith, "taking the cross" for a noble cause was appealing. Added to this was the allure of going on a pilgrimage to the very center of the Christian tradition (the Seljuk Turks had put an end to Christian pilgrimages by harassment and murder) and in the process they would defeat God's enemies and rescue the holy places. Together with these enticements there was also the exciting prospect of travel and adventure for many who had never ventured more than a few miles from their homes. The response was enthusiastic. The crowd shouted, "Deus vult" ("God wills it"), which became a battle cry, and some tore strips from their clothing to place the sign of the cross upon themselves, the badge of a crusader.

Such was the enthusiasm of the people that many of them refused to wait for the campaign to organize, and about fifty thousand peasants, including entire families with small children, followed the leadership of two strange characters, Walter, "the Penniless," and Peter, "the Hermit." Peter was an unlikely leader, an ascetic who rode a small donkey, and of whom it was said "He was short and swarthy, sweated profusely, never bathed or changed his clothes, and consequently had an odor as strong and impressive as his personality and his message."[23] As they proceeded through Germany they inquired at each town whether it might be Jerusalem, but as they went they also ravaged the countryside, incurring the hostility of the residents. Their vendetta against the infidel found expression in the massacre of thousands of Jews in Speyer, Mainz, Worms, and Cologne. In Bulgaria the disorganized crusaders were mercilessly attacked by fellow Christians whom they had despoiled. When the remnant appeared before Constantinople, Alexius I was appalled at this "help" from the West. He transported them across the Dardanelles where the Turks put an end to the Peoples' Crusade.

The main army of the First Crusade was in four groups, which were to meet at Constantinople. Godfrey of Bouillon, Duke of Lorraine, and his brother, Baldwin of Flanders led one group; Robert, count of Flanders led another; Count Raymond of Toulouse led a group from southern France; and Bohemond of Taranto led the Normans. There was no overall general, which obviously was a shortcoming, but the pope's legate, Adhemar of Puy, was the convener. These groups arrived at Constantinople in 1099. The residents of the city looked with some amusement on this band of unlikely warriors, drawn mostly from French farms. The emperor's daughter, Anna Comnena, has left us her impressions of Byzantine's would-be saviors: "The whole of the West and all the barbarian tribes . . . had migrated in one body and were marching into Asia . . . making the journey with all their household . . . and persons of intelligence felt they were witnessing a strange occurrence."[24] The Franks were overwhelmed by the glitter of the city, its churches, statues, wide streets, fountains, and the accumulated culture of centuries. Finally they moved on, and in June 1097 they recaptured Nicea, though the defeated Turks insisted on surrendering to the emperor rather than fall into the hands of the crusaders. From there they pushed on toward Antioch, which they took in 1098 after a long siege. No sooner had they taken it than they were besieged in turn by the Turks. The fortuitous discovery of the lance that had pierced Christ's side gave them the courage to sally forth and rout the besiegers. After some dissension the leaders agreed that the city should go to Bohemund. Meanwhile, Baldwin had gone over to Edessa near the headwaters of the Euphrates River, where his forces seized the city, and he succeeded to the throne by marrying the prince's daughter. In this way two of the crusader states were established, the Principality of Antioch and the County of Edessa. The initial objectives of the crusade, removing the military threats to Constantinople and capturing Jerusalem, were giving way to the creation of personal fiefdoms. At this point the pope's legate, Adhemar, who provided the only semblence of unity, died. Only a remnant finally arrived in Jerusalem, which was captured in July 1099, taking the holy city amidst carnage and destruction. A letter to Pope Paschal II describes the event. "He (God) delivered the city and His enemies to us . . . and if you desire to know what was done with the enemy who were found there, know that in Solomon's Porch and in his temple our men rode in the blood of the Saracens up to the knees of their horses."[25] One chronicler of the Crusade, Fulcher of Chartres, maintained that ten thousand Turks were killed. Godfrey of Bouillon was named "Protector of the Holy Sepulchre," insisting that no temporal ruler of Jerusalem should take the title of king where Jesus had worn the crown of thorns. But Godfrey died shortly thereafter, succeeded by his brother Baldwin, who had no scruples about assuming the title of King of Jerusalem. Jerusalem became the third crusader state. The fourth crusader state, the County of Tripoli, was established by Raymond of Toulouse. The pope's representative became the Latin Patriarch of Jerusalem, replacing the existing Greek Patriarch, and he subdivided the entire territory captured by the crusaders into eight archbishoprics and sixteen bishoprics. Collectively these four crusader states were known in Europe as *Outremer* or the land "beyond the seas," and for two centuries they were Christendom's eastern perimeter. However, the crusaders had succeeded only in establishing themselves along a narrow strip of Palestinian coastline. Inland the Turks were still in control, providing a constant threat to the new Latin states.

In order to meet this threat and to protect the many pilgrims who now flocked to Palestine, two new religious orders emerged. The Knights of the Temple, or Templars were founded (so called because their headquarters was near the temple) in 1118 by Hugo of Payens to defend Jerusalem against a recapture by the Muslims. In 1128 Bernard of Clairvaux gave them a form of rule patterned after the Cistercians. They combined the ideals of the military with monasticism, as they were under the vows of monks. Because of the great wealth they amassed, the Templars became the victims of the cupidity of King Philip IV of France who suppressed them in 1307. The Knights Hospitallers were organized to defend pilgrims and to tend those who became sick. A third order, that of the Teutonic Knights, was founded in 1189. During the late Middle Ages this order was primarily responsible for the evangelization and organization of Prussia.

Once the crusaders had settled down in the East, generally recreating the feudal structures they brought with them from the West, the inevitable process of cultural assimilation began. Having left homes in frigid climates, they were attracted to the more temperate life of the Mediterranean, including the casual styles of the resident Muslims. They adopted flowing robes, became fond of steam baths, wore turbans, and through social contacts and intermarriage learned to know and respect their erstwhile enemies. Fulcher of Chartres complained that "He who was a Roman or Frank has become a Galilean or Palestinian. We have already forgotten our birthplaces."[26] When later crusaders arrived they were shocked and chagrined at the indifference toward the Turk displayed by the earlier campaigners, and more often than once the first generation warriors sided with the Muslims against their zealous nephews who arrived some years later. The First Crusade alone of all the crusades came close to accomplishing a positive objective, freeing Jerusalem and establishing a Christian presence, and that without providing help for the Byzantine emperor. All subsequent crusades were attempts to maintain or strengthen the Christian presence in the Holy Land, and in this they were all failures.

Europe was galvanized into the Second Crusade when Edessa fell in 1144. Kings Louis VII of France and Conrad III of Germany led the expedition, which had been popularized through the preaching of Bernard of Clairvaux. Despite such impressive support it accomplished nothing except the capture of Lisbon in Portugal by some German sailors who seized this opportunity of fighting Muslims nearer home. In Europe the blame for the Crusade's failure was attributed by Bernard of Clairvaux to the sins of Christendom and to the lack of support by the Eastern emperor.

In 1187 a powerful Saracen leader, Saladin, recaptured Jerusalem, and Europe's three strongest monarchs were moved to lead the forces of counteraction. Frederick Barbarossa from Germany drowned en route to the Holy Land and his forces were scattered; Philip II of France became disgusted at the indifference of the first generation crusaders and returned home; while Richard I, "the Lion-hearted," of England managed to negotiate a truce which permitted pilgrims to visit the holy places unmolested. En route home Richard was also captured and held for ransom in Austria. The one important battle was at the Horns of Hattim, near Tiberius, where Saladin decisively defeated the Latins, which was followed by the loss of much of the Holy Land. Jerusalem, which had been in Christian hands for less than a century (1099–1187), was never regained.

Following this Crusade Europe tired of these ventures. The West itself was expanding internally and intellectually, and the emergence of a new urban culture at home attracted more attention. Byzantium gained little from the Crusades except a brief respite from Turkish attack. The behavior of the Franks in Asia Minor led some Byzantines to ask whether the Turks themselves may not be more desirable as neighbors, but the Franks in turn had reason to complain of the duplicity of the Byzantines. The most tragic of all Crusades for its long-term effect was the fourth. Pope Innocent III succeeded in gathering an army to recapture the holy places, but the Venetians whose ships were to transport the army convinced the Latins to divert their course to Constantinople, which in 1204 they pillaged for three days. They forced the Byzantines to accept a Latin Patriarch and to observe Latin rites until 1261, when the Greeks finally drove them out. One respected historian of Byzantium and the Crusades insists that the disaster of the Fourth Crusade led directly to the fall of Constantinople two centuries later. "It is hard to exaggerate the harm done to European civilization by the sack of Constantinople. The treasures of the city, the books and works of art preserved from distant centuries, were all dispersed and most destroyed. The Empire, the great Eastern bulwark of Christendom, was broken as a power. . . . The conquest by the Ottomans (in 1453) was made possible by the crusaders' crime."[27] Eastern Christianity to this day bears the scars of this unhappy event.

The tragic debacle of the Children's Crusade in 1212 saw thousands of children from northeastern France and the Netherlands make their way across the Alps to Italy. Many died along the way, and of those who survived, most were dispersed and some were sold into slavery in Egypt. In 1229 the colorful Frederick II succeeded in negotiating a truce with the Sultan of Egypt whereby Jerusalem, Bethlehem, and Nazareth were once again open to Christian pilgrims. The irony of this agreement was that Frederick was under excommunication at the time, and the most successful "crusade" after the first was undertaken by one out of favor with the church, and without shedding a drop of blood.

Two attempts at recovering the holy places were organized by King Louis IX of France. Both in 1248 and in 1270 he sought to defeat the

Muslims by attacking Egypt, the center of their power at that time. In the first venture he was captured, and ransom was paid for his release; in the second he died of dysentery at Tunis. In 1291 the forces of Islam captured Acre, the last stronghold of the Christians in the Holy Land, and the period of the Crusades came to an end exactly two centuries after it began.

Today historians generally agree that the Crusades produced few positive results and many that were negative. They failed in their original purpose, they did not halt the advance of Islam, and instead of helping the Eastern empire, which was the occasion for the initial impulse, they hastened its demise. The disastrous Fourth Crusade hardened the schism between East and West that continues to this day.

Although the Crusades were preached as the fulfillment of spiritual ideals, the crusaders themselves were usually impelled by baser motives and behaved in ways that disgraced their religion. Some observers suggest, perhaps with a touch of cynicism, that Europe's civil strife was reduced by the exodus of large numbers of quarrelsome landless nobility, many of whom failed to return.[28] The Papacy benefited by leading an activity which represented a united Western Christendom, even though popes were critical of the excesses of the crusaders, especially those of the fourth. This enhanced prestige deriving from the twelfth century was one of the contributing factors that led to the zenith of papal power in the thirteenth century. The crusading ideal persisted, albeit in a distorted form, when it was applied to heretics, schismatics, and political opponents. Even today the concept of a crusade as embodying action in support of a cause perceived as righteous remains a part of our vocabulary.

New Religious Movements

The monastic reform movement which began at Cluny was spectacularly successful, especially in recalling the monks to a more serious effort of practicing the austerities of the *Rule* of St. Benedict. The ideals of Cluny were especially a force for reform during the Gregorian period, although the extent to which they completely endorsed the investiture program remains a disputed question.[29] By the beginning of the twelfth century, however, Cluny had been so successful that its ideals were compromised, or so its critics claimed. Many monasteries attracted satellite groups to their vicinity and, in time, villages and towns grew up around them. The monks became more and more involved in society and in the feudal system in general by serving as administrators, overseers, teachers of children, and businessmen (through the sale of surplus goods). At the same time there was a general movement in society toward a return to the simplicity of life portrayed in the gospels, the *apostolica vita* or apostolic poverty. This corresponded with an urban and commercial renaissance associated with the rise of capitalism and a monied economy. The monasteries were faced with the choice of leaving the rural districts and moving their work to the cities, remaining as they were, or divesting themselves of all the distractions of worldy entanglements and returning to the primitive ideal of poverty and simplicity. Many monks chose the latter course, which can accurately be described as a "back to the desert movement," from 1050–1150.

Peter Damian (1007–1072) from Ravenna, exercised the single greatest influence on the new eremitical life. We have already taken notice of his contribution to the Gregorian reform, but he also advocated the hermit's life as the most perfect way for all people to follow Christ. His influence was largely limited to Italy, where the new movements began.

One of the first houses espousing the new austerity was that of the Camaldolese, between Pisa and Florence, founded about 1012 by Romuald of Camaldoli. Peter Damian had been a member of this group before he became a cardinal. Romuald had earlier founded numerous hermitages modelled on those of Egypt and Syria; "desert" was his favorite term for the monastery. The Camaldolese emphasized the anchoritic life (i.e. living alone as a hermit) and almost complete silence. Their austerities attracted large numbers of pilgrims, including Otto III of Germany (983–1002) who prostrated himself before Romuald. Their isolation, however, was not such as to inhibit missionary journeys to Prussia, Poland, and Russia, and the founder himself died on such a journey to Hungary.

Another order, this one known as the Vallambrosians and founded in 1036 by John Gualbert, also arose in the territory between Pisa and Florence. It was a mixture of cenobitic and eremitic life, being strictly contemplative, observing perpetual silence and remaining cloistered, meaning the monks were required to remain in the monastery at all times. An important aspect of the Vallambrosians was the distinction made between choir monks and lay brothers, or *conversi*. The conversi took the same vows as the choir monks, who were also ordained priests, but their work was mostly manual labor and care for the upkeep of the monastery, freeing the other monks for prayer, study, and intellectual activities. The conversi were generally less educated than the choir monks and often illiterate. By 1200 the order had more than fifty abbeys, and by 1500 had more than eighty.

The conversi represent something new in monastic life. If the vocation of the monk is to focus on prayer and contemplation apart from entanglements with the world, some arrangement must be made for the physical upkeep and necessities of the monastery. The conversi, who were also under vows, answered this purpose. They were usually drawn from the lower social strata for whom life in the monastery was a way to better themselves socially. Some monastic scandals were caused by conversi who had no appreciation of the purpose of the monastic life or its obligations.

The Grandmontines were founded by Stephen of Muret in the late-eleventh century with similar requirements of silence and especially poverty. But unlike the other new foundations which were basically Benedictine, they followed their own rule. They were French, and their history came to an end during the French Revolution. Another French foundation, the Order of Fontevrault, founded by Robert of Arbrissal about 1100, likewise required austerities common to the new movement, but they were unique in constructing double monasteries. These were houses for monks and nuns situated contiguously, or nearly so, separated by a church. We find such arrangements already in the fourth and fifth centuries, with the interesting feature that the two houses were ruled by only one superior who was usually the abbess. Within fifty years of its founding Fontevrault became best known as a nunnery for aristocratic women.

The Carthusians or Poor Brothers of God were one of the foremost of the new religious orders, named from their motherhouse at Chartreuse in the Rhone valley. There, amidst snows that were almost perpetual, Bruno of Cologne and six companions established themselves in 1084. They resembled the Egyptian anchorites, each monk in his own hut living a life of prayer, mortification, and silence. We have a description of their life from Peter, "the Venerable" (d. 1156), Abbot of Cluny. They wore hair shirts, fasted continuously, abstained completely from meat, ate dairy products only on Sundays or Thursdays, and engaged in prayer, reading, manual labor, and writing books.[30] Today the Carthusians present much the same type of monastic life as eight centuries ago, and it is said they are the only religious organization that has never required reform.

Of all the new orders, the Cistercians were the most famous in numbers and influence They were founded in 1098 by Robert of Molesme in reaction to the laxity that he perceived elsewhere, especially among the Cluniacs. An Englishman, Stephen Harding, was responsible for drawing up the foundational documents of the order. They rejected all forms of luxury and wealth, as well as ostentation of any kind, which included works of art. This austerity was also reflected in pruning what they perceived as embroidery from the liturgy, which under the influence of Cluny had become ornate. They made their habits of cheap undyed wool which gave them an off-white color from which their name, "White Monks," was derived. They permitted no crosses of silver or gold, but only of wood. Rather than extend the services of worship, they emphasized the *lectio divina* and manual labor. They refused all sources of wealth except that produced by their own hands. Feudal entanglements such as mills, fairs, courts, and serfs were to be avoided, as well as churchly revenues. No oblate children were admissable to the monastery, and the minimum age for the novitiate was set at fifteen. Food, clothing, and even rest were limited to the absolute necessity. Ailred of Rivaulx, an English Cistercian abbot, describes this life in 1144: "Our food is meager, our clothing of the rougher sort. Our drink is from the running spring; our sleep, often upon our book. And under our wearied limbs is a mat that is anything but soft. When the bell sounds, even though sleep were far sweeter, we must rise. There is no place for self-will; no time for ease or dissipation."[31] This same Ailred referred to the Cistercian monastery as "a school of love." As to the physical hardships endured by the monks, a modern authority belives that, "the discomforts of the monastic regime were no worse than those a peasant had to endure in the outside world, and the living quarters were vastly superior."[32] In order to facilitate their separation from society to pursue their ideals, they followed a policy of establishing their houses far from places of habitation, and in so doing pushed back the internal frontiers of Europe. It was they who ventured deep into the primeval forests where no one else dared go, who began to build polders (land reclaimed from the North Sea) and became the pioneers of Holland, and who drained malarial marshland for their habitations.

Stephen Harding drew up the charter document, the *Carta Caritatis*, which created the machinery of the order.[33] Each monastery maintained some independence, being directly under the local bishop. The Abbot of Citeaux was also responsible to visit each house (canonical visitation was a periodic on-site inspection of the spiritual and physical well-being of a religious institution) and all abbots were required to visit houses established by their monastery. The Abbot of Citeaux was to be visited by its four principle foundations, La Ferte, Pontigny, Clairvaux, and Morimund. Whereas the "Black Monks," or traditional Benedictines, continued to operate with manors, tenants, schools, and serfs, the Cistercians made a resolute attempt to be completely independent and self-sustaining. Land was often given to a monastery which was at a considerable distance from the main house. These lands were called granges, and in the Cistercian economy of things, rather than fall back into feudal entanglements by having tenants farm the grange, conversi under the supervision of a few monks would administer the property. The lay brothers, although bettering themselves socially, remained illiterate by Cistercian rule, did not sing with the monks in choir, but contributed their manual labor. As stated before, however, monasticism in general sanctified manual labor itself by elevating it (as contrasted with the late Roman empire) to an honored ascetical sacrifice to God.

The Cistercians grew rapidly, an expansion ably described by a contemporary, Conrad of Eberbach: "Like a great lake whose waters pour out through a thousand streams, gathering impetus from their rapids, the new monks went forth from Citeaux to people the West."[34] Within fifty years of its founding there were 343 Cistercian abbeys, 68 founded by Citeaux itself, and by 1500 there were 738 men's abbeys and 654 for nuns.[35] Part of the popularity of the order was its appeal to peasants and artisans for whom it was an opportunity to live the ascetic life, and to its demanding regimen. But equally compelling was the towering figure of Bernard of Clairvaux, the most influential theologian of the twelfth century and the best known ascetic of the Middle Ages, who joined the order with thirty companions in 1112, and three years later became the Abbot of Clairvaux.

For thirty years Bernard of Clairvaux (d. 1153) was the uncrowned leader of Western Christendom, mentor to four popes, one of whom, Eugenius III (1145- 1153) came from Clairvaux. He preached the Second Crusade; wrote a Rule for the Knights Templar; sided with Innocent II (1130–1143) in a disputed papal election; fought strenuously against the alleged heresy of Gilbert de la Poree, Arnold of Brescia, and Peter Abelard; and offered counsel to kings, princes, bishops, and popes. His authority lay in his charismatic appeal, his ascetical rigors and saintliness, and in his powerful sermons, of which we still have 332. One of his most significant works is the *De Consideratione* written for Pope Eugenius III in which he deplores the amount of time the pope spent with lawyers and litigation, urging that more time be spent with the law of God than that of men. His *De Diligendo Deo* was a masterpiece of mysticism, and in the *De Gratia et Libero Arbitrio*, he revealed a strong dependence upon Augustine in the aphorism: "Remove free-will and there is nothing to be saved; remove grace and there is no means of saving. The work of salvation cannot be accomplished without the cooperation of the two." But he also denied any hint of the Pelagian notion of humans contributing to their salvation: "The merits that God required of men were those that he, by prevenient grace, had already given to them."[36] Bernard's fame as a theologian rested on his classical expression of the new piety. Whereas others had worshiped Christ as a king and transcendent God, Bernard devoted himself to Jesus, the man, in his humility, obedience, suffering, and death. He maintained that if one meditated on Christ's holiness and God's wrath, one would become aware of one's sinfulness. But gazing upon God's mercy, one became certain of forgiveness, and in response it was possible to imitate the life of Christ. The goal of the mystical life was the complete surrender of the will of the individual to the will of God. Bernard placed such an emphasis upon the grace of God that he became known as *Augustinus redivivus* (Augustine revived). His philosophy was "to know Jesus and Jesus crucified."[37] He is traditionally cited as the author of "O Sacred Head Now Wounded," "O Jesus, King Most Wonderful," "Jesus, the Very Thought of You," and other hymns that reflect his devotion to Christ's suffering and the deep emotion which it evoked.

During Bernard's lifetime a dispute arose between the Cistercians and the Cluniacs over which of their monastic customs was most authentically Benedictine. The controversy was ignited when Bernard's own nephew left Citeaux for Cluny, finding the life at the former too difficult. The result was a protracted literary exchange between Bernard and Peter, "the Venerable," Abbot of Cluny (d. 1156), in which condemnations and charges were hurled. In the end, we can see that they were each defending different monastic ideals, each legitimate. "It is well to recollect that two quite distinct cases were being tried, though the disputants rarely made the distinction."[38]

About 1154 some hermits living on Mount Carmel in Palestine, near the modern city of Haifa, organized a new order, Our Lady of Mount Carmel, under the direction of Berthold. According to their tradition they were in continuity with Elijah and the sons of the prophets (2 Kings 2). They adopted the ideals of rigid asceticism, including extreme poverty. The two best known Carmelite mystics in later years were Teresa of Avila (d. 1582) and John of the Cross (d. 1591). The Carmelites were one of the four orders of mendicant begging friars, together with the Dominicans, Franciscans, and Augustinians.

A religious institution that gained prominence in the eleventh century and thereafter was that of canons. These were priests living a communal life in a parish, either in a cathedral or as the staff of a large collegiate church, who were under the jurisdiction of a bishop or archdeacon. This movement goes back as far as Eusebius of Vercelli (d. 371), who produced a Rule for the clergy of his parish. St. Augustine adopted the same usage for his priests at Hippo. The custom gradually declined until it was revived by Chrodegang of Metz (d. 766) and, under the Carolingians, canons reappeared as the center of clerical educational reform under the direction of a chancellor. Around 1100 C.E. the Canons Regular of St. Augustine appeared (known also as Austin Canons), inspired by Ivo of Chartres, who brought them under a more strict monastic regimen which required the renunciation of private property, vows, and a strict communal life. About the same time William of Champeaux established the Canons of St. Victor, who became known especially for their interest in mysticism. A meeting of the canons was known as a chapter, as it was with monks in community. The cathedral chapters of canons gained the rights of episcopal election in due time, as collegiate chapters gained supervision over education entrusted to them. It is from the latter we derive the word college today. A canon was supported by a prebend, which meant revenues that came to him from sources other than the church he was serving. Although this system worked well for a time, it was also liable to abuse, in that canons could be tempted to collect a number of prebends, which may include the revenues of several churches, a practice known as accumulating pluralities. The canon, who was therefore the official priest at several churches, would hire a vicar at a minimum salary to serve the church while he kept most of the revenues. In the Middle Ages this organization of secular priests into a community was prompted by the growing monastic ideal and the attempt to bring all clergy under its influence by requiring them to observe a Rule (*canon*). The term canon today usually refers to the ministerial staff of a large church.

CHAPTER FIVE

THE CHURCH AND THE NATION-STATES

The Growth of Papal Government

Gregory VII had no interest in administration. In his struggle with Henry IV he had relied heavily on traditions of papal primacy, on various political alliances, and on his own charisma; but at his death the machinery of papal oversight of the church was in disarray. It was Urban II (1088–1099) who laid the foundations for the centralization of the papacy. The compromise with the empire formalized by the Treaty of Worms (1122) would concede the right of the church to supremacy in the area of spiritual life. Although this lay in the future, Urban anticipated its outcome by organizing the Roman See to prepare itself to govern, and to this end he reconstituted the cardinals to serve as his advisory council and to assist him in the oversight of the church. Whereas before this time the cardinals were largely symbolic, through the election decree of 1059 they gained the right to elect popes, and under Urban they became bureaucrats in the administration. This is evident in the appointments of cardinals to supervise various departments in the papal machinery of government.

Among these was the establishment of the *camera*, or department of financial management, which in the next century would expand to become a truly powerful instrument of papal influence, responsible for the collection of tithes, taxes, and fees. The *chancery* was established, directed by a cardinal, which not only created papal correspondence, decrees, and contracts, but kept an accurate file of all such instruments. "Without [the chancellors] the rapid expansion of the central administration in the twelfth century would scarcely have been possible."[1] This is dramatically illustrated by the increase in correspondence under successive popes. Under Leo IX (d. 1054) we have on average 35 letters per year, which remains constant for popes until 1130. After that there is a sharp rise to an annual average of 72 under Innocent II (d. 1143), 130 under Adrian IV (d. 1159), 179 under Alexander III (d. 1181), 280 under Innocent III (d. 1215), 730 under Innocent IV (d. 1254), rising to 3,646 per year under John XXII (d. 1342).[2] This exuberance of papal letters reflects the growth of the daily conduct of business in the papal chancery.

Under the successors of Urban II, notably Paschal II (1099–1118), Callistus II (1119–1124) and Innocent II (1124–1143), the centralization of the Papacy accelerated. By far the most significant development was that of canon law and the study of law in general, spurred by the rediscovery of the Roman law of Justinian's *Corpus juris civilis*. This was not only limited to the Papacy but was a central interest of secular governments as well.[3] We have already taken note of a collection of laws by Burchard of Worms (1012) and of a "Collection in 74 Titles" (1050), but these were overshadowed by the work of Gratian, a lawyer from Bologna, who tried to bring conformity to the contradictory and doubtful texts which had come down. His work, which dates from 1140, was called the *Concordia discordantium canonum* (concordance of contradictory canons) or simply the *Decretum*. It soon became the principal authoritative collection of ecclesiastical law studied in the schools and was frequently cited. What made this collection significant for the Papacy was its decided advocacy for papal primacy and for church law over secular law. Since it was incomplete and required periodic updating with new material, a five-book supplement, known as the *Decretales*, was prepared by Raymond of Penafort under the direction of Pope Gregory IX in 1234. A sixth book, or *Liber Sextus*, was added by Pope Boniface VIII, and in 1314 Clement V added the *Clementinae*. The entire collection was completed with the *Extravagantes* in 1484. In 1500 this material was systematically arranged and published as the *Corpus Juris Canonici*, or body of canon law, which remained the official exposition of church law until a revision was made in 1917. Canon law was crucial to the centralization of the Papacy in the Middle Ages and in the rapid growth of papal power.

The papal court quickly attracted litigants from all over Europe. Basically the court was appellate, that is, the court of final appeal from lower courts, whether those of bishops, archbishops, or archdeacons. Since the church claimed jurisdiction in a wide variety of cases, including those of marriage, divorce, vows, wills, ordination, sacraments, patronage, canonization, electoral procedure, legitimization of children, inheritance, and the like, the potential number of claimants seemed infinite. The business of rendering judgments grew, not because the popes fostered it, but because litigants believed it was to their advantage to seek papal justice.[4] It was not unusual, considering the flood of appeals, that in time many litigants sought to bypass the lower courts and go directly to Rome, which resulted in the papal curia becoming a court of first instance. As the number of petitioners grew to the thousands, the papal court system expanded similarly. This was especially true under Alexander III (1159–1181), of whom it was said he sat in judgment hearing cases with the cardinals every day of the week. It was to this situation that Bernard had written earlier to Pope Eugenius III, "Why do you sit from morning until evening listening to litigants? What fruit is there in these things? They can only create cobwebs."[5] It has often been observed that most of the popes of the twelfth century were lawyers, and not one has ever been canonized.

But it was not possible for all plaintiffs to make the long journey to Rome, and so delegate-judges were created to bring papal justice to the people. These usually consisted of three local churchmen who were given authority to dispense papal justice, subject to the approval of Rome. In the course of time there were hundreds of such judges throughout Europe, vested with papal authority to hear cases and render a decision. Naturally the flood of new legal decisions created a complex collection of new precedents or laws (there lies a fine line between such legal decisions and the creation of legislation), necessitating periodic additions and updates to the collection of canon law, as indicated above. The increase of litigation also created a new office in the papal curia, that of canon lawyer. There were probably upwards of one hundred such experts in Rome at any given time in the twelfth and thirteenth centuries. Most religious orders, bishops, and secular princes did not wait for litigation, however, before they sought advice. They hired representatives in Rome to look after their interests in the maze of papal procedures, much like having a lawyer (or a lobbyist) on a retainer in today's government center.

But justice did not come without a price. There were fees to be paid at every turn, as well as favors and gifts, but such emoluments usually did not find their way to papal coffers; they went instead to the oiling of the large and complex judicial machinery. Advice from a monk at Canterbury to his fellows who were in Rome in litigation against the archbishop reads, "We cannot rival the archbishop's party in the quantity of gifts . . . but our cause cannot be conducted without gifts; . . . show a cheerful face to the legate's clerk and load him with promises."[6]

The writer says that one's poverty ought not prevent him from making lavish promises.

While the juridical machinery tended to pay for itself, the church leaders in the service of the Roman curia also required a means of support. This was facilitated through the practice of papal provisions, which meant that the pope reserved to himself the right to appoint one of the prelates in his service to a vacant benefice, usually a church, with the right of receiving its income. In turn the prelate so beneficed would secure a vicar to do the actual work at the church while he retained most of the income. In its beginnings this arrangement appeared to benefit all concerned, but the potential for abuse was great. Under Hadrian IV (1154–1159) this practice became a policy, and thereafter it was often employed. As the century moved toward its close, popes added to the situations in which they retained the rights of appointments to vacancies, thereby further centralizing their power, but often at the expense of bishops who traditionally had enjoyed the rights of appointment.

Another way in which papal influence was spread throughout Europe was that of the office of papal legate, who was the pope's ambassador and representative to the courts of kings and princes. Not only did they serve as a local presence of the Roman pontiff, but they in turn served as his eyes and ears, reporting back to Rome what was happening in the court and country of their residence. In this way the curia at Rome was usually current on political, economic, and social conditions throughout Europe. The increase of papal centralization, however, had a devastating effect on the power of bishops. Canon law favored a strongly centralized power in Rome, and litigants could either bypass the episcopal courts or appeal from them to Rome. Delegate-judges, invested with papal authority, took precedence over bishops. Papal legates could and did lecture bishops about their responsibilities. Rights of appointment to vacant parishes or other institutions, traditionally the prerogative of the bishop, were increasingly taken over by the pope. This subordination to papal control is more evident in smaller dioceses in Italy than in the much larger bishoprics in northern Europe and England, where papal influence was often challenged or resisted.

The church council was another instrument of papal centralization. Such councils had served as deliberative organs of the church ever since the assembly at Jerusalem in the first century (Acts 15). When a council was considered to be representative of all Christendom, East and West, and binding upon all, it was considered *ecumenical*. The first seven such councils were held in the East but were **also** concurred in by the West. Those falling within the time frame of the Middle Ages are the fifth at

Constantinople (553) which condemned Nestorianism and Monophysitism; the sixth at Constantinople (680–681) against Monothelitism; and the seventh at Nicea (787), which condemned Iconoclasm. These, together with the first four ecumenical councils, are the only councils that remain authoritative for both East and West today.

Pope Callistus II called a council in 1123, the year after the Treaty of Worms, in order to assert his newly won independence from the emperor and to solidify the gains of the Investiture Controversy. It was the first council ever to be convened by a pope, for which over three hundred bishops met at the Lateran Palace in Rome. Simony, nicolaism (marriage of clergy), and lay control of clerical persons and property were condemned, and the council was followed by six regional synods in England, France, Spain, and Italy repeating these prohibitions. It was clearly a declaration of papal independence. A Second Lateran Council was called by Innocent II in 1139 to heal the schism caused by his election and to condemn Arnold of Brescia. The Third Lateran Council was convoked in 1179 by Alexander III, and declared that henceforth the pope must be elected by a two-thirds majority of all cardinals, thus eliminating the possibility of contested elections and anti-popes which had plagued the church. Also, every cathedral was to provide a school for clergy, whose minimal age for ordination was set at twenty-five, while that for bishops was established as thirty. The Fourth Lateran Council will be discussed below. By their participation in the four Lateran councils the bishops of the West acknowledged the primacy of the pope and the fact that he was the Vicar of Christ, a title which he assumed from the middle of the twelfth century, and which represented a considerable inflation in dignity from his previous designation as Vicar of Peter.

In 1198 Lothar of Segni was elected pope at age thirty-seven (while only a deacon and not yet a priest), and as Innocent III (1198–1216) was the greatest of all medieval popes, under whose guidance the Papacy reached the summit of its temporal power. The young pontiff sought to free the Papal States from all outside interference, to combat heresy, to extend Christianity by fighting against the Muslims, and to establish clearly the primacy of spiritual authority over temporal rulers. He succeeded in building up the Papal States to become an Italian principality of size and strength. In combating heresy he was active in opposing the Albigensians and Waldensians, and in his desire to expand Christianity eastward he supported the Fourth Crusade until it came to its disastrous end. He clearly stated his attitude toward papal relations with temporal powers. In his decretal *Venerabilem* he claimed the right to decide between two pretenders to the German throne. "If the votes of the princes are divided in an election, we can favor one of the parties . . . [since] consecration and coronation are demanded of us"[7] In a dispute between King Philip of France and King John of England, the pope intervened on behalf of John. When the French king protested unwarranted interference by the pope, Innocent replied that a sin had been committed, and "it pertains to our office to rebuke any Christian for any mortal sin and to coerce him with ecclesiastical penalties if he spurns our correction."[8] By responding this way, the pope revealed an enigmatic side to subsequent historians, because despite his theoretical claims to supremacy over temporal lords, Innocent III never intervened in a temporal dispute simply on the basis of a theoretical claim to primacy. The reason he gives for his right of intervention—*ratione peccati*, by reason of sin—is new to the Papacy. His claim, as we have seen in the dispute between the kings of England and France, is that being the chief spiritual authority in Christendom, he had a right to become involved in any issue when a sin had been committed.[9] In the dispute referred to above he also claimed that an oath had been broken and that by virtue of his office he was required to defend the peace. He asserted this despite the fact that he also laid claim to a purely theocratic authority over all secular rulers, as in the famous statement that just as God established two great lights in the heavens, a greater to preside over the day and a lesser to preside over the night, the sun and the moon represent papal and royal power: "Just as the moon derives its light from the sun and is indeed lower than it in quantity and quality, in position and in power, so too the royal power derives the splendor of its dignity from the pontifical authority."[10] Innocent III successfully applied this worldview to the kings of his day, entering aggressively into German affairs, threatening the king of France in his domestic life, excommunicating the king of England, and asserting himself in Spain and Hungary. Within the life of the church itself, one of his greatest and most lasting contributions was convening the Fourth Lateran Council in 1215.

By Western reckoning the council ranks as the Twelfth Ecumenical Council, "and just as it was the most largely attended so it was the most important of all the councils of the Middle Ages . . . the most important assembly of the Roman Communion before the Counter-Reformation."[11] The assembly is said to have brought together 412 bishops, 800 heads of monastic houses, and a large number of representatives of absentees, and envoys from kings, the emperor, and municipalities. Altogether seventy canons were passed. The first is a credal statement somewhat modeled on the Nicene Creed, and which states that there is only one Universal Church, "outside of which there is absolutely no salvation."[12] Of great importance is the claim that in the Eucharist, "the bread being changed (*transubstantiato*) by divine power into the body, and the wine into the blood . . . which no one can effect except the priest who has been duly ordained." This is the first official use of the term *transubstantiation*. Canon 3 is against the Albigensians, and lays down procedures for their subjugation and a list of penalties. Also included is the inquisitorial procedures to be followed by bishops. Canon 13 forbids any new religious order from being formed, and Canon 21 mandates that all the faithful must make confession of their sins and receive the Eucharist at least once each year, at Easter. The same canon upholds the privacy of the confessional, and if any priest by word or signs makes known the sinner to others, he is to be deposed and do penance for the rest of his life. Many canons are directed against clerical abuses—incontinence, intemperance, hunting, worldly occupations, carousing. Canon 62 opposes the abuse of devotion to relics, and Canon 66 condemns clergy who charge fees for burials, weddings, and "similar things." Warnings must precede excommunication (Canon 47) and excommunications should not be lifted for a fee (Canon 49). Usury (payment of interest) should be left to the Jews, but it should not be excessive (Canon 67). Canon 68 decrees that Jews and Saracens must be distinguished in public from other people by a difference of dress.

Assessments of the pontificate of Innocent III vary widely. The verdict of history is that his pontificate reveals the medieval papacy at its most powerful, but there are those who believe this is an illusion, or that the pope never intended to weaken temporal rulers, or that his success was due to circumstances.[13] One interpreter suggests that Innocent's claims to plenitude of power were exaggerated and were never accepted by secular princes, that his resources were not sufficient to enforce his threats, and that he failed to match his ideals with execution. His successes largely depended upon his allies and on circumstances. "His interpretation of the relations of empire and papacy was repudiated in Germany, while his interference in England had the paradoxical result of stimulating the growth of national sentiment in the English church."[14] Whatever factors went into the creation of his pontificate, however, his eighteen years as head pastor of the Western church were remarkable for their ideals, accomplishments, and precedents. Later popes foundered in trying to live up to Innocent's image, realize his visions, or emulate his success.

Divine Right or Human Custom?

The possibility of tension between church and state was inherent in the very nature of Christianity (although the designation "state" is anachronistic if by its use we impose images of a modern nation onto antiquity, yet the term may still be useful). The followers of Christ were encouraged to separate themselves from the world while they lived in the world. In the early centuries the church developed its own structures of government, which stood apart from but yet were based on the Roman political system, and the church's teaching that Jesus Christ is Lord was sometimes at variance with Roman custom. The persecuted church believed that God, rather than humans, ought to be obeyed, although St. Paul's warning, "Let every soul be subject to the governing authorities (Rom. 13:1)," was also respected.

The conversion of Constantine (312) dramatically altered this situation. Because of imperial patronage and support the church's position was reversed, and from a persecuted minority it changed rapidly to a dominant majority in society. In 392 Emperor Theodosius declared Christianity the only legal religion in the empire. The church's success during the fourth century sharpened the debate between church leaders and secular rulers over their respective roles in society. The church in the East tended to acquiesce in imperial domination, whereas ecclesiastical authorities in the West held either to a strict separation of the two institutions, or in some cases believed that the church should dominate the state. The theocratic idea (that the church or its leaders should rule) in the West was accelerated by the removal of the imperial capital to Constantinople in 330, leaving no effective check on the growth of ecclesiastical power. On the other hand, the presence of the emperor in Constantinople inhibited any claims to autonomy on the part of the church in the East.

The medieval struggle between the popes and the kings was more than a conflict of personal ambition. It was an attempt to reconcile the spiritual claims of the church with the temporal, or the doctrine of redemption with that of creation. Both parties in the struggle relied heavily on biblical material to buttress their position. Those who contended for a strict separation of church and state relied on such passages as "Render unto Caesar the things that are Caesar's, and to God the things that are God's" (Luke 20:25), and reminded their opponents that Christ himself had said that his kingdom was not of this world (John 18:36). Most important for the development of the Papacy were Christ's words to Peter, "You are Peter, and on this rock I will build my church, and the power of death shall not prevail against it. I will give you the keys of the kingdom of heaven, and whatever you bind on earth shall be bound in heaven" (Matt. 16:18–19, RSV). Although medieval writers unanimously agreed that the powers conferred on Peter were transmitted to the pope, they disagreed about the nature of these powers and their role in temporal government. From the eleventh century on the "two swords" theory was popular on both sides. Derived from Luke 22:38, (RSV) "Look, Lord, here are two swords," and he said to them, "It is enough," the controversialists used this slender basis for supporting either a separation of powers or the primacy of one over the other.

Papal theory in general proposed that the secular order was inferior to the spiritual and must therefore be controlled by it. Following the thought of Augustine, government had basically a negative role in society, because earthly rulers were established primarily to curb the results of the sinful nature of humanity, to punish evildoers, and to maintain order. Since the existence of the state was a consequence of sin, it followed that the state was inferior to the church, which was God's remedy for sin through the forgiveness it dispensed. In 494 Pope Gelasius I enunciated this relationship: "There are indeed, most august Emperor, two powers by which the world is chiefly ruled, the sacred authority of the popes and of the royal power. Of these the priestly power is much more important, because it has to render account for the kings of men themselves at the divine tribunal."[15] This same pope, however, also maintained a separation of the two powers. He pointed to Melchisedeck (Gen. 14:18) as a symbol of the union of the powers of kings and priests. Since Christ was the new Melchisedeck, Christ united royal and priestly powers in Himself. After Christ's ascension the two powers were to be separated, "that the humility of each order would be preserved, neither being exalted by the subservience of the other, and each profession would be especially fitted for its appropriate function."[16] Isidore of Seville (d. 636) taught that Christ gave the rulership to kings in order to guard the church and to assist it in the maintenance of justice. It was up to the church to determine the nature of justice since ethics was the church's business, and the king was to carry out its objectives. Pope Gregory I (d. 604) introduced a theory that gained popularity in the Middle Ages, in which he maintained that terrestrial society was modeled on a celestial pattern. Just as heaven followed a hierarchical order with God at the apex, so the earth was to be governed by God's vicar, the pope, at the top. To rebel against this immutable law was to bring chaos. Other theorists supported papal primacy on the dualistic concept of body and soul. The soul, being spiritual, was superior to the body; therefore clergy, whose province was the care of souls, were superior to earthly rulers, whose province was physical. Many of these ideas were contained in the forged *Donation of Constantine* and the *Pseudo-Isidorian decretals* coming from the eighth century.

Opposed to the concept of papal/clerical superiority was that of royal theocracy, the idea that kings derived their authority directly from God without the mediation of the pope. The origins of this veneration of the sovereign prince derive from the ancient conception of divine kingship, from Germanic tribal traditions, and from biblical precedent (the examples of David, Solomon, and Paul's letter to the Romans were often cited.) The king was considered sacred, and royal consecration was included among the sacraments in the early Middle Ages. Kings were said to possess miracle-working powers. They typified Christ, and just as He ruled in heaven, kings claimed the right to rule on earth. At the time of the Investiture Controversy one royalist wrote, "Our kings and emperors take the place of the highest Lord in this earthly life and rightly stand before all other pastors."[17]

Supporters of royal supremacy also used the Christological argument, as did the papalists, but they turned it around. They agreed that Christ was both king and priest, but the kingly role was superior. The church was the Bride of Christ the king, not of Christ the priest, and temporal kings were superior to their "brides." Hugh of Fleury, an early twelfth-century cleric and royalist, wrote that "Within the boundaries of his land the king seems to take the place of God the Father, and the bishops that of Christ," and he continues by suggesting that bishops should be subordinate to the king as the Son is to the Father.[18] An anonymous writer of York offered a clear statement of royalism: "The king is not to be called a layman, for he is the anointed of the Lord, a god through grace, the supreme ruler, supreme shepherd, master, defender, instructor of holy church."[19] When Europe became synonymous with Christendom the stage was set for the Investiture Controversy and its aftermath, continued tensions between popes and secular rulers.

England and the Papacy

From the earliest days of the evangelization of England there had been close relations between rulers and bishops. Indeed, Christianity owed its success in large part to the support it received from the newly converted princes. The Anglo-Saxon rulers who reigned from the sixth century to 1066 appointed bishops and abbots as their chief advisors in the witan (king's council), and throughout England the bishops sat as judges in the county courts together with the counts and sheriffs. The rulers, however were not passive recipients of clerical advice.

England's champion against the Norse invaders of the ninth century, King Alfred of Wessex (871–899), was also famous for his zeal in the reform of the church and of monasticism. In 878 he concluded a peace treaty with the leader of the Danes (as the Norse were called) whereby the invader agreed to receive Christian baptism and cease his depredations. Alfred himself translated into Old English the *Pastoral Care* of Gregory I, the *History of the Church* by Orosius, and *The Consolation of Philosophy* by Boethius. He also instituted the *Anglo-Saxon Chronicle*, next to Bede the most important source for English history before the eleventh century.

In 1066 Duke William of Normandy, "the Conqueror," invaded England, ending the Anglo-Saxon period and beginning that of the Normans. This was not undertaken without pretexts, for he was the cousin of the last king of the Saxons, Edward, "the Confessor" (1042–1066), who allegedly had promised him the throne. The witan legitimized the conquest by electing him king. William separated the civil from the church courts; but of much greater significance, he issued a decree in three parts: (1) no pope would be recognized in England without the king's permission; (2) none of the king's immediate vassals could be excommunicated without the king's permission; and (3) no conciliar decrees of the church could be promulgated in the realm without his sanction. It is one of the ironies of history that William (king 1066–1087) gained control over the English church during the same time that Gregory VII was contesting the German king's identical actions over against the church in the empire. "King William and his advisor, Archbishop Lanfranc of Canterbury, tightly controlled the church in England. But since they appointed suitable men to be bishops and abbots and were in favor of the moral reform of the clergy as long as it did not decrease the king's power, Gregory avoided a direct challenge to William's power."[20] In 1079 the pope made a determined effort to get both English and Norman representatives to his forthcoming Lenten synod, but William refused to allow any of his bishops to attend, although they were canonically required to be present.

When William was asked to do fealty to the pope for England, he refused. In 1072 Lanfranc was invited to spend Christmas at the papal court, but turned down the invitation, pleading overwork. These examples seem to indicate a studied attempt by both king and archbishop to distance themselves from Rome.[21] The *Anglo-Saxon Chronicle* says of the Conqueror: "He was mild to those good men who loved God, but severe beyond measure toward those who withstood his will. He founded a noble monastery on the spot where God permitted him to conquer England, and he established monks in it (Battle Abbey)." He also built a number of monasteries, including one at Canterbury, and religion flourished in his day.[22] William's son and successor, William II ("Rufus," 1087–1100) completely ignored the rights of the church. From 1087 to 1095 he refused to recognize any pope in England (mostly this fell on Urban II, pope from 1085 to 1099), and for four years he deliberately kept the see of Canterbury vacant, declaring that he would be his own archbishop. Before Lanfranc died in 1089 he exercised considerable influence on the king, and there is evidence that the archbishop was in communication with the anti-pope, Clement III, who had been installed by Emperor Henry IV.[23] In 1093 William finally appointed Anselm of Bec to Canterbury, but because of his allegiance to the pope and attempts at reform, Anselm was forced to flee England. The next king, Henry I (1100–1135), another son of the Conqueror, invited him back, but in 1103 Anselm again had to leave England because he refused to do homage to the king and consecrate bishops whom Henry had chosen.

During Anselm's second absence a compromise was negotiated through the efforts of Ivo of Chartres and Hugh of Fleury, who made a distinction between the spiritual and temporal offices of bishop. Anselm returned to England in 1107 and ratified a settlement wherein the king gave up the practice of investing bishops with ring and staff, but retained the right to receive feudal homage for the lands attached to the bishop's churches. This agreement set the precedent for the German-Roman settlement at Worms in 1122.

From 1135–1154 England was torn by a civil war, and during the disorders the church regained a large measure of its independence. The anarchy was ended by Henry Plantagenet (Henry II, 1154–1189), a grandson of Henry I and one of England's greatest kings. He was the first of the house of Anjou to ascend the throne, inaugurating the Anjevin succession of kings. At age twenty-one he was simultaneously the King of England, the Duke of Normandy, and the ruler of Anjou, and when he married Eleanor of Aquitaine he became the ruler of a vast continental empire which stretched from Ireland to the Pyrenees. For the next two centuries the English kings ruled half the territory of France as well as England.

The issue of church-state relations during the reign of Henry II turned largely on his struggle with the Archbishop of Canterbury, Thomas à Becket. The king attempted to regain the liberties which the church had acquired during the civil war by restating the principles which had been laid down by William, "the Conqueror." To facilitate this he appointed Thomas à Becket, his close friend and chancellor of the realm, to the archbishopric of Canterbury; but no sooner was Becket installed than he began to champion the cause of the church. In 1164 the king drew up statements of the customs of the realm, called the Constitutions of Clarendon, which were ratified by the clergy as well as by the archbishop, who in the end refused to affix his seal to them. The Constitutions are sixteen statements in which Henry II insisted on returning to the old patterns of church-state relations that had existed under his grandfather, Henry I. The most important of these were the prohibition of appeals to Rome without the king's consent and the king's right to try clergy guilty of criminal acts in the king's court. He also insisted that when church offices (archbishop, bishop, or abbot) fell vacant, and if it involved royal land (demesne), the revenues from those lands were to go to the king. Also, all newly appointed prelates "shall do homage to the Lord king as to his liege lord, for his life and his limbs and his earthly honor."[24] Becket responded, "Kings receive their power from the church, not she from them but from Christ. . . . You have not the power to give rules to bishops, nor to absolve or to excommunicate anyone."[25] Soon after these Constitutions were adopted Thomas left England. The pope, however, took a middle position, exhorting the archbishop to "be discreet, and we warn, advise, and exhort you to show yourself wary, prudent, and circumspect. . . . Do nothing hastily. Forbear with the king."[26] The pope, Alexander III, could ill afford a complete breach with the king. King Henry convened an assembly of nobles at Northampton intended to force the archbishop to do his will, but in a dramatic midnight escape, Thomas and his servants fled to France, where he remained in exile for six years. The pope, meanwhile, under pressure from Emperor Frederick I and the anti-pope, left Rome for France, where he lived for four years while dealing with Henry and Frederick, two powerful and potentially mortal enemies. A modern study of Thomas suggests that under these circumstances he was "a vexatious and gratuitous nuisance" to the pope.[27] Becket spent most of his exile at the Cistercian house at Pontigny. The pope met several times in person with both Henry and Thomas, but to no avail. Henry meanwhile had his son crowned as heir to the throne by the Archbishop of York, clearly an infringement on the ancient prerogatives of Canterbury. After Becket excommunicated two bishops and threatened all of England with an interdict (a region under interdict meant that no services or worship could be held or sacraments celebrated, with some exceptions), a reconciliation was effected. He returned to Canterbury on November 30, 1170.

When he refused to reinstate the deposed bishops, King Henry uttered words in a fit of rage which four noblemen believed gave them license to act independently, and on December 29 the archbishop was assassinated by them in his cathedral. In the short term this was a disaster for Henry. He was faced with rebellions and threatened with excommunication. The pope placed his French dominions under the interdict. The king was forced by public outrage at his alleged complicity in the murder to do penance by suspending several clauses in the Constitutions of Clarendon, promising to join a crusade, pledging obedience to the pope, and establishing monasteries. In 1174 he did public penance at the tomb of Becket, who had been canonized one year earlier. But in the long term, conditions returned to the pre-Becket years. Henry continued his control of English ecclesiastical affairs as before, with one significant difference. Whereas king and archbishop had been inflexible and absolute, "flexibility was restored without calamitous difference to either party. Canon law was implicitly recognized as having a status, and reasons had to be shown, or at least devised, for breaking it."[28] It was not a matter of church against state but two authorities, acknowledged as legitimate by the entire population, who claimed complete control of that population, having to make accommodation and compromise for the good of all.

In the midst of his struggles with Becket, Henry II supported the first foray of the English into Ireland. At the request of Dermot, the Irish king, Henry sent a force to assist him, which resulted in the Earl of Pembroke subduing parts of Ireland. In 1171, while the reaction to the murder of Becket was at its height, Henry traveled to Ireland to receive Pembroke's homage, and thereafter included "Lord of Ireland" among his titles.

One of Henry's sons, King Richard, "the Lion-hearted" (1189–1199), is best known as the adventurer of the Third Crusade. During the last six years of his father's life he had governed Aquitane, the English lands in France, and after he became king he resided in England for only four months out of his ten-year reign. Richard's absence for nearly a decade gave the nobility, including leaders of the church, the freedom to govern as they saw fit without royal intervention. This taste of independence was a primary factor in the tensions between king and nobility when King John attempted to assert royal prerogatives. Richard made good on his father's pledge to lead a crusade, but his enmity with Philip of France contributed to its failure, and en route home he was held for ransom nearly two years by Leopold of Austria, a ransom grudgingly raised by the English. The negotiator in the ransom was the Cistercian Abbot of Les Dunes, the chief agent of the Queen of England, whose monastery also owned a fleet of ships, indicating the extent to which monks were engaged in commerce and temporal pursuits.

King John of England (1199–1216) is especially known for his struggle with Innocent III over the selection of the Archbishop of Canterbury, and as the signer of the Magna Carta in 1215, the document that established the principle that the king is subject to the law. As to the first, the pope voided two earlier elections and in Rome appointed Stephen Langton as Archbishop of Canterbury. The king refused to receive him, and so he was excommunicated by the pope, and England was placed under an interdict (1208). John gave in after five years, recognized Langton as archbishop, and became a papal vassal. "The papal interdict caused great distress in the country, especially as papal taxation demands had exacerbated the sentiments of the English towards the papal curia."[29] Although the pope prevailed, in the long run this further alienated the people from their loyalty to Rome. It was during the five years of interdict that the nobility forced the king to sign the Magna Carta (1215), which in its clause relating to the church declared that "the church of England be free, and have her rights intact, and her liberties unimpaired." The charter was annulled by Innocent III, who also suspended the archbishop and excommunicated the "rebels" who had drawn up the charter but without effect.[30]

Henry III (1216–1272) ruled for over a half century, a period known especially for the growth of representative government forced by the barons. The king's primary concern seemed to be raising taxes to finance various papal projects, which the barons refused to pay. The tensions finally erupted in a civil war which ended when the king, confronted by lay and spiritual lords united, extracted from the king an agreement to conduct business together with a council of twelve elected nobility, lay, and clergy. This parliament of 1265 has been hailed as the introduction of the middle class into representative government. A highly respected church leader, Robert Grosseteste, Bishop of Lincoln, sided with the barons in opposing further papal taxes. The papal legates played a large part in fostering good government under Henry III. Edward I, son of Henry, succeeded his father (1272–1307), and his reign is noted especially for his attempts to subdue and incorporate Wales and Scotland into his realm, in which he succeeded only to a degree. In 1301 the papal claim that Scotland was a papal fief was met with derision and scorn by king and parliament.[31] Edward continued to oppose the papal provisions by which foreigners were appointed to English benefices, and he confronted Pope Boniface VIII directly in opposing *clericis laicos* (1296), the document in which the pope forbade clergy to pay taxes to laymen. The king declared that any clergy who refused to pay taxes to the state was an outlaw. The Model Parliament of 1295 was a landmark in the growth of representative government, for it established a precedent of including representatives of the "commoners," the knights and burgesses, together with lay and ecclesiastical lords. Clerical influence was represented in this parliament by two archbishops, eighteen bishops, and twenty-seven abbots who sat in the House of Lords. The clergy were known collectively as the Lords Spiritual, and in this way the mutual interests of church and state were addressed through one institution of government, and the king as well as lay lords with knights and burgesses participated in making ecclesiastical decisions.

France and the Papacy

The relationship between kings and churchmen in France before 1300 was never as strained as in other areas of Europe. One reason for this was the weak condition of the monarch under the early Capetian kings, who were generally dominated by their more powerful vassals. Another factor was the genuine fidelity of the French rulers to the Papacy. On several occasions popes found hospitality in France, "the eldest daughter of the church," when residence in Rome became difficult. We have already seen examples of this with Urban II and Alexander III, and earlier it was the policy of Leo IX to shun Rome and to spend much of his pontificate in France. By 1108 the investiture question had been settled in France under terms similar to those in England (1107) whereby bishops and abbots were to be elected according to canon law, but the king retained the right of investing with the temporalities of office.

The story of France in the twelfth century begins with Louis VI (1108–1137), the son of King Philip I (1060–1108) and the fifth king in the line founded by Hugh Capet (987–996). He was the first of the line successfully to challenge and overcome the feudal nobles in the Ile-de-France, laying a foundation for successors to build upon. It became apparent in his time that the primary point of contention between England and France was between two families, the Capets and the Plantagenets, the former being the royal line in France and the latter combining the kingship of England with claims to a large part of France as well. Ever since the conquest of England by Duke William of Normandy the potential for conflict was great, because henceforth the King of England was also the Duke of Normandy. This meant that in England he was sovereign, but in Normandy and in other territories in France he was the vassal of the French king and owed him allegiance. Throughout the medieval period there would be a duel between them to decide which was to predominate. Louis VI, whose reign was basically co-terminus with that of Henry I of England, spent much energy in fighting him over Normandy, with no lasting results. It was during his rule, however, that Suger, Abbot of St. Denis (d. 1151), became prominent. He was the principal emissary of the king to the Roman curia, attended the Lateran Council of 1123, and was the influential advisor of the French crown. One of his most notable accomplishments was the beginning of Gothic architecture in his rebuilding of the church of St. Denis in 1144, of which he has left a detailed description. A modern historian writes of him that "in part he controlled the government, the earliest of the class of clerical first ministers who were to fill such a place in French history, the class to whom Richelieu was to belong."[32]

Louis VII (1137–1180) was pious and deferential to the church. He returned from the disastrous Second Crusade and divorced Eleanor of Aquitane, who then married Henry II of England, thus enriching the English king with vast areas in the south and west of France. When Louis died he was succeeded by his son, Philip (1180–1223), often called "Augustus," who was determined to expel the English from France. Early in his reign he participated in the Third Crusade, the ill-fated venture in which he joined with Richard, "the Lion-hearted," of England. Through a series of wars and alliances he re-conquered Normandy in 1204 and Aquitane in 1208, and at the battle of Bouvines in 1214 he routed John of England and his allies. "Bouvines had a tremendous result in France; it marks both the end of the feudal period . . . and the entrance of the French monarchy into the front rank of important European policy."[33] The most important confrontation of Philip with the pope occurred when Innocent III, under threat of interdict, forced Philip to take back his wife, Ingeborg, whom he had divorced. Philip was also useful to the pope by threatening an invasion of England in order to force King John to accept Stephen Langton as his archbishop, and by announcing a crusade against the Albigensians in southern France, an enterprise in which Philip had no interest and from which he remained aloof. By the end of Philip's reign it seemed as though the Capet's had won in the battle against the Plantagenets, embodied in the English king. Normandy had been regained, Flanders was restored to the realm, seven other major fiefs were annexed, Brittany was ruled by a Capet, and Burgundy was under a Capetian regency. Only one area in France remained outside the royal domain—that encompassed by Gascony and Languedoc in the south. It was under these circumstances that

Innocent III resolved to launch a crusade against the Albigensians, who were concentrated in southern France.

Philip II was succeeded by Louis VIII, who died prematurely after three years, and then by his grandson, Louis IX (1226–1270), who at age twelve was under the regency of his mother, Blanche of Castille. It was an opportune moment for the Plantagenets to recover their continental possessions in western France, but Louis defeated King Henry III of England in 1242 as well as another alliance of northern vassals intent on gaining their autonomy. In the 1259 Treaty of Paris Henry renounced all hereditary claims to land in France and genuine peace prevailed between the two countries until the outbreak of the Hundred Years' War in 1337.

Louis IX (Saint Louis) endeavored to measure up to the ideal of the "Most Christian" king, a title already applied to him in his lifetime. He was austere in his private life and insisted that people of every station should have access to the king's justice. His biographer, Joinville, wrote of him, "The rule of his land was so arranged that every day he heard the hours sung, and a requiem mass without song; and then, if it was convenient, the mass of the day or of the saint. At night he heard complines. He would seat himself in the woods of Vincennes, and lean against an oak, and make us sit around him. All those who had any cause in hand came and spoke to him without hindrance."[34] The king's piety did not prevent him from being one of France's strongest monarchs, and although he was a loyal supporter of the church, he wrote to the pope in 1247 that in cases of national emergency it was the king's right to confiscate the treasures of the churches and all their temporal possessions. It is said that he was fond of recalling the words of an ancestor, "In remembrance of the benefits which God has given to me, I would rather lose my rights than dispute with the servants of Holy Church;" nonetheless, he refused to listen to the angry bishops who accused him of having despoiled them.[35] Reference has already been made to the two crusades he led in 1248 and 1270. He acquired what was supposed to be Christ's crown of thorns from Baldwin II, for which be built the Sainte-Chapelle Church in Paris. His integrity and discretion received wide recognition throughout Europe, and several times he was invited to arbitrate differences between Henry III of England and his barons, and between Frederick I and the pope. Further, he offered Innocent IV a haven in France, although he refused to recognize the pope's deposition of the emperor. It was during the time of Louis IX that a special dependency of the Papacy on France began, which would reach its culmination in the next century. Pope Urban IV (1261–1264) was a Frenchman who appointed French cardinals, and it was he who gave southern Italy and Sicily to Charles of Anjou, brother of Louis IX; Clement IV (1265–1268) was also a Frenchman. In 1297 Boniface VIII canonized Louis IX.

Philip III (1270–1285), son of Louis IX, was not as capable as his father, and during his reign his uncle, Charles of Anjou, wielded more power. As ruler in Sicily and southern Italy, Charles assumed the leadership of the Guelph or pro-papal faction. The Sicilians rebelled against the severity of his rule, an event known as the Sicilian Vespers in which thousands of Frenchmen were killed on March 30, 1282. The Sicilians offered the throne to Peter of Aragon, who accepted despite a papal excommunication. Through various alliances and systems of land holding the French also became involved in the controversy between the Papacy and the empire.

The Empire and the Papacy

The Concordat of 1122, signed by Emperor Henry V and Pope Callistus II, did not end the controversy between the Papacy and the Germans. Henry died two years later without an heir, ending the Salien (Franconian) line of emperors. Under the guidance of the Archbishops of Cologne and Mainz, the magnates chose Lothair II (1125–1138), who was faced with a civil war among the German barons. As a result of the controversy with the Papacy, Germany had become a decentralized collection of fractious nobles who resisted the idea of a strong central monarch. Lothair was succeeded by Conrad III (1138–1152) who was likewise occupied with incessant revolts. His rule was marred by near anarchy and by a massacre of Jews living along the Rhine; but, prompted by Bernard of Clairvaux, he participated in the Second Crusade. It was during this time that a great feud broke out between two powerful German houses, the Hohenstaufen Dukes of Swabia and the Welfs of Bavaria. In Italy the allies of each party became known as the Guelphs who allied themselves with the Papacy to thwart the ambitions of the emperors and who favored decentralization, and the Ghibbelines (after a favorite residence of the Hohenstaufen), who supported control of the church and a strong imperial government. When Conrad died, Frederick of Swabia was selected with the hope that his election would end the civil strife, as his father was a Ghibbeline and his mother a Guelph. These dynastic rivalries, however, continued for several centuries.

Frederick I (1152–1190), also known as "Barbarossa" because of his red beard, claimed for the empire the same sacred origin and dignity as

that of the church, and to underscore his claims he coined the designation Holy Roman Empire, the first to refer to the empire in this way. The
revival of Roman law by Irnerius at Bologna around 1100 provided a
theory of temporal sovereignty which elaborated on Justinian's Code,
which had stated that "God set the imperial dispensation at the head of
human affairs . . . and the emperor is not bound by statutes."[36] The
popes of the twelfth century also used Roman law, but in their case it
was used to develop ecclesiastical law into a system which made possible the unprecedented growth of administrative unity in the church
under a strong papacy, which was the objective of Gratian's *Decretum.*
Both papal and imperial parties were more formidable antagonists
because of the precedents of Roman antiquity than were those during
the Investiture Controversy of a century past.

In 1155 Frederick arrived in Rome on the first of six Italian campaigns. He was preoccupied with Italy and, while he made these peri
odic visits to the south, the German nobility pursued their own
independent course. In return for rescuing the pope from the control of
Roman factions, Adrian IV crowned him emperor, and Frederick demonstrated his dedication to Catholic Christianity by burning Arnold of
Brescia as a heretic. Irritated by Frederick's imperious attitude toward
him, the pope contracted a military alliance with the Normans of southern Italy. Two years later an incident occurred at a great imperial Diet of
1157 in Besancon in Burgundy which fanned the papal-imperial ani-
mosities to fever pitch. The papal emissary, Roland, the future Pope
Alexander III, read a letter of Pope Adrian IV to the emperor. It was
translated aloud for the sake of the nobles who did not understand
Latin. "You should not forget, my most glorious son, how graciously the
Holy Roman Church lately conferred upon you the imperial crown. . . .
We should rejoice to confer even greater *beneficia* upon you, if that were
possible."[37] These were dangerously ambiguous words. When the assembly heard the word *beneficia* a tumult ensued, for in imperial language a benefice was a "fief," and that implied that the emperor was a
vassal of the pope. Frederick called it a "false and lying statement. We
hold this kingdom and empire through the election of the princes from
God alone. Therefore whoever says that we hold the imperial crown as
a benefice from the pope resists the divine institution and is a liar."[38]
Cardinal Roland made clear that his intention had been exactly what
Frederick feared it was when he said, "From whom else, then, does the
emperor hold the empire if not from the pope?" The pope explained
that he had intended the term simply in its literal sense, meaning good
deed.

When Adrian IV died in 1159, the College of Cardinals elected Alexander III, but a small faction supported Victor IV. The papal election decree of 1059 did not specify whether unanimity, or a simple majority, or even a majority of the *sanior pars* (wiser ones) was required for a valid election, and Frederick decided to support the minority faction. The schism, in which two rival popes contended for recognition, lasted almost twenty years until the emperor recognized Alexander in 1177. Frederick entered another arena of conflict when he convened a council in Pavia, since "in my office and dignity as emperor I can convoke councils, as did Constantine, etc." Only imperial representatives attended and Victor IV was declared the true pope, though Sicily, Spain, France, and England recognized Alexander III. It was probably due to Alexander's need for English support that he tended to side with the king against Thomas à Becket in that struggle which was then current. When Frederick marched to Rome in 1166 to install his anti-pope, Alexander III fled to France, where the Becket affair was awaiting his attention.

Frederick's two most dangerous enemies were the north Italian cities and the Normans in the south. In 1158 the imperial armies crushed the northern opposition, and at the Diet of Roncaglia the towns were denied the right of self-rule. Milan refused to accept the king's representative, and in retaliation it was reduced to ashes. The relics of the Three Wise Men were removed from Milan to the cathedral at Cologne, where they remain to this day. By 1168 the towns had formed the Lombard League, which allied itself with the Papacy against the emperor. When Frederick returned to Germany from his second Italian expedition, he found it necessary to make his way through Lombardy disguised as a peasant. His attempt to reconquer the towns ended at the battle of Legnano in 1176, which was a complete victory for the Lombard League, said to be the first major defeat in medieval history of feudal cavalry by infantry.

As a result of this loss he found it necessary to recognize Alexander III as pope, and to celebrate this recognition the pope convened the Third Lateran Council of 1179. In order to prevent confusion in future papal elections, the decree of 1059 was tightened at this council by declaring that a valid election required a two-thirds majority of the cardinals. In the Peace of Constance in 1183 Frederick fully recognized the autonomy of the north Italian municipalities, and they in turn supported the emperor against the pope. This was because in their struggle for freedom, they were equally opposed to episcopal lords as well as to imperial oversight, and a strong current of anti-clericalism ran through the communes. Having pacified the north, Frederick turned to the south, where his son and successor, Henry VI, married Constance, heiress to Sicily, thus effectively surrounding the papal states with Hohenstaufen influence. In 1188 the old emperor joined the Third Crusade, but en route to Jerusalem he drowned while bathing in Cilicia. In subsequent years he became a legendary figure, and during nineteenth-century German nationalism *der alte Kaiser*, the great Barbarossa, became a romantic symbol of the medieval glory of the Germanies.

Henry VI did not live long enough to pursue an effective policy, and when he died in 1196 he left a three-year-old son, Frederick II, as a ward of the pope. His death brought on a civil war in Germany (1198–1215) between his brother, Philip of Swabia, and Otto IV, son of the most powerful baron, Henry, "the Lion," essentially a Guelph-Ghibbeline conflict. It was at this moment that Innocent III came to the papal throne (1198–1215). His position of strength was undoubtedly enhanced by the fact that he faced no strong German emperor during his entire reign. He crowned Otto IV emperor, who thereupon reneged on his promise not to interfere in German ecclesiastical affairs. With the help of Philip II of France the pope stirred up the German barons against Otto IV. In alliance with John of England, Otto attacked France but was routed at the battle of Bouvines in 1214. Thereupon the pope championed the cause of his young ward, Frederick II, the grandson of Barbarossa.

Frederick II (1215–1250) was by character and upbringing a Sicilian. Although he was king both in Sicily and in Germany, he left the princes north of the Alps to themselves while he concentrated his attention in the south. In fact, he visited Germany only once during the last thirty years of his life.

Without question Frederick was one of the most gifted monarchs in European history. He was accomplished in statecraft, architecture, mathematics, philosophy, art, sculpture, natural sciences, and he spoke nine languages. It is no wonder that his contemporaries called him the *stupor mundi*, wonder of the world. In matters of religion he was a skeptic. He maintained a harem of Saracen women and he employed Muslim mercenaries in his wars against the Christian cities of Italy. It is not surprising that he was unimpressed by papal claims to be vicars of Christ.

Frederick was crowned emperor by the pope in 1220, and in return for this favor he promised to lead a crusade to the Holy Land. For the next six years, however, he concerned himself primarily with organizing his Sicilian estates and with attempting to unite all of Italy by placing it under his control. The pope, viewing this program with alarm, excommunicated Frederick in 1227 for failure to keep his crusader's vow. Two years later he finally led a crusade, but since the excommunication was still in force the pope found it necessary to oppose the crusade. Upon arriving in Palestine, Frederick negotiated a settlement with the Muslims instead of making war. Many Western Christians considered such diplomacy as treachery, and when Frederick was crowned King of Jerusalem, the pope placed the Holy City under the interdict. In 1230 a truce was negotiated with the pope, and the excommunication was lifted.

Upon his return from the crusade Frederick energetically sought to unite the Lombard towns of northern Italy to his own holdings in the south. His vision was that of reviving Rome's ancient greatness. "Our hearts have ever burned with the desire to reinstate . . . Rome herself, that the blood of Romulus may revive, the ancient Roman dignity be renewed and an inseparable bond by our grace be tied between the Roman empire and the Roman people themselves."[39] Pope Gregory IX, who vigorously opposed these designs, was also the best canon lawyer of his day. He kept up a constant struggle with the emperor and in 1239 excommunicated him a second time because of his Lombard policy. The propaganda on both sides became heated and lively. The pope declared, "This king of Pestilence has proclaimed that . . . all the world has been deceived by three deceivers, Jesus Christ, Moses, and Mohammed, of whom two died in honor but Christ upon the cross . . . and Frederick maintains that no one should believe anything unless it can be proven by reason."[40] Frederick responded in kind by saying that he was like Elijah rooting out the prophets of Baal, claiming that anyone who opposed the emperor was anti-Christ. In 1241 the pope called a council to depose the emperor, but Frederick managed to capture the ships that were carrying the bishops to the meeting. This capture of an entire ecumenical council scandalized even the most ardent imperialists.

Finally in 1245 the pope managed to slip away from Rome and convene a council at Lyons in France. There Frederick was deposed from office for perjury, sacrilege, and heresy—charges which were no doubt well founded. His response to the news of his deposition was said to be, "I have been the anvil long enough, now I shall be the hammer," and he proceeded to launch an attack against wealthy clergy, maintaining that "all true religion is choked by their surfeit of riches and power. Hence to deprive such men of the baneful wealth that burdens them to their own damnation is a work of charity."[41] Frederick died in 1250, and assessments of his life have been divided ever since. To a modern he was "a colossus of impertinence, curiosity, and skepticism"; he was the only medieval emperor Dante consigned to hell in his *Divine Comedy*, while a cleric of his day eulogized him, "Blessed art thou amongst kings, that is, over all kings."[42]

After his death there were twenty-three years of civil strife until a Diet in 1256 established the procedure of selecting the emperor through election by seven prominent ecclesiastical lay lords, known as the "electors." They chose Rudolph of Hapsburg as emperor in 1273, thus inaugurating the Hapsburg dynasty, which continued until 1918.[43]

The revival of Aristotelian studies, especially his *Politics*, served the interests of the state in the struggle with the church. For centuries, at least since Augustine, it had been assumed that the state's sole purpose was to curb sin, that is, a negative function of law and order to keep the effects of sin from disrupting society. This placed secular rulers at a disadvantage, since the assumption was that they were therefore subservient to the church, which alone could define sin. Aristotle, however, said that political organization was a characteristic of human nature. What this meant in religious terms was that, had Adam and Eve never fallen into sin, some form of social organization would still have been necessary. The "Aristotelian conception of the *societas humana* provided the early fourteenth-century challenge to hierocratic thought, and provided the framework out of which the modern nation-state could arise."[44] Thomas Aquinas, following this trend, wrote that, "It is natural for man, more than any other animal, to be a social and political animal, to live in a group."[45] The stage was set for another round of conflict in the final two centuries of the Middle Ages.

CHAPTER SIX

RENAISSANCE IN THEOLOGY AND LEARNING

From about 1050 until 1250 European society experienced a regeneration of intellectual and cultural life which sets it apart from the rest of the Middle Ages. In practically every arena of human endeavor—artistic, literary, architectural, musical, scholarly, scientific, and theological— there was a new self confidence and a vigorous pursuit of hitherto neglected resources. This period has come to be known as the twelfth-century Renaissance, implying a rebirth of ancient culture. The revival ocurred because of the rediscovery of the church fathers and the early Christian traditions as well as a reclamation of Graeco-Roman culture and literature. We have already discussed the growth of legal studies, which revived after the discovery of Justinian's Code from the sixth century. But this period also produced much that was original and creative, either through reworking old materials, or through pressing on to new and uncharted horizons. The reasons for the revival have often been discussed, but no single factor emerges as a cause. The rediscovery of Aristotle, the end of the wars of the Papacy versus the empire, the rise of the urban middle class, the increased standards of living as a result of revived commerce, as well as the recovery of the Mediterranean from pirates all played their part. During this time pilgrimage routes throughout Europe were filled with people going to Rome or Santiago in northwest Spain or some other shrine in numbers which have not been equalled since, exchanging ideas along the way. Here we will explore the way in which this revival affected the church and its theology. Although its origins were in France and northern Italy, the revival spread throughout Europe. South of the Alps the Renaissance was largely urban and lay, with its interests focused on medicine and law. North of the Alps the movement came from monasteries as well as cathedral schools, with interests focused on theology and philosophy.[1]

The Theological Revival of the Twelfth Century

The mental awakening began with a new method of inquiry by means of Aristotelian logic called dialectic. The new form presented a problem as a question (*quaestio*), to which arguments, both for and against, were presented (*disputatio*), and finally a tentative solution was proposed (*sententia*). In short, this is the method known as scholasticism, which was essentially the application of reason to revelation, with the object of harmonizing the two, or "the rational attempt to penetrate the revealed data of faith through a logical apparatus."[2] The development of scholasticism was also accompanied by the question of universals, or the reality of "ideas," a philosophical approach to reality that was Platonic in origin. These "ideas" or universals were general concepts representing the common elements belonging to things of the same species. Thus "humanity" belonged to all humans, "goodness" belonged to the good angels, "brightness" to all light, and so on. At issue in this approach was whether universals exist apart from their objects; that is, could there be "humanity" apart from people (*universalia ante rem*), or did universals exist only as they are manifest in things (*in re*)? Or were they merely names describing the collective quality of things (*universalia post rem*)? The question had serious ramifications for theology. For instance, could the church exist without people, as an inevitable entity in the mind of God (invisible church)? Was there such a thing as an evil principle existing in nature? Could God exist apart from God's manifestations in nature, or was God in nature? Those who held to the reality of universals apart from things, following Plato, were called Realists. Those who took the position that universals were merely words describing things, were called Nominalists (*nomen* = merely a name). Those in the latter group were inclined to acknowledge as true only that which could be proven from observable data, and the extremists placed reason above revelation. Much of the ferment in medieval theology henceforth would be a conflict between these two extremes, between reason and revelation, with most theologians ranging themselves somewhere in the center.

The first significant name in theology in the early days of scholasticism was Berengar of Tours (d. 1088). A pupil of Fulbert of Chartres (d. 1028), Berengar made the School of Chartres the most illustrious center of theology in the twelfth century. Its leading masters insisted on the authority of Scripture and the church as the final arbiter of truth, but Berengar broke from tradition by suggesting that reason and not authority should take precedence. One consequence of his position was to challenge prevailing eucharistic piety which, following Radbertus, held that in the Eucharist an actual change in elements took place. Berengar espoused the "symbolic" view that Ratramnus had suggested, but he was opposed by Lanfranc (d. 1089) who later became the famous Archbishop of Canterbury under William, "the Conqueror." Berengar was excommunicated in 1050, and although he recanted, he never abandoned his view. The conflict shows that although the eucharistic question remained dogmatically undefined, popular leanings were strongly in favor of transubstantiation, that is, that in the Eucharist the bread and wine were substantially changed into Christ's body and blood.

There was considerable opposition to the use of dialectic, one of its most outspoken critics being Peter Damian (d. 1072) who looked upon it as "worldly, beastly, and devilish. That which is from the argument of dialecticians cannot easily be adapted to the mysteries of divine power; that which has been invented for the benefit of syllogisms . . . let it not be obstinately introduced into divine law. . . ."[3]

The School of Bec in Normandy sought to follow a middle ground between the extremes. Anselm (d. 1109), who succeeded Lanfranc as Archbishop of Canterbury, is often called the "Father of Scholasticism." He suggested the proper use of reason in his celebrated *Proslogion: Fides quarens intellectum* (Faith in Search of Understanding): "For I do not seek to understand that I may believe, but I believe in order that I might understand (*credo ut intelligam*)," which Augustine had also said long before.[4] By the use of reason alone one could arrive at truths which had been revealed, one of which was the existence of God, for which Anselm employed his famous ontological argument: "And assuredly that, than which nothing greater can be conceived, cannot exist in the understanding alone. For, suppose it exists in the understanding alone: then it can be conceived to exist in reality, which is greater."[5] Anselm saw no tension between faith and reason, as they each proceeded from the same source—God. Therefore in the *Proslogion* and the *Monologium* he sought to prove the Christian faith without reference to Scripture or other received authorities.

His most influential writing, *Cur Deus Homo,* (Why the God-Man?), has to do with salvation and his theory of the doctrine of Atonement. Up to his time a popular conception was that humans were saved because God, in Christ, had made a contract with the devil whereby a ransom had been paid to Satan for the release of all the condemned.

Basing his theology on St. Paul, Anselm showed that in the Christian scheme of redemption, satisfaction was owed to God, not Satan. He taught that God had created humans in order to fill the vacancy left by the fallen angels; but by falling into sin, humans had thwarted God's purposes. Humans were now required to satisfy God's justice or honor (a thought influenced by feudal ideas of kingship) either through holiness of life or by suffering eternal damnation. This placed God in a dilemma. God could not simply forgive humanity's sins, for this would violate justice; and God could not punish humans forever, for this would violate mercy and thwart the original plan. If the original plan was thwarted, it would prove God to be less than all-powerful. The solution lay in the sending of God's Son who was both God and human, who would render the satisfaction which was due to God. As a human being Christ owed God a perfect life, which he gave; this however, held no merit for anyone other than himself, for all people owe God a perfect life. But in his deity Christ did not owe God anything, and since the divine nature also died, this became the ransom which God accepted for the sins of all people. Anselm elaborated a juridical explanation of the Atonement with the death of Christ as the single most important act of salvation. The influence of this interpretation of Christ's death on the medieval mind can be seen in the dramatic increase of the use of the crucifix in the twelfth century and in the importance given to Good Friday. Anselm's satisfaction metaphor continues to have a powerful influence on the Christian imagination today.[6]

Despite his high estimate of reason, Anselm remained a loyal follower of the church, devoted primarily to Scripture and the tradition. This can be seen in his conflict with Roscellin (d. 1125) whose Trinitarian doctrine, under the influence of nominalism, insisted that either the Father, Son, and Holy Spirit were identical or they were three separate entities. He was accused of tritheism at Soissons in 1092 but denied the charge. Roscellin objected to a theology based upon Realism, which was indispensable for the defense of traditional views on the Trinity and the Person of Christ. He was also opposed by William of Champeaux (d. 1181), founder of the School of St. Victor in Paris and a trusted friend of Bernard of Clairvaux.

Peter Abelard (d. 1142), Roscellin's most famous pupil, was also undoubtedly the most brilliant theologian of the twelfth century. He developed such a following of students in Paris that he is sometimes credited with being the catalyst for the University of Paris's foundation. Most of what we know of him is from his autobiography, *Historia Calamitatum*, the story of his adversities, and from his correspondence with Heloise after they were forcibly separated. "Scintillating, sardonic, and intellectually arrogant, Abelard went through life making friends and enemies with equal facility."[7] His whirlwind love affair with Heloise, his pupil, came to an end when she was secluded in a nunnery and he was forcibly emasculated by thugs hired by Fulbert, Heloise' uncle. After the affair with Heloise he entered the monastery of St. Denis (named for Dionysius the Areopagite), from which he was expelled after demonstrating that St. Denis was not St. Paul's contemporary but a fifth-century mystical theologian. Abelard adopted a modified form of nominalism which led him to cast doubt on traditional Christian formulations. His explanation of the Trinity bordered on tritheism, and on the Atonement he believed that the chief value of Christ's life and death was to provide an example of obedience and holiness. He also denied the traditional teaching on original sin, stating that sin consisted in contempt for God, placing emphasis on the intention which lies behind an act, rather than on distinguishing between good and evil acts in themselves. The task for theology is, "by doubt we come to inquire, and by inquiry we arrive at the truth."[8] Sometimes he is said to have reversed Anselm's motto, "I believe in order that I may understand," to "I understand in order to believe," but there is no such statement in his writings. He was a critical thinker who refused to accept traditional formulae simply without examination. He opposed the legacy of Augustine by insisting on a complete freedom of the will which made it possible for every person to grow in holiness by following the example of Christ.

Abelard's most influential writing was his *Sic et Non* (Yes and No), in which he collected and systematized 157 *sententiae* or doctrinal propositions, and under each listed divergent authorities including Scripture, the Fathers, and philosophers, dramatically demonstrating thereby the contradictions among authorities. This method was already in use by others, notably Gratian's famous *Decretum*, but it had never before been used in theology. His critics claimed that Abelard's use of this method cast doubt on ecclesiastical authority; but in his prologue he explained that all authorities varied in their value, depending upon many circumstances. His "rules of exegesis" are today followed by most biblical scholars. The *Sic et Non* exercised a decisive influence on the scholastic method. "This work was the first comprehensive exposition of theology as a science rather than as a meditation; it prised theology away from authority and exposed it to the scrutiny of reason."[9] His teachings were condemned at Soissons in 1121, but he resumed his teaching in Paris. In 1140 some of his propositions were condemned at the Council of Sens. Abelard's most formidable antagonist was Bernard of Clairvaux, who was instrumental in his later condemnation. The hostility between these two theologians was one of the hallmarks of the age, with Bernard usually being cast as overzealous in his defense of orthodoxy. Some believe that it was essentially a personal dispute, while others point to a basic ideological difference at the root of their quarrel on the relationship between faith and knowledge.[10] Abelard considered himself a faithful Christian, and when he died in the arms of Peter the Venerable at a Cluniac monastery, he was reconciled to the church. After his condemnation in 1140 he wrote to his beloved Heloise, by this time an abbess: "I will never be a philosopher, if it is to speak against St. Paul; I would not be an Aristotle, if this were to separate me from Christ. . . . I have set my building on the corner-stone on which Christ has built his church . . . if the tempest rises, I am not shaken; if the winds rave, I am not fearful. I rest upon the rock that cannot be moved."[11] David Knowles observes that, "Abelard remains, both as a teacher and as a thinker, one of the half dozen most influential names in the history of medieval thought. It would be difficult to instance any other theologian, accused so often and unjustifiably of error, who has given so much of method and matter to orthodox thought."[12]

Peter Lombard (d. 1160), a student of Abelard, used his master's methods, but the end product, *Sententiarum libri quatuor* (Four Books of Sentences) was accepted as orthodox. He was a friend of Bernard, and in 1159 he became the Bishop of Paris. His four books arranged topically were on the Trinity, Creation and Sin; the Incarnation and Virtues; the Sacraments and Last Things. He used the same dialectical method as Abelard, ranging authorities for and against each proposition. He was one of the first to fix the number of sacraments at seven in order to distinguish them from lesser rites, but it was not until the Council of Florence in 1439 that the church formally affirmed this list and fixed number. The *Sentences* became the standard theological textbook of the Middle Ages until the sixteenth century, and a commentary on them was one of the requirements for all students (including Martin Lutehr) who wished to become masters of theology.

Thirteenth-Century Synthesis

Since its encounter with Hellenism in its formative years, Christianity in its worldview and presuppositions had received large injections of Plato's ideas, whom Justin Martyr confidently asserted was a Christian before Christ. Aristotle was almost unknown until the twelfth century, when his dialectical writings began to appear in the West, giving rise to the early scholastics we have considered. Beginning in the thirteenth century, Aristotle's philosophical writings appeared, containing ideas that contradicted both the Platonic and the Christian traditions. This was due in part to the fact that his writings had been preserved by the Arabs, whose glosses and commentaries accompanied his works. It was particularly via Spain that Aristotle entered the West, and of the Arab transmitters, Avicenna (d. 1037) and Averroes of Cordoba (d. 1198), were preeminent. In addition to them, Maimonides (d. 1204), a Jewish philosopher from Cordoba whom Thomas Aquinas held in highest regard, produced commentaries on Aristotle. The Arabic editions of Aristotle, which had come from the earlier Greek manuscripts, now needed to be translated into Latin, and Toledo became a center of this activity. Two such early translators were Dominic Gundisalvi and Gerald of Cremona, but the greatest of them was a Flemish Dominican, William of Moerbeke (d. 1286), who had access to the primary Greek texts and came to know Thomas Aquinas.

Some of the new ideas that challenged the Christian tradition were Aristotle's belief in the eternal nature of the world, the concept of a universal soul rather than one's individual soul, and a universalism that called in question the particularity of Christianity. In his theory of knowledge, Aristotle taught that all our understanding comes from external impressions, i.e. the soul is a blank slate which receives stimuli; whereas Augustine (from Plato) believed that knowledge can be derived from inner illumination provided by God: things external to the soul do not cause knowledge. So disturbing were these new ideas to some that in 1210 a ban on Aristotle was declared in Paris—a ban that was largely ignored. By 1200 the theological scene found various schools of thought jostling for attention. The Augustinian-Neoplatonic tradition, representing the older and more conservative thought, was espoused by the Franciscans, while the Dominicans tended toward the newer Aristotelian ideas. The Franciscans were also inclined toward voluntarism, meaning the will rules over one's actions; whereas, the Aristotelians believed that the intellect was of primary importance in that it influenced the will. These divisions were not hard and fast, and Dominican theologians could be found who were Augustinians, while Aristotelians ranged somewhere between realism and nominalism. The "synthesis" of the thirteenth century has to do with efforts at achieving some harmony among these competing thoughts and the basic question of the relationship of faith to knowledge.[13]

Representing an earlier, mystical, Augustinian and Neoplatonic tradition was the School of St. Victor in Paris, founded by William of

Champeaux (d.1141). Hugh of St. Victor associated the pursuit of truth with that of virtue. His *De sacramentis christianae fidei* is the first attempt to give a comprehensive view of theology in all its branches, and he is credited with a classic description of faith, "The will to assent to things unseen with a certitude greater than that of opinion and less than that of direct knowledge."[14] Richard of St. Victor (d. 1173) followed Anselm in his belief that adequate and convincing arguments to prove the mysteries of the faith can be found; but his fame rests largely on two treatises of mystical theology, *Benjamin Major* and *Benjamin Minor*, which were long used as textbooks on contemplation. He reflected Augustinian thought but more powerfully the influence of Pseudo-Dionysius. Walter of St. Victor (d. 1180) was intensely opposed to the new dialectic, as we can see in his treatise against *The Four Masters of Confusion* (Abelard, Gilbert de la Poree, Peter Lombard, and Peter of Poitiers). His verdict on Peter Lombard was, "May your grammar be your damnation."[15] Adam of St. Victor (d. ca. 1192) was especially known for his hymns.

The Franciscan school in Paris produced three great theologians who consistently followed Augustine. Alexander of Hales (d. 1245), the first Franciscan theological master, wrote *Summa universae theologiae* ("Heavier than a horse and not his at that," groused Roger Bacon), which was a commentary on Peter Lombard's *Sentences*. Following Augustine's theory of illumination, Alexander of Hales taught that a knowledge of God is inherent in every person from birth and that, later, more enlightenment comes by grace through infused faith. He believed that human will also played a part in receiving such illumination. Bonaventure (d. 1274), a student of Alexander and General of the Franciscan Order when he died, subordinated philosophy (knowledge) to faith. All rational thought springs from faith, and truth must be revealed; it cannot be gained through external stimuli. As opposed to Aristotle, he taught that the creation of the world in time could be demonstrated by reason and that all intellectual activity and human learning should be subject to theology. He was especially devoted to mystical theology and in subsequent years was given the title of "Seraphic Doctor." With Albert and Aquinas, he opposed the growing movement toward belief in the immaculate conception of the Virgin Mary. His theology is best revealed in his *Commentary on The Sentences* of Peter Lombard.

A third Franciscan who continued opposition to the idea that the intellect governs one's actions in place of the will was Duns Scotus (d. 1308), a teacher at Oxford and Paris. He emphasized the supreme sovereignty of God's will, and said that most of God's acts are outside the realm of human comprehension. It is in Scotus that philosophy and theology, which heretofore had been almost synonymous, began to fall apart. Scotus gave the intellect limited capacity to understand God's actions. He believed that we cannot know God's will, predict it, or satisfactorily explain divine actions.

Albertus Magnus (Albert, "the Great," d. 1280) was the first to master the entire body of Aristotle's writings, and it was his goal to make them intelligible to the Latin West. He was born in Swabia, became a Dominican in 1223, and taught in Germany for seven years until he went to Paris for a time. He spent most of his life in Germany, at Cologne. His productivity was enormous, filling thirty-eight volumes in a Paris edition of 1890 devoted almost entirely to commentaries on Aristotle and theological treatises based on Aristotle. His interests were primarily in philosophy and in making Aristotle known; but in theology he laid the foundations for the task of harmonizing faith and reason, specifically Aristotle with the Christian tradition. He saw philosophy as a legitimate study for its own sake apart from theology. Albert is perhaps best known for his famous pupil, Thomas Aquinas, whom he met in Paris and who returned with him to the newly established *studium generale* in Cologne, where he studied Aristotle for four years.

Thomas Aquinas (d. 1274), *Doctor Angelicus* and the prince of the scholastics, achieved a synthesis between Augustine and Aristotle, a harmony between reason and faith. No theologian in the Latin church since Augustine has enjoyed such a wide influence. "St. Thomas' system is the most lasting testimony to knowledge in the service of belief. It was directed to proving the truth of revelation. Indeed, the safety valve of Thomism was his refusal to stretch reason beyond its limits. When the two seemed equally probable, there could be no final judgment by reason. It then was left as a matter of faith."[16]

He was a native of Aquino, a village between Rome and Monte Casino, and he resided at that famous monastery for a time before joining the new order of Dominicans, under protest of his family. After studying at Naples he became the student of Albert at Paris and Cologne. It was here that his fellow students referred to him as the "dumb ox," a reference to his corpulence and to his reserve. He taught in Paris, at various places in Italy, and in Rome, prodigious in his literary output and in his involvement with the church. He died in 1274, not yet fifty years old, en route to the Council of Lyons to which he had been invited by the pope. The principal modern edition of his works is in twenty-five volumes.

Three major theological treatises can be used as mirrors to reflect his principal thoughts. The *Summa contra gentiles* was written for Dominican missionaries to Muslims, Jews, and heretical Christians in order to commend the truth of Christianity to the "gentiles," i.e. those outside the faith. In it he proposes that truth has a single source, God, but that it comes to us both through faith and reason. Since truth is one, there can be no contradictions between them. "Although the truth of the Christian faith surpasses the capacity of reason, nevertheless that truth that the human reason is naturally endowed to know cannot be opposed to the Christian faith."[17] On the basis of Scripture he accepts the Trinity, Incarnation, the creation of the world in time, original sin, the resurrection of the body, etc., but such doctrines are shown not to be contrary to reason. In short, his treatise is a defense of natural theology against non-Christians. Truth is one. Grace does not destroy nature; it perfects nature.

The *Summa Theologica* was his greatest and most influential theological work. It was his attempt to bring all knowledge, both secular and sacred, into an orderly rational system. It is written in three parts; thirty-eight sections offer answers to 630 theological questions by citing authorities and by reasoned argument. He follows a type of "Sic et Non" methodology, when for each question raised he ranges all the possible arguments for and against the proposition. Then he addresses each objection in a logical, clear, and analytical way, concluding with the conviction that the statement as it stands must be correct. In the process he answers some ten thousand objections to propositions of Christian truth. Instead of being suspicious of reason, he sets out to demonstrate the compatibility between human knowledge and revelation, theology and philosophy, faith and reason, Plato and Aristotle.

In the *Compendium Theologiae* Aquinas presents a short capsule of the Christian faith for beginners, a work which his death left incomplete. He speaks of the Trinity, the person and work of Christ, and repeats exactly Anselm's argument for Christ's atonement as it was expressed in *Cur Deus Homo*.

Aquinas was not as positive as Anselm and others that all biblical truths could be explained by reason. Christianity still contained "mysteries" which were revealed by Scripture and only accessible through faith. However, although such truths lie beyond the capacity of reason, they are not contrary to it. Following Aristotle, he believed that all natural knowledge begins with sensory perception, and in this way he suggests five proofs for the existence of God based on arguments of causality. He begins in this way: "Whatever is put into motion is put in motion by another, for nothing can be in motion except it is in potentiality to that towards which it is in motion. For motion is nothing else than a reduction of something from potentiality to actuality. But nothing can be reduced from potentiality to actuality, except by something in a state of actuality," and that, he suggests, is God.[18] It was he who introduced the Aristotelian distinction between substance and accident in the Eucharist, and because Christ's body and blood were entirely present in either the bread or the wine, he afforded justification for communion in one kind (The practice of communion under one kind—receiving only the bread—was not approved until 1415 at the Council of Constance). Fallen humanity can be restored only through the free grace of God. This grace is infused into humans through the sacraments, and it enables the recipient to respond in obedience and love. Although the grace is unmerited and given alone by God, it is also imperative that the recipient exercise this enablement to live a life of obedience. The sacraments convey such grace, *ex opere operato* (by the act performed). Following Peter Lombard, Aquinas numbered seven sacraments, of which the Eucharist was given preeminence. It may be that Thomas composed the office for the newly instituted Feast of Corpus Christi. On the sacraments he wrote: "Now remedies must be of some visible signs. God provides for man according to his condition. Man's condition is such that he is brought to grasp the spiritual through the senses. Therefore spiritual remedies had to be given to men under sensible signs. Also, because men fell into sin by clinging unduly to visible things, but that one might not believe visible things are evil, it was fitting that through the visible things themselves the remedies of salvation be applied to men."[19]

Imposing as his theological synthesis was, Aquinas nevertheless aroused strong opposition from those who believed that he had undermined the Augustinian tradition. Just as these critics represented a conservative reaction to his theology, so also there were others on the intellectual left who believed that he had not gone far enough. These were the Latin Averroists, led by Siger of Brabant and Boethius of Dacia who taught in the Faculty of Arts in Paris. They accepted more of Averroes and Aristotle than was considered orthodox, such as the eternity of the world (denying creation in time), denial of the immortality of the soul, and emphasis on free will and moral responsibility. When pressed to respond to their obvious heresy, the Averroists proposed a "double truth" theory, which maintained that a statement could be philosophically true but theologically false. In such a case they insisted that theology must prevail. Thomas Aquinas had written a treatise opposing this form of circumlocution, but he had also opened the door to the separation of philosophy and theology. In 1277, Etienne Tempier, Bishop of Paris, at the request of the pope had condemned 219 propositions, mostly of Averroists, but including one against courtly love poetry, some against dialecticians, and several against Aquinas, without mentioning him by name. The Archbishop of Canterbury, Robert Kilwardby, a fellow Dominican, repeated the condemnation verbatim, followed by John Peckham and Raymond Lull, influential Franciscans. "The condemnation (of 1277) attacked the rights of philosophy; it denied to philosophy an existence independent of theology, and to reason a life apart from faith."[20] As a result, all philosophical inquiries aimed at rationalizing theological traditions became suspect, a trend which is readily apparent in John Duns Scotus's emphases on God's inscrutability, freedom, and sovereignty, a trend which will find its culmination in William of Occam in the next century. "The marriage of reason and faith was broken forever."[21] The way was open for the rise of Christian mysticism on the one hand and on the other the emergence of a thoroughly secular Renaissance which sought to supersede the "Age of Faith"[22]

The Rise of the Universities

Up to and beyond the Carolingian period (750–1000) most people were illiterate and there was no need or incentive for formal learning. The one exception to this was in monasticism, because the monks by virtue of their vocation were required to know the Rule of St. Benedict, the liturgical books of worship, and the church fathers. Indeed, the Rule required that all monks learn to read. Since monasteries were dependent for their continuation on new recruits from outside, it was necessary to educate novices in the rudiments of reading and writings, which was usually assigned to one master or *scholasticus*, and in this way monastic schools developed. These were primarily for those intending to take monastic vows, although on occasion it was likely that sons of local nobles were permitted to attend. The minimum age for entrance was ten years, and it was not unusual for parents to bring such young children into the service of the monastery as their "sacrifice," for which reason these boys were called *oblates* (sacrifice). The monastic schools were relatively isolated from the surrounding world because of their intention to educate for a monastic life, for which reason the curriculum was focused more narrowly on learning and maintaining ecclesiastical tradition and worship life. We have already taken note of the basic curriculum of studies inherited from Roman times, the *trivium* (grammar, rhetoric, logic), and the *quadrivium* (arithmetic, geometry, astronomy, music).[23] Monastic education was primarily concerned with grammar and rhetoric, with a view toward understanding and reproducing the traditions of the past, but with minimal interest in creativity, originality, or questioning that tradition.

Alongside the monastic schools other centers of learning developed in towns with cathedrals. These cathedral schools were primarily for the instruction of secular priests, often only those attached to the cathedral and possibly to an occasional child of the urban aristocracy. The large majority of priests, mostly in rural areas, remained uneducated, with just enough knowledge of Latin to say Mass and conduct minimal parish duties. The cathedral schools were taught either by the bishop himself or by a master (*scholasticus*), but there was no uniform curriculum, and the contents of the education depended primarily upon the interests of the teacher. One difference between these schools and monastic schools, however, was that in the urban centers students were preparing for a life in the world, in the secular arena, and they tended toward greater independence, mobility, and innovation. This can clearly be seen in the popularity of Peter Abelard, who taught at Notre Dame in Paris, attracting large numbers of students to this lectures. The same was true for Peter Lombard. The first half of the twelfth century was an age of "wandering scholars" who moved from place to place, often taking students with them. The migratory nature of a twelfth-century scholar has been described by Fulbert of Chartres, who mentions six different schools attended by one Gilbert of Liege.[24] Schooling was not yet formalized to the granting of degrees and examinations, but with the rise of urban centers and the increasing complexities of life, including the need for literacy to engage in commerce or law, such formalization was soon in coming.

In 1179 Pope Alexander III required that a master be appointed at every cathedral school to provide advanced education, and by that time at Notre Dame in Paris the chancellor of the diocese was authorized to grant teaching licenses to masters. In addition to the cathedral school, Paris also had a school at the monastery of St. Genevieve and at the canonry of St. Victor, which together became the future university. There were also independent masters who were not attached to any school. Among the masters there developed a guild, similar to other guilds of craftsmen such as bakers or carpenters, who determined admission to their ranks as well as protection from hostile townsmen or even students. "University" (*universitas*) came to refer to the totality of a group banded together to serve its own interests, and was applicable to any guild, much as today we may refer to a labor union.[25] Then, as today, there were often tensions between the students and townspeople, the former being seen as strangers and foreigners. One estimate is that in the High Middle Ages, Paris had between five thousand to seven thousand students, most of them between fourteen and twenty years of age. Brawls and misunderstandings were frequent. After such a conflict between "town and gown" in 1200, King Philip II of France exempted the university from the royal provost, and in 1215 the university was further organized under the papal legate who regulated academic dress, fees, length of lectures, and other items. Another violent incident occurred in 1229, and the masters responded by calling a "strike" and leaving the city for two years. Despite the tensions, many Parisians had come to depend upon the university for their economic welfare, and the problem was resolved when Pope Gregory IX gave the school a charter, making it a *stadium generale*, self governing under papal protection. In their struggle against the control of the chancellor, the masters won the sole right of conferring degrees. During the exodus of 1229, King Henry III of England wrote to the scholars at Paris, "We want your university to know that if you desire to transfer yourselves to our kingdom of England and abide there for the sake of study, we will assign to you whatever villages you choose," and he further promised them their "liberties and tranquility."[26] The economic power of the university was used as leverage in other cities as well, notably the exodus of three thousand scholars from Oxford in 1209, some of whom formed Cambridge University. It was five years later that studies were resumed at Oxford. Over fifteen hundred masters and students left the University of Prague in 1409 to start their own university at Leipzig.

The university was divided into four faculties: arts, canon law, medicine, and theology. The arts curriculum was a preliminary requirement before one was permitted to enroll in the other three advanced disciplines. The masters in Paris were divided among four "nations": French, Normans, Picards, and English. The names simply represented the dominant group in each, because virtually every master of arts was a member of one of the four nations. The guild of arts was by far the most numerous, and in the course of time the elected leader of this guild, or rector, became the head of the entire university, including the masters of the three advanced studies. Paris became the center for theological studies in Europe and the seat of orthodoxy.

Meanwhile, Bologna in northern Italy was developing as the center for the study of canon and civil law with some marked differences from the university in Paris. Because the study of law was an advanced discipline, the students in Italy were more mature than those at Paris, which resulted in more control by students. Indeed, in Bologna it was the students who formed a guild which controlled the masters, to the point of levying fines on the masters for incompetent or overly long lectures, for missing lectures, or failing to get through the syllabus. Twenty different student nations were brought under two corporations, one for Italians and one for students north of the Alps. Another difference with Paris was that the study of law, whether canonical or civil, came from practical concerns resulting in no small part from the Investiture Controversy of the early twelfth century. Civil law attracted a large number of laity who were interested in commerce, drawing up documents, and pleading in the courts, all of which generated a growing demand for legal knowledge. A modern scholar points to the basically secular nature of Bologna as a continuation of its Roman roots and educational traditions, which had never died out, to the wide diffusion of literacy demanded by commerce, and to the needs of a new professional class of judges, clerks, assessors, and legal advisors.[27]

In Paris the arts course consisted primarily in the *trivium* of grammar, rhetoric, and logic, with Aristotle taking pride of place in the latter. The *quadrivium* was also taught, especially mathematics, more so in England and Germany than in Paris. The baccalaureate (bachelor's) degree took about eighteen months to two years, and it was directed by the student's nation, but it was conferred by the faculty of masters. This entitled the candidate only to begin studying for the master's license (degree) and the right to teach anywhere (*jus ubique docendi*) which could require between four to six years. The age of twenty was minimal for reception of the master's license in arts. For theology the lowest age for completing the master's license was thirty-four, and for a doctorate about forty. There was a close relationship between inclusion into the merchant and craft guilds and that of the university master's guild in that candidates were required to produce a "masterpiece," which consisted of engaging in solemn disputations or, in later years, a dissertation.

At Bologna the course of studies for canon law included Denis, "the Little" (c. 515), who first codified ecclesiastical law (and, incidentally, was responsible for dividing historical epochs into B.C. and A.D.), the Pseudo-Isidorian decretals, and above all Gratian's *Decretum* and later additions to it. For civil law the texts included Theodosius' *Code* and Justinian's *Corpus Juris Civilis*. At Paris students in theology, considered the "queen of sciences," studied the Scriptures, the church fathers, and (after 1160) Peter Lombard's *Sentences*, on which doctoral candidates were required to write a commentary. In the fourteenth century, Thomas Aquinas rivalled and ultimately superseded Lombard as the premier theologian to be mastered. Although Paris, Bologna, and Oxford were the most significant universities at the beginning of the thirteenth century, Salerno in Spain was established before them, with its primary focus on medicine. In later years, however, it was eclipsed by Montpelier. By 1500 there were about seventy universities in Europe, and although at first many of these centers of study owed their establishment primarily to the church, those founded after 1450 were all begun by lay princes who recognized the prestige and material benefits of having a university in their territory.

The basic medium of instruction was the *lectio*, the lecture or reading by a master, which was a running commentary on a traditional authority, whether the Bible, Gratian's *Decretum*, Lombard's *Sentences*, Justinian's *Corpus*, or any other acknowledged authority. Another form of inquiry was the *quæstio* which simply meant asking questions of the text; but more interesting was the *disputatio* in which the "Sic et Non" method was employed. In it several authorities and logical arguments both for or against a proposition were ranged alongside each other, the issue was disputed, and the master gave his *determinatio*. At times "open questions" or *quaestio quodlibetalis*, on which there was no accepted orthodox answer, would be debated by many disputants, including students, masters, and visitors. These could include questions of current social, political, or theological interest, and we can imagine that such occasions engaged the interest and challenged the imagination of all concerned.

At first students who came to a university town had to shift for themselves regarding meals and lodging, which was a challenge to boys fourteen years of age. In the course of time colleges grew up, which were simply residences for students, one of the earliest being that founded by Robert of Sorbonne of Paris in 1257, which in time gave the name "Sorbonne" to the entire university there. Such collegiate hospices eventually developed their own libraries and tutorial systems, and today the educational institution itself has assumed the name "college." As to the student life, we read that "The lack of discipline was one of the chronic ailments of medieval educational institutions. . . . As shown by the eternally repeated prohibitions, authorities were absolutely unable to keep the students off the streets: from idling around the squares, spending hours in the taverns drinking, dicing, and gambling, and visiting other 'dishonest' places."[28] On the other hand, Jacques de Vitry, a cardinal, observed that, "almost all the students in Paris did absolutely nothing except to learn to hear something new."[29] The university was entirely a creation of medieval Europe, largely but not exclusively developed from cathedral schools. There was nothing like it in antiquity, and in general structure and organization, in degrees, nomenclature, officers, method of instruction, rituals, and symbols, including "town/gown" tensions, the legacy has remained intact to this day.

The Friars

The twelfth-century revival in commerce resulted in the rise of urban centers, which offered freedom from feudal obligations and new opportunities for personal advancement. The church, however, like most other institutions, was based on an agrarian economy. Neither the monasteries nor the parish churches exercised the influence they had enjoyed in earlier times. The rise of universities also brought a new challenge, that of intellectual inquiry, disputation, and criticism. Although Christianity was born in the cities, established its first churches there and attracted its earliest converts from urban areas, Europe was for much of the medieval period almost entirely rural. It remained a largely rural society from the fall of Rome in the fifth century until 1100. The emergence of an urban middle class after 1100 called for some new directions. At this critical juncture the church received help from the new religious orders, notably the Franciscans and Dominicans. Preaching and pastoral care had fallen to a low estate among the secular clergy, and the universities, especially in Italy, fostered a secular gospel which called into question truths that had been held to be absolute for nearly a millennium. Even in Paris, the theological center of Europe, the newly discovered Aristotelian logic and the high value given to disputation caused disquiet among many. The clergy and hierarchy were embroiled in a struggle with powerful nobles and kings to keep a firm hold on their old agrarian estates. The Papacy, too, was in conflict with the growing power, centralization, and laicization of the emerging national states. The friars represented a new form of ministry to meet the needs of the time.

These needs were met in part by the democratic ideals of the new orders. Whereas the earlier monastic houses had largely attracted only men and women from the aristocracy (recall how many houses had utilized illiterate *conversi* as servants), the new orders, especially the Franciscans, appealed to all, including the poor. Also, the new cities brought with them ghettos of the sick and homeless, whose needs the parish churches were not equipped to address. Although preaching had fallen to a low level, and lay preaching had always been suspect, the friars were able to take on this task with papal approval. Finally, as exempt orders—directly answerable to the pope and operating with his blessing—the friars were free from the bishop's authority wherever they traveled, which gave them a great amount of independence, but also brought upon them resentment and hostility from parish clergy.

Francis of Assisi (d. 1226), son of a wealthy merchant, became dissatisfied with his aimless life of leisure, and during a serious illness determined to devote the rest of his life to the service of the poor. At one time he stripped naked in public in Assisi and exchanged his fine clothing for the mean rags of the poor. During a trip to Rome he took on the appearance of a beggar and spent the day begging for alms. He was undecided on how his adoption of apostolic poverty should be expressed when one day while attending mass at the small church of Portiuncula outside Assisi he heard the Gospel of Matthew, "Preach as you go, saying, 'The kingdom of heaven is at hand.' Take no gold nor silver nor copper, no bag for your journey, for the laborer is worthy of hire."[30] Francis understood this to mean that in addition to identifying with the poor, he was called to preach. A number of men followed Francis in his search for allegiance to Lady Poverty, his ideal. They went about helping farmers with their harvest, occasionally preaching (although they were laymen), visiting lepers, and being especially attentive to nature. At one time Francis preached his famous sermon to "my little sisters, the birds."

In 1209 Francis and his followers traveled to Rome where they sought the approval of Pope Innocent III to confirm their rule of poverty, which he did with some reluctance and only verbally. The espousal of poverty (or at least the extreme self-denial demanded by Francis) as the primary ideal was something new in the religious life, as the Benedictine Rule laid its main emphasis on obedience. "He and his followers were to be the most abject, the most wholly deprived, of the poor. He saw wealth as something corrupt. Poverty shone as an ideal of purity and romance."[31] The new order took the name of "friars minor" or little brothers (O. F. M. = *ordo fratres minores*) and from the color of their original habit they have also become known as Greyfriars. The Second Rule of the Franciscans (1223) further defines their ideals. "[Let those who wish to join us] sell all their goods and strive to distribute them to the poor. . . . The brothers shall appropriate nothing to themselves, neither a house nor place nor anything. And as pilgrims and strangers in this world, serving the Lord in poverty and humility, let them go confidently in quest of alms, nor ought they to be ashamed, for the Lord made himself poor for us in this world."[32]

As the order grew, Francis' ideal of personal as well as corporate poverty became more problematic, as they required churches in which to preach, houses in which to live, and places from which to distribute alms. In 1230 Pope Gregory IX permitted them to appoint a "spiritual friend" to hold money on their behalf and to distribute it according to need. But the tension went unresolved, and within twenty-five years of Francis's death the order was divided between the "Spirituals" who believed in a strict interpretation of poverty and the majority who were called "Conventuals" who adopted a more moderate policy. Under Bonaventure, who was general from 1257 to 1274, there was peace, but the division over strict vs. moderate interpretations of poverty reached a crisis in 1322 when the extreme Spirituals were condemned; the discussion over poverty continued into modern times.

Francis' missionary impulses found expression in his own journey to Spain, and then to Egypt on the Fifth Crusade, but he was shipwrecked on his attempt to get to the Holy Land. Meanwhile his followers spread over Europe and England, Hungary, Tunis, Morocco, Egypt, Guinea, Congo, and then to Central Asia, Tibet and China. In 1212 his ideals were espoused by Clare, a noble lady of Assisi, who founded the Poor Sisters of Clare or second order of women Franciscans. Shortly before he died Francis received the Stigmata, that is, a reproduction of the five wounds of the Passion of Christ in his own body. The order was significantly changed not only by the principle of admitting wealth, circumscribed though it was, but also by admitting priests into the fraternity and by establishing houses in the great universities. At Paris the Franciscan school included such luminaries as Alexander of Hales, Adam Marsh, Roger Bacon, Duns Scotus, William of Occam, Nicholas of Lyra, John Peckham, and above all, Bonaventure.

Francis' ideals still attract countless admirers—poverty, simplicity, and harmony with nature, especially as expressed in his *Canticle to Brother Sun*, in which he hails the joyous unity of all creation with the Creator.[33] He was canonized in 1228, only two years after his death.

Dominic of Guzman (d. 1221) was an Augustinian canon from Castille in Spain, whose life took a different direction when he saw how ineffectual a bishop and three Cistercian monks were in combatting the Albigensian heresy. These ecclesiastics traveled with a retinue of servants and all the pomp of high office, a fact which did nothing to dissuade the people from following those who had adopted the apostolic life (*vita apostolica*) even though they were doctrinally suspect. In 1215 Dominic gathered around himself a few others to combat the heresy, and they received lodgings from Bishop Fulk of Toulouse, the city that would become the center of their struggle for orthodoxy. Their goal was to win over the heterodox and the wavering through preaching and by living a simple life. Dominic attended the Fourth Lateran Council (1215) hoping to gain papal endorsement for his new order, but the council forbade the establishment of more Rules, and he was advised to select an existing Rule for his group. He selected the one he was already following, that of St. Augustine, and in 1217 Pope Honorius III confirmed the establishment of the Order of Preachers (*Ordo Praedicatorum*, O. P.), known also as Dominicans or Blackfriars (they wore a white habit with a black scapular or wide cloth which hung down from the shoulders). They shifted their center of operations away from southern France to the universities of Paris, Bologna, Oxford, and Spain, a clear indication that Dominic was determined to pursue his goals through an educated clergy and by influencing centers of learning. At this time their total number was only sixteen, and they came from seven different nationalities, but, small as they were, they were intent on a vocation of global mission.

Dominic possessed rare gifts of organization (something that Francis had lacked) and in his constitution for the order he offered a completely novel form of democracy. Priors of houses were elected by the chapter, together with one of their own members, who was to accompany the prior to the provincial chapter and report back on their own superior's conduct. The order was divided into regional provinces, whose head was elected by the heads of individual houses and two other representatives of each house. The general chapter held annually was the supreme deliberative and legislative forum. The head of the order was elected for life, although he was answerable to the general chapter and could be corrected or deposed. "Here then was a completely articulated system of representative government, which apparently sprang fully fledged from the mind of St. Dominic and his successor, Jordan of Saxony."[34]

As with the Franciscans, the Dominicans intended to live by begging, but they also found this to present difficulties, and in 1475 the pope permitted the order to hold property and enjoy other sources of income. The Dominicans were eminently successful in their mission, which was education, preaching, and global outreach. Most prominent among their scholars stand Albert, "the Great," and Thomas Aquinas. Both Dominicans and Franciscans, says a modern historian, "put excitement back into scholarship that had been lacking since the mid–twelfth century. . . . All the greatest names in medieval theology from 1250 to 1350 are the names of friars."[35] Popes gave the Dominicans responsibility for preaching later crusades and for organizing the papal inquisition. Their zeal for the purity of the Catholic faith and opposition to heresy earned them the nickname of "watchdogs of the Lord" (*Domini canis*). Both orders of mendicants enjoyed immediate and widespread popularity. By 1400 there were about ten thousand Dominicans in six hundred priories, and twenty-five thousand Franciscans living in eleven hundred houses. Much of their following came from their engagement with people, which cloistered monks were unable to do. They were not as welcome, however, by many parish priests, because friars often outshone the priests in their skill at preaching, pastoral care by way of the confessional, and piety. An anonymous treatise gives vent to a cleric's complaint: "Here are men who seek to forestall the clergy in their ecclesiastical function. They claim to administer the sacraments of baptism, penance, and extreme unction of the sick, and also to bury the dead in their own churchyards." He continues by saying that there is scarcely a Christian alive who does not appear on their registers of confraternities, i. e. associations of lay persons who imitate them in their piety, and support their work.[36] Both orders from the beginning also established second orders of women religious, although at times with reluctance. The ideals of apostolic poverty and mendicancy were emulated by a number of groups during the thirteenth century, but besides the Franciscans and Dominicans, only two survived the Middle Ages with their ideals intact: the Carmelites and the Austin Friars.

The Growth of Heresy

Southern France, or Languedoc, had always displayed a sense of independence from the north, both in language and culture. Perhaps its warmer climate and proximity to the Mediterranean contributed to a greater toleration for new ideas and a more leisurely approach to life. It was here that a type of thinking flourished during the twelfth and thirteenth centuries whose adherents were called Albigensians, after the town of Albi, although the centers of their strength were in Toulouse, Narbonne, Beziers, and Carcassonne. The more generic term Cathari (pure ones) was also applied to them. They taught that the creator of the world was an evil spirit, the Demiurge, or Satan, and that this spirit was the author of the Old Testament. People's souls, however, were created by the good God, the Father of Jesus Christ. Although souls were perfect when God created them, through bad choices they had become imprisoned in fleshly bodies. The goal of redemption, according to the Cathari, consisted in the release of the soul from the body following the teachings and the example of Jesus. It was his message that the true nature of humanity's predicament was enslavement to the flesh, and the way of release was through asceticism. Since the flesh was evil, it was impossible for Christ to have become human, and his suffering and death were not real but only apparent, an ancient heresy known as Docetism. The Cathari taught a rigid morality, perpetual chastity, abstention from all animal food, nonviolence, and general deprecation of the body. Sinners were condemned to further enfleshment through the transmigration of souls, that is, after death their souls would enter another body, and that possibly in a lower form of life. The Albigensians were organized into two classes, the Perfect who were the leaders, and the Believers who lived a less austere life.

The heresy presented a challenge, both in terms of theology and as constituting a formidable rival to the church's hierarchy. The Cathari were condemned at the Second Lateran Council 1139, and Bernard of Clairvaux was dispatched to preach against them. Innocent III was favorable to the new Dominican Order as a way of combatting them and gaining conversions through preaching. When that effort failed, a crusade was launched, touched off by the murder of Peter of Castlenau, a papal legate, in 1209. Philip II, King of France, refused to cooperate in the Crusade, believing that the enterprise was an infringement on his royal prerogatives. He perceived, rightly so, that under the guise of contending for the Catholic faith the northern barons would transform the Crusade into a war of conquest and plunder. In this he was proven to be correct. The Albigensians were completely routed, and the northern extremists established themselves in the south with full rights of oppressing the population in the name of religion. "It was an atrocious war, full of fanaticism and pillage—a veritable invasion, which in a few years destroyed the characteristic civilization of Languedoc, and whose fury far surpassed what the Holy See had foreseen or wished."[37] The Crusade was more against the rulers of southern France than it was was against religious aberration. In the Treaty of Meaux in 1229, the last Albigensian count, Raymond of Toulouse, was forced to marry his daughter to a brother of the French king. Through this marriage the boundaries of France were extended on the south to the Mediterranean Sea, but this ocurred at the expense of the church in two ways: (1) It displayed the inability of the pope to control unruly barons who subverted what had begun as an altruistic cause to their own rapacious ends, the same as in the Fourth Crusade. (2) It was in the pope's interests to prevent the emergence of strong secular states ruled by powerful monarchs, but with the Albigensian Crusade, called and supported by Innocent III, France emerged as a powerful rival to the Papacy. This became painfully clear within fifty years, when King Philip IV literally captured the pope.[38]

France was also the home of another group of people who advocated a return to apostolic poverty and a church unencumbered with ecclesiastical organization or hierarchical structure. These became known as Waldensians, named after Peter Waldo, their leader, a rich merchant of Lyons.[39] In 1173 he distributed his wealth to the poor and established a lay order known as the "Poor Men of Lyons." At first Peter's program consisted primarily of living a life of poverty, but after he became acquainted with the Bible in the vernacular he began publicly to explain the Scriptures. His followers openly criticized the immorality of the clergy and their indifference to the expectations of their calling. Although Waldo's activities were not heretical, since he did not challenge church teaching, it was contrary to canon law for laypeople to preach. At the Third Lateran Council (1179) the Poor Men of Lyons received authorization for their vow of poverty, and were given permission to preach provided they received authorization from local church authorities. When they found it difficult to receive such authorization, they ignored the council's restrictions and began publicly to expound the Scriptures. Along with the Albigensians, they were condemned for this at the Council of Verona in 1184 and expelled from Lyons. They fled to Spain, Lombardy, the Rhineland, Bohemia, Hungary, and northern France, and as they went they came into contact with more radical heretical groups who influenced them into adopting more extreme beliefs which challenged the church's traditions.

In opposition to the church, the Waldensians denied the existence of purgatory, the efficacy of indulgences, and prayers for the dead. Lying was considered an especially grievous sin, and they forbade the shedding of blood and the taking of oaths. In an age when society was bound together by a system of feudal oaths as well as ecclesiastical and marital vows, such a prohibition appeared threatening to the social order. They also condemned war and capital punishment. From preaching they turned to hearing confessions, absolving sins, and assigning penances. When they were condemned at the Council of Verona they were charged with refusing obedience to the clergy, usurping the right of preaching, and opposing the validity of masses for the dead. Although the Waldensians could not be accused of any classical doctrinal aberrations (Christological or Trinitarian), which was not true of the Albigensians, they opposed the entire sacerdotal system, declaring that the authority to exercise priestly functions was not derived from ordination but from the merit of individual piety. This reflects the heresy of Donatism, which was condemned in the fifth century.

Like the Albigensians, they divided themselves into two classes, the Perfect and the Believers. The Perfect were bound by vows of poverty and celibacy, led an itinerant life of preaching, and depended upon the Believers for their support. The requirements for the Believers were less stringent, and they continued to lead normal lives in the world, even attending Catholic masses, but they could receive penance only from Waldensians. After they were dispersed they split into two groups, the one under Waldo seeking reconciliation with the church and the other settling in Italy where they continue to this day, numbering approximately thirty thousand and supporting a Waldensian Theological College in Florence. "They were the first dissenting group in the west to develop an organization which enabled its members to preserve their identity after the death of their founder."[40]

The early Waldensians, appearing about thirty years before Francis of Assisi, asked for no more than he—living a life of poverty and the right to preach. Even up to their condemnation in 1184, they had not yet opposed any teachings of the church. The Albigensians, on the other hand, were decidedly aberrant in their beliefs in the evil of matter, denial of Christ's incarnation, and the transmigration of souls. But they also appealed to people's minds as well as their hearts, and for this reason it has sometimes been suggested that the Franciscans and Dominicans succeeded in combatting these heresies only by bringing their central themes—poverty, preaching, and the life of the mind—into the service of the church.

Joachim of Fiore (d. 1202) was a Cistercian monk and, briefly, an abbot, from Calabria in the "heel" of southern Italy. He is chiefly remembered for his apocalyptic writings in which he divided history into a three-fold pattern according to the Trinity. The age of the Father, or the "order of the married," was that period covered by the Old Testament under the Law; the age of the Son, or the "order of clergy" was that covered by the New Testament under grace, extending into his own time; the consummation of history would take place in the age of the Spirit under the "order of monks," ushering in a "spiritual church." This period was to begin about 1260. Some of Joachim's ideas were condemned after their death because of their implied threat to the role of the clergy and the structure of the church. The Spiritual Franciscans believed themselves to be the embodiment of the spirit-filled monks who were to govern the world after 1260. Joachim's apocalyptic periodization of history continued to attract interest to the present day.[41]

Arnold of Brescia (d. 1155) in Italy attacked the worldliness of the church, insisting that no clergy should own land, that sacraments of immoral priests were invalid, and that confession should be made only to lay Christians. At the Council of Sens in 1140 Bernard of Clairvaux secured Arnold's condemnation, but Arnold refused to recant, joined a civic uprising against the pope in 1146, and for nearly ten years his party controlled Rome. He was captured by Frederick, "Barbarossa," in 1155 who had him hanged. Peter de Bruys (d. c. 1140), a contemporary of Arnold of Brescia, opposed infant baptism, mass, church buildings, prayers for the dead, and the authority of the clergy; he also refused to accept much of Scripture. His followers, the Petrobrusians, encouraged priests and monks to marry. He was condemned at the Second Lateran Council in 1139 and burned to death the next year by a mob in Nimes when he preached against venerating the cross.

From earliest times Christianity was concerned about uniformity of belief, partly as a guarantor of truth. After Constantine such unity was also considered essential for the unity of the empire, and coercion was used to secure it. Justinian's *Code* (V, 16, 18) defended the use of force, and it may have been the rediscovery of Roman law in the twelfth century equating heresy with treason that encouraged a revival of inquisitorial procedures. Although there were sporadic instances of doctrinal dissent in the early Middle Ages, the volume of dissenters rose appreciably, and the authorities, both lay and clergy, felt the need to respond. In 1022 thirteen Albigensians were burned at the stake by order of King Robert of France, the first time execution by fire was used against heretics. In 1051 some Cathari were hanged. These eleventh-century deaths were prompted by outbursts of the people, with the clergy advocating leniency. By the end of the twelfth century, however, Catharism was so widespread in southern France that the existence of the church seemed to be threatened. In 1184 at the Council of Verona it was decreed that every bishop was to make a formal inquest in each diocese to root out heretics, thus inaugurating the episcopal inquisition. In 1227 each parish was to appoint *testes synodales* to make diligent inquiry and to report suspects to the bishop. These measures were not effective. It was the murder of the pope's legate to southern France in 1209 that touched off the Crusade against the Albigensians. In 1233 Pope Gregory IX issued two bulls establishing the papal Inquisition, which in theory was to root out heresy but in practice was often an instrument of papal control. The Dominicans and Franciscans were generally chosen as papal inquisitors, answerable only to the pope.[42]

The inquisitor was surrounded by numerous assistants who kept careful records, and it was the preservation of these records that promoted the success of the Inquisition, some suspects being apprehended years afterward and far from the original trial. The list of offenses was long, including anticlericalism, association with heretics (including close relatives), moral offenses, sorcery, witchcraft, and harboring incorrect beliefs. It was rare for anyone to escape punishment, because a mere accusation was considered a sign of something amiss. The accused were not permitted to cross-examine their accusers, although they were permitted to draw up a list of any enemies who might gain from their conviction. The inquisitor-judge pronounced sentences at a public exhibition (*auto da fe* = act of faith), which all residents of a given locality were required to attend. Sentences varied from death by fire to imprisonment of varied duration, confiscation of goods, pilgrimages, and lesser penances. Punishment was carried out by civil officials. Recent assessments of the Inquisition have suggested that it was far less bloodthirsty and oppressive than it is often represented as being. "The vast majority of those whom it found guilty were dismissed with canonical penances; . . . the number burned at the stake was small."[43] Whether the number of victims was great or small, the medieval church did not consider religious toleration a virtue. The Spanish Inquisition at the end of the fifteenth century was of an entirely different nature, being primarily an instrument of the state in which many respected and orthodox churchmen were singled out for punishment.

CHAPTER SEVEN

ORGANIZATION, WORSHIP, PIETY, AND SOCIETY

By 1100 much of Europe had been evangelized, although there remained pockets of pagan resistance primarily on the periphery. It is also difficult to determine to what extent former pagan practices remained among those who professed to be Christians, and how deeply the new faith had its roots in European soil. That vestiges of former nature and tribal religious practices persisted is clear, but it is also true that by 1100 we can basically refer to Western Christendom and Europe as synonymous, except a large part of southern Spain which was still under Muslim control.[1] This chapter seeks to explore the inner life of the church, its organization, worship, piety, and relationship to society, with a primary focus on the average peasants who constituted the vast majority of the population. Not only were there class distinctions which made for a variety of expressions of Christianity, but there were significant variations in time also, as beliefs and practices developed over the years. Christianity in society was far different in the early Middle Ages from that of the twelfth century. Taking into account such variations, the descriptions that follow will basically be a vignette of European church life in the twelfth century.

Church Organization

The basic unit of church organization was the parish (*parochia*) which was often coterminus with the manor, and was served by a priest. The priest himself was often a son of the manor who knew intimately those whom he served (and vice versa). He was directly responsible for the spiritual welfare of the people in his parish, which was geographically defined. He administered the sacraments except for ordination and confirmation, which were reserved for the bishop. His education was usually shallow, and derived from another parish priest or a monastery nearby. Candidates for the priesthood sometimes lived in the bishop's home during their preparation, as in the early church. In later years the study of theology was available in northern universities, but this was rarely available for most parish priests. Seminaries as we know them today did not come about until the sixteenth century. The priest's duties were to say mass, visit the sick, teach the Creed, the Lord's Prayer, and the Ten Commandments and, if able, to give boys a rudimentary instruction in letters. The age for orders was fixed at thirty for the priesthood, twenty-five for the diaconate, and twenty for the subdiaconate. Priests who lived in towns enjoyed a greater variety of service and opportunities for advancement. In larger churches several priests would live in a semi-monastic community according to a rule (canon) from which they derived the name canons. These priestly communities were called *collegia* and the churches came to be referred to as collegiate churches. Canons were also associated with cathedrals, in which they served as the bishop's assistants. In the course of the twelfth century the cathedral canons (collectively known as the *chapter*) came to play a decisive role in the selection of new bishops.

Priests who served in large urban churches were supported by endowments of income-producing land called *prebends*. Some canons abused the system in the late Middle Ages when they went about collecting the rights to several prebends, from which income they hired substitutes (*vicars*) to fulfill their duties. Regulations were enacted which stipulated that every priest must spend at least one third of each year in residence at his parish. The rise of towns and even large cities beginning in the twelfth century, together with the emergence of universities, considerably increased opportunities for education and clerical advancement.

Parish churches were usually a small frame building, but after 1200 stone buildings came into general use. The land around the church, including a cemetary, was considered sacred, and only those who died as members in good standing were permitted burial in this space. Within these precincts acts of violence were forbidden, from which practice arose the right of sanctuary whereby someone in danger of physical harm could flee to the church for protection. Such rights were not always respected, as in the case of the murder of Thomas à Becket at his altar. Churches normally did not have pews, and people stood (or walked about) during the liturgy. Churches also served as social centers for the parish: children played in their cool interiors, secular business was conducted there, and dances were held in the courtyard or dancing pavement (*choraria*) at the main entrance. Occasionally one reads of grain being stored and animals being lodged in churches. It was not lack of reverence which prompted such use of sacred space but rather a consciousness that God was close and friendly; whereas in the later Middle Ages, God became more remote, and God's home a place of awe and silence.

Every parish belonged to a territorial unit governed by a bishop called a *diocese*, at first coterminus with old Roman provinces or the *civitas* (city-state). During the period of economic decline which followed the fall of Rome it was often the presence of the bishop and his household which alone kept towns alive and continuing to function as an administrative center. Dioceses varied greatly in size, from small ones in Italy to large tracts of land in northern Europe and England. The bishop's throne (*cathedra*) gave the name "cathedral" to the church where it was located, usually in the largest town of the diocese. As indicated above, canons assigned to the cathedral formed a chapter with the archdeacon as its leader, and it was a rare bishop who did not experience tension between himself and this influential official. The archdeacon usually served as the judge of the bishop's court.

In the early church bishops were elected by the clergy and people of the diocese. In later years cathedral canons gained control of episcopal elections, but the king's "consent to elect" (*concessio regalis*) was required. Because bishops were also involved in land holding and secular duties, sometimes including military activity, kings and lay lords had a vested interest in their selection. It is estimated that by 1100 over two-thirds of the bishops and abbots in France were selected primarily by lay lords, hence the tensions of the Investiture Controversy. In theory the consecration of a bishop took place following his confirmation by the archbishop, whose jurisdiction included several dioceses. The *Decretum* of Burchard of Worms (c. 1012) stated that bishops should be "elected by the clergy, asked for by the people, and consecrated by the metropolitan (archbishop)." It was only later in the fourteenth century and beyond that popes claimed the right of intervention in episcopal elections, and only since the sixteenth century that such claims have been put into practice. At his consecration the bishop received the symbols of his office: the pastoral staff, the ring, and (after 1100) the mitre, a shield-shaped headress. The lay lord retained the right, even after the settlement of the Investiture Controversy in 1122, of investing the bishop with his "temporalities" or land holdings.

The bishop's primary responsibility was the supervision of all churches, monasteries, revenues, and ecclesiastical justice within the diocese. He was required to conduct visitations to every church or monastery under his care once every three years. We possess a number of records of such visitations. A typical account is that of Archbishop Eudes of Rouen in Normandy, made in February 1248: "We found that the priest of Ruiville was ill-famed with the wife of a certain stone carver, and by her is said to have had a child; he does not stay in his church, he plays ball, and he rides around in a short coat (the garb of armed men); The priest of Ribeuf frequents taverns and drinks to excess. Simon, the priest of St. Just, is pugnacious and quarrelsome."[2] In a large city church, Eudes discovered that "the canons talk and chatter from stall to stall, and across each other, while the divine office is being celebrated. They hasten through the psalms too quickly."[3] In another place the bishop discovered priests who were deficient in their knowledge of Latin verse. This Register covers over twenty years of visitations (July 1248 to December 1269) and in English translation is over seven hundred pages.[4] Although some bishops undoubtedly were delinquent in this task, Eudes was typical of most in his conscientious attention to propriety and decorum within his jurisdiction.

Bishops engaged in a multitude of responsibilities. They baptized, preached, heard confessions, aided the poor and oppressed, founded and supervised welfare agencies, and acted as arbiters; they maintained a court, administered the properties of the diocese, engaged in correspondence, attended church councils, advised princes, and occasionally wrote theological or devotional treatises. A large diocese was subdivided into archdeaconries over which the archdeacons had direct supervision, and were responsible to the bishop. Since the Council of Chalcedon in 451 (Canon 19), each bishop was required to hold two annual diocesan synods to adjudicate cases and to announce decrees of councils and of the pope.

At the pinnacle of church governance stood the pope, the bishop of Rome. The theoretical claims for papal power were a legacy from the early church, based primarily on an interpretation of Christ's words to Peter (Matt. 16:13-19) that the church was built upon Peter, whose successor the popes claimed to be. Although the theory of papal infallibility was not made dogma until 1870, popes were in fact the final authority in matters of dogma and discipline. They created cardinals, ratified the election of bishops, authenticated relics, canonized saints, and absolved grave sins. The growth of papal authority was gradual, increasing over the centuries. For a time in the tenth and eleventh centuries papal prestige was at its lowest point; it was then that lay princes, notably the Emperor Henry III (1039–1056) called for reforms. Medieval papal power and prestige was at its height under Innocent III (1198–1216).

During the early Middle Ages popes were chosen by the clergy and nobility of Rome, with the agreement of the cardinals and the assent of the emperor. In 1059 Nicolas II sought to remove secular influence from elections by a decree that henceforth the cardinals alone should elect.[5] In 1179 this was revised to stipulate that "he shall be considered Roman pontiff who shall be elected and received by two-thirds of the cardinals."[6] The following account of a papal election (from 1400) indicates the efforts that were required to keep the cardinals from outside influences. "The conclave is set apart to the cardinals for the election of the pope; and it must be shut in and walled in on all sides, so that, excepting a small wicket for entrance, which is afterwards closed, it shall remain strongly guarded. And therein is a small window for food to be passed to the cardinals, at their own cost. After the first three days they have but one dish of meat or fish daily, and after five days bread and wine, until they agree."[7] The cardinals, or pope's advisors, made up the *curia* or court, and a deliberation of the pope with the cardinals was called a *consistory*. The office that drafted documents and maintained correspondence was the chancery; it was the chancellor who affixed the papal seal (*bulla*) on official documents, from which term the documents themselves derived the name "bull."

Papal presence and influence was extended throughout Europe by the use of *legates*, who were ambassadors assigned to the courts of leading princes and monarchs or appointed for a special task, such as Boniface in evangelizing the Germans. They were given authority to act in the pope's name, subject to his approval. "A legate, acting within his commission, might exercise all the administrative and judicial functions of the pope, often with no possibility of appeal."[8] Since legates made regular reports to Rome about conditions in their assigned posts, the pope had access to current information about social, political, and religious circumstances throughout Europe.

The church was also the principle financial institution in society. Since the time of Gregory, "the Great" (d. 604), it was the custom that parish income was to be divided four ways: to the bishop, to the poor, for the upkeep of the church, and for the support of the priest. Since many lay lords controlled churches for the purpose of increasing their own funds, this division of income was not always observed. The lower echelons of the church had four main sources of income: tithes, perquisites, donations, and benefices. All Christians were expected to contribute one-tenth of their income to the church, either in money or in kind, which was difficult to collect. Priests went about the parish gathering whatever they could—grain, animals, cloth, produce— to be stored in the tithe barn. We read of priests who were beaten or even killed in their attempt to gather the tithe. Perquisites were gifts to the church for special pastoral services which in time became fixed charges. Donations were special gifts prompted by sincere piety, and benefices included all the properties held by the church. Bishops and abbots often possessed considerable revenue-producing real estate.

In addition to the gifts of the faithful, the papacy received income (*census*) from its estates in Italy. These holdings continued to grow so that by 1200 the papacy was the feudal lord of one-third of Italy. Peter's Pence was contributed annually by the monarchs of England, Poland, Hungary, and Scandinavia. The pope also received fees for *exemptions*, the right of monasteries, churches, and religious orders to be free from the jurisdiction of bishops and come directly under papal supervision (i.e. Cluny, Premonstratensians, Cistercians, Knights Templar). High church officials paid fees for the confirmation of their appointments, and archbishops paid to receive the *pallium*, a circular band of white wool worn on the shoulder, their insignia of office. In the late Middle Ages newly consecrated bishops paid the *annate*, a sum equivalent to one year's revenue of their diocese. There were also fees for papal documents, charters, and the use of papal courts.

In the fourth century, Constantine conferred judiciary rights upon bishops when he decreed that, "anyone desiring to transfer his case to the Christian law and to accept its judgement, he shall be permitted, even if the case has already been before the judge. Whatever may be settled by a sentence of bishops shall ever be held as sacred."[9] During the barbarian invasions of Europe the bishop's court was often the only institution for justice available. By 1100 a large percentage of the population came under the jurisdiction of ecclesiastical courts and law.

The lowest church court was that of the dean, who was a priest exercising the oversight of an area about the size of a county. He held a monthly court (*Kalends*) which also had disciplinary and educational functions. The next highest court was that of the bishop (or his archdeacon) from which appeals could be made to the papal court. Part of the secret of Rome's primacy in the West was the judicious use of the court system. Thousands of litigants flocked to Rome as the court of omnicompetence, and papal judge-delegates were sent throughout Europe to make papal justice more easily available. Ecclesiastical courts claimed jurisdiction in all cases touching persons in holy orders (priest, deacon, subdeacon, acolyte, exorcist, lector, doorkeeper) including all students, crusaders, and household servants of ecclesiastics. Cases which came under church jurisdiction were those involving violation of oaths (which under feudalism included all breaches of contract), orphans, widows, marital disputes, physical injury to churches or clergy, and a host of infractions of moral law. Innocent III insisted that any case which involved sin (*ratione peccati*), should be heard by the church. Had this idea been rigorously carried out there would have been no need for civil courts. One reason for the popularity of church courts was that they tended more toward clemency than was the case with the civil courts. The church took into account intentions, motivation, and mitigating circumstances, whereas the civil courts were more rigid. It was from medieval church courts that jurisprudence developed the practice of assessing crimes in terms of degrees. As we have seen, the legal code of the church which governed litigation was canon law, which grew in volume during the late Middle Ages and was finally published in 1500 as the *corpus juris canonici.*[10]

A central feature of church organization was the council, a deliberative assembly of clergy (or bishops) convened either at regular intervals or for a specific task to address the needs of the church. The most significant of these assemblies were those designated as ecumenical, which meant that their decisions were accepted as authoritative by all (or most) Christians, in both the East and the West. Only the first seven of these councils are today recognized universally by the church, beginning with the First Council of Nicea in 325 A.D. and ending with the seventh, the Second Council of Nicea in 787 A.D. All of these were held in the East, were convened by the emporer, and attended by the five patriarchs of Christendom or their representatives (Rome, Alexandria, Antioch, Constantinople, and Jerusalem). After the schism between the church in the East and West, (1054 A.D.), the Latin church continued to hold councils, which it considered ecumenical but which were not recognized by the Greeks. These were called by the popes who presided at them and ratified their decrees. Four medieval gatherings called Lateran Councils, named after the papal palace where they were held, met in 1123, 1139, 1179, and 1215. In addition to these, four other councils in the late Middle Ages were considered ecumenical in the West: Lyons (1245), which excommunicated Emporer Frederick II and called for a Crusade against the Saracens; Lyons (1274), attended by more than fifteen hundred dignitaries, which effected a temporary reunion with the Greek church, which temporarily agreed to the *filioque* in the Nicene

Creed; Vienne (1311), which condemned the Knights Templar, Beghards, Beguines, and Fraticelli for heresy and called for a reform of the clergy; and Constance (1414-1418), which ended the papal schism and condemned the heresies of John Wycliffe and John Huss, although it was not considered ecumenical until it was ratified by Pope Gregory XII.

All of the foregoing councils were impressive gatherings of bishops convened by popes to deal with urgent matters of the church. But ever since the first ecumenical council at Nicea (325) it had been decreed that two gatherings of clergy in every province (diocese) should be held annually, at Lent and in the autumn, to discuss matters of local concern. In addition to these councils, which were intended to occur on a regular basis, there were other gatherings on a regional level, such as a series of eighteen Spanish councils in the seventh century and reform councils called by Boniface for the Frankish church in the eighth century. Through the use of these deliberative assemblies the church addressed the needs of the day.

Patterns of Public Worship

From the beginning Christians understood themselves to be different from other religions in that they did not worship idols or venerate one sacred shrine above all others. God was omnipresent and could be worshiped anywhere and at any time, but to be a Christian meant to be incorporated into a group, the church or "the body of Christ." The principle reason for coming together was to worship God in Christ, and the central act of worship was the Eucharist or, as it came to be called, the mass. There one received Holy Communion, or the body and blood of Christ in the forms of bread and wine. The liturgy or basic form of worship was fairly well fixed in the West by the time of Gregory the Great (600), although there were variations of the basic structure. In addition to the Roman Mass we find the Ambrosian in Milan, the Mozarabic in Spain, and the Gallican in France. Worship in the large city churches was much more elaborate than in the country parishes, where most of the people lived. What follows is a description of a papal Mass in Rome around 800 C.E. From this basic structure we can move forward several centuries to see what changes had taken place by 1200.[11]

The service was at the cathedral church of Rome, the Church of St. John Lateran, and it was surrounded by Byzantine court ceremonial borrowed from the emperor's retinue. The presider was first vested in garments identical with those still in use today: a linen alb with cinture, an amice or linen cloth over the shoulders, two linen dalmatics or over-garments, and finally a chasuble (a garment like a tent with a hole for the head). Then he received the pallium, a cloth around the neck and maniple, a napkin in his right hand. There is at this time no mention of a stole, pectoral cross, pastoral staff, tiara (bishop's distinctive hat), or ring, all of which would be added by 1200. In the church men and women were divided, men on one side and women on the other. This practice may reflect a caution we find already in Hippolytus (c. 200), that at the kiss of peace men should share only with men and women with women. Candles were lit on seven candlesticks, and the procession began, led by a thurifer with incense, followed by assisting clergy, with the presider coming last. Meanwhile the choir was singing the *Introit* (entrance) psalm, ending with the *Gloria Patri* (Glory to the Father), and the presider went to his chair (throne) during the singing of the *Kyrie eleison* (Lord have mercy). He faced eastward during the *Gloria in excelsis* (glory to God on high), followed by his greeting, "Peace be to you," after which he prayed the Collect or Prayer of the Day. Readings from the Bible (either from the Old or the New Testament) by a sub-deacon followed, after which a singer responded with a psalm verse (the *Gradual* and Alleluiah). A deacon, after receiving a blessing, read the Gospel, accompanied with candles and incense. There is no mention of a sermon at this point, as sermons fell out of use in the ninth and tenth centuries, to be restored in the twelfth century. Neither was there a creed, which did not enter the liturgy until the eleventh century. This ended the Service of the Word. In ancient times the catechumens, those not yet baptized, were dismissed at this time, but by 800 almost all adults had been baptized as infants, and there was no dismissal. The Offertory procession began the Service of The Eucharist, but only offerings of bread and wine were permitted, which were gathered as the choir sang an Offertory psalm.Those who received these offerings washed their hands, including the pope, and the clergy in the chancel arranged themselves according to rank as the pope began the Great Thanksgiving. He presided facing the people from behind the free-standing altar. By 1200 the altars had been moved to the east end of the church, with the presider having his back to the people. The liturgy followed the ancient order of Hippolytus, which has remained constant in most Christian churches throughout the world, East and West, even to the present day: "The Lord be with you," "And also with you," "Lift up your hearts," "We have lifted them to the Lord," "Let us give thanks to the Lord, our God," "It is right and just to give him thanks." There followed the consecration of bread and wine through the use of a Eucharistic Prayer, but as yet there were no elevations or genuflections, which were added by 1200. In the West the "moment of consecration" was believed to be the recitation of Christ's words of institution, but in the East the crucial action was the *epiklesis* or prayer for the Holy Spirit. This central prayer came to be recited in an inaudible whisper by the priest, further accenting the mystery but also contributing to the alienation of the people. The Lord's Prayer followed the prayer of consecration, in the belief that "give us this day our daily bread" referred to the Eucharist, and during the *Agnus Dei* (Lamb of God) the clergy broke the bread into small pieces, which the people received into their hands. The congregation at these masses did not participate in any of the chants. By 1200 regular leavened bread was no longer in use, being replaced by wafers similar to those in use in some churches today. Whether people came forward to the altar to receive Communion or were served in the nave is not clear, but they did receive both the bread and wine. After 1200 the people's reception was limited to the bread only, and due to the concept of a "worthy" or "unworthy" reception, most people feared the latter and did not commune often. The Fourth Lateran Council in 1215 stipulated that all Christians must commune at least once each year, and that at Easter. By the eleventh and twelfth centuries the mass was far more a priestly ceremony at which the laity were present, and being in Latin, was unintelligible to most people. The mass ended with the deacon calling out, "Go, the mass is ended," and the people responding, "Thanks be to God;" the pope proceeded in a solemn ceremony back to the sacristy, giving his blessing to the congregation on the way.

This papal service was far different from the simple eucharistic rites described in the second and third centuries, and the embellishment with ceremonial grew even more in the high Middle Ages. The same was not true for the average parish church served by a single presbyter (priest). The mass was often reduced to its bare essentials—readings from the Bible, prayers, the Lord's Prayer, the consecration of bread and wine, the Communion, and the dismissal. Despite its rudimentary nature, the Sunday Mass was the primary act of corporate worship in which the people found spiritual edification. In many parts of Europe the parish was "a small box with a tiny chancel, the whole being no larger than a moderately large living room in a modern house. Here the priest and people were far closer than in most modern churches."[12] And yet it was not solemn. We read of cats, dogs, and hawks taken into the churches, and numerous sermons remain in which the preacher admonishes the hearers to cease chattering and listen.

By 1200 the practice of priests saying private mass, a custom begun in the monasteries, triumphed throughout Christendom. Masses were celebrated with no congregation present, and the emphasis shifted from a communion of the people to the sacrifice offered by the priest. By this time communion itself was so infrequent and the participation of the people so restricted that they were reduced to spectators at the divine drama being enacted by the priest. Because of the multiplication of private masses, numerous side altars appeared in the larger churches to accomodate the demand. The act of the priest in offering sacrifice, even apart from people or communion, was believed to be acceptable to God and efficacious for various intentions, including benefits for the faithful departed in purgatory.

The Roman mass (or Gregorian) was made obligatory in the Franko-German kingdom by Pepin III, father of Charlemagne, when the pope crowned him king in 754. Charlemagne later requested an authoritative version of the liturgy from the pope, but his minister, Alcuin, found it unsatisfactory and after careful study made emendations. Meanwhile, toward the end of the ninth century the office of Roman bishop fell into unworthy hands, who did not fulfill their liturgical duties. "The clergy of Rome and the Roman people lost all interest in the liturgical life of the Church."[13] The work of restoring a vibrant worship life in Rome began with the the the reformers of the eleventh century. But during the nadir of the tenth century, "it would be no exaggeration to say that during this critical period, the Franco-German Church succeeded in saving the Roman liturgy not only for Rome itself but for the entire Christian world of the Middle Ages."[14]

The revival of preaching, which is one of the distinctive characteristics of the High Middle Ages, can be traced to three sources: the Crusades, Scholasticism, and the Friars. Bernard of Clairvaux "won a great reputation as a speaker preaching the Cross and working to convert the heretics in Languedoc."[15] Scholasticism contributed to the popularity of homilies in the university chapels, which were often not far removed from the disputations of the lecture hall, but attracted many hearers nonetheless. The Friars were noted especially for their zeal in preaching, both to convert the heretics and to revive the faithful. Collections of sermons were made for those priests who were deficient in the art. Honorius of Autun (d. 1130) maintained that preaching was the priest's primary responsibility, but that the sermon should not be too long; it must entertain as well as edify, and it must avoid rhetoric which detracts from its contents. The typical medieval homily has been described as having, "a style that was animated, familiar, uninhibited, and sometimes little more than trivial or clownish. The parish priest would not gloss over petty scandals or even grave ones. A sermon was a kind of melodrama at which the audience wept or laughed."[16] Honorius of Autun wrote a collection of sample sermons, the *Speculum ecclesiae*, for clergy who could not write their own, including a general sermon (*sermo generalis*) which could be shortened, lengthened, or adapted as conditions warranted. In it he recommends where to place humor and even when to take a brief respite so that people could answer the call of nature.[17]

Although hymn singing was not observed in many parts of the medieval church, thousands are extant from this period.[18] The same Honorius mentioned above urged that every mass begin with *Veni Creator Spiritus* (Come Holy Spirit). Among the most loved of all medieval hymns was one dedicated to the Virgin Mary, *Stabat Mater Dolorosa* (The Mother stands in sorrow), and a Passiontide hymn, *Pange lingua* (Sing my tongue), by Venantius Fortunatus, who also wrote *Vexilla Regis* (The Royal Banners Forward Go). Theodulf of Orleans (d. 821) wrote *Gloria, laus et honor* (All glory, laud, and honor) which remains the principle Palm Sunday hymn for most of Western Christendom to this day. Another favorite was the solemn dirge of a thirteenth-century Franciscan, *Dies Irae* (Day of Wrath). Thomas Aquinas composed a popular Eucharistic hymn, *Pange lingua gloriosi corporis mysterium*, and Bernard of Clairvaux wrote, *O Sacred Head Now Wounded*; *Jesus, the Very Thought of You*; *O Jesus, Joy of Loving Hearts*; *Wide Open Are Your Hands*; and *O Jesus, King Most Wonderful*.

The average Christian looked for the reassurance of religion especially at the central events of life: birth, marriage, death, and crises. The rites through which divine presence was communicated were the sacraments, whose number remained flexible during most of the medieval period because there was no dogmatic definition of the nature of a sacrament other than that of Augustine, "a visible sign of an invisible grace." Hugh of St. Victor counted as many as thirty. Peter Lombard listed the seven which have become traditional, although the church did not officially agree to this until the Council of Florence in 1439. We have already discussed the weekly Sunday worship, the mass, which was the one central communal expression of faith, although by 1200 it had increasingly become the priest's service while the people looked on or occupied themselves with private devotions. *Baptism* stood at the head of the sacraments because by it new Christians were made. Although in the early church the number of adult baptisms was large, by 1200 most adults had already entered the church, and baptisms were primarily of children. Under Charlemagne the large baptistry for adults gave way to a smaller font, and immersion was replaced by pouring, but infants were still immersed in large fonts as late as the sixteenth century. The rite was accompanied by the use of symbols—water, candle, white gown, salt, and oil. At a later age the child received *Confirmation*, which was an affirmation of Baptism. This sacrament has had a checkered history; it was never observed in the Eastern churches, which conferred Chrismation immediately following baptism. Today Confirmation is seen as an integral part of the inseparable triad of baptism/chrismation/Eucharist. Only the bishop was authorized to confirm. Eudes of Rouen was said to be beloved by his people because, unlike other bishops, he dismounted from his horse when he confirmed children. *Holy Orders* (Ordination) was the rite by which a man entered the priesthood. The route progressed through a series of suborders, leading to the diaconate and then to ordination. As we have seen, the education of priests had not yet been regularized, but the final decision on the suitability of a candidate was by the bishop, who alone was allowed to ordain. Through *matrimony* the church elevated and hallowed the marriage bond. By 1200 it was customary for the ceremony to take place outside at the church doors, as marriage itself was not by "grace" but by "nature," followed by the church's blessing at the altar. Medieval marriage customs and ideals are not consistent in an age where celibacy was more highly prized, where many unions were arranged by parents, and where there was no clarity as to whether the oath or the consummation constituted a marriage. At the hour of death the church fortified the faithful by annointing them with holy oil, *extreme unction* usually accompanied with the Eucharist (*viaticum* or food for the way.) "The whole process of requiem mass, committal and tending the grave . . . was something which impinged very much on the consciousness of the laity;"[19] this in a world with an extremely high infant mortality and low life expectancy in a culture with limited medical understanding or resources. These five sacraments were nonrepeatable. The mass, of course, was weekly, although reception of communion by the laity was infrequent. *Penance* was also repeatable, consisting of remorse of the heart, confessing to a priest who pronounced the absolution, and who enjoined an act of piety which allowed the penitent to demonstrate remorse for sin or satisfaction to one who had been wronged. Penitents tended to view the act of satisfaction as reparation for sin, an abuse which had far-ranging consequences by the sixteenth century. The mechanical calculation of penances according to some rigid numerical system was another potential abuse, but the possibilities were also present for a wholesome, evangelical, and personal attention to the nurture of the penitent.

The Piety of the Faithful

While theologians were disputing scholastic issues and priests were engaged in pastoral duties, what kind of religious interests engaged the common people who made up the overwhelming majority of the population of the church? What follows includes the piety of the scholars and clergy as well, but it was through the popularity of saints, relics, and the cycles of the church year that the people identified with the faith and lived their lives.

The veneration of saints began with the cult of martyrs in the second century, the earliest being that of Polycarp of Smyrna (d. 155). We are told that after his death his disciples buried his body and celebrated the Eucharist at his grave at the annual anniversary of his death.[20] Already in the New Testament we read of a "cloud of witnesses (Heb. 12:1)" which Christians are to imitate, and of the martyrs who pray before the throne of God (Rev. 6:9). Confessors, those who suffered but did not die for the faith, came to be included in the growing number of those so honored. Saints were not only to be emulated in holiness of living, but it was believed since Origen (d. 254) that the prayers of the saints are efficacious for those who follow in their steps. The first attempt to control the number of those so honored was by an African council in Carthage in 401 which said that the sanctity of some so honored was suspect.[21] Early canonization of saints was by local bishops, but with the growth of papal authority there was an attempt to control the canonization process. The first documented papal canonization intended for the entire church took place in 993. In 1172 Pope Alexander III unequivocally stated that canonization was an exclusively papal prerogative. Yet there were (and are) many saints revered locally without such papal sanction. Indeed, each diocese had its own calendar of saints. According to the teachings of the church the saints reign together with Christ and offer their prayers to God on behalf of humankind. In this they served as intermediaries, and in the course of time several saints gained specialties. Sailors and fishermen addressed prayers to St. Nicholas, St. Genevieve cured fever, St. Blaise was known to relieve toothache, St. Hubert guarded against madness, and St. Jude was the saint of last resort. Each season was under special protection: spring, St. Mark and St. George; summer, St. John the Baptist; autumn, St. Martin; winter, St. John the Evangelist. We know from the life of Luther that in his earlier years he prayed to St. Ann, patron of miners. Each parish church was under the protection of a saint from whom it derived its name. St. John's was literally the possession of St. John, and any violators of its precincts or privileges would be directly answerable to the saint. Because of the multiplication of saints, the special feast of All Saints' Day (November 1) was inaugurated as early as the fifth century to commemorate all uncanonized as well as canonized saints. Elements of pagan origin played a role in medieval veneration of saints in that sometimes they simply became the surrogates for old tribal deities, but a recent study insists that "it is an exaggeration to conclude that popular veneration of these saints constituted a form of religious experience that was alien to the church and to Christian life."[22] Interest in saints resulted in multiplied accounts of their lives, or *hagiographies*, which were usually accounts of the miraculous and fanciful interspersed with reliable historical data. Medieval people understood them as evidence of the supernatural realm, pointing beyond themselves to a transcendent world of new possibilities and the rewards of faith and virtue. Modern scholars have amassed a collection of stories which include more than twenty-five thousand saints venerated in the Middle Ages. The authoritative lives of saints today is the *Acta Sanctorum* in sixty-seven folio volumes.

Veneration of saints was defended as integral to a doctrine of the church and of salvation in that the church transcends time and place to include God's reign over the departed faithful who are now at rest (the church triumphant). What caused difficulties in later years, however, was the role of saints as mediators. While some claimed that Christ was the only mediator, others believed in the intercession of the saints, and especially in the concept that their merits could be applied to other believers, living or dead. Alexander of Hales (d. 1245) first defined the "treasury of merit" (*thesaurus meritorum*) as a treasury of spiritual merits accumulated from the abundant merits of Christ and the saints which suffice to pay the spiritual debts of the living. It was from this treasury that the medieval church granted indulgences, the remission of temporal punishment for sins.

The most favored saint of all was the Virgin Mary, who as Christ's mother was believed to have direct access to her divine Son. Days commemorating her life increased, including the Annunciation (March 25), her birthday (September 8), and her Assumption into heaven (August 15). Both the liturgy and the iconography of the great cathedrals are evidence of her role in salvation, either in holding up her son for adoration or her advocacy on the day of judgment. A debated issue was whether she was conceived sinless, that is, preserved from the stain of original sin (Immaculate Conception). Aquinas and the Dominicans argued against the idea, but Duns Scotus and the Franciscans supported it; it was declared to be a dogma of the Roman church in 1854.[23]

The cult of saints fostered an intense preoccupation with their relics. The practice began as far back as 156 when Polycarp's disciples retrieved his body, "more precious than fine gold." But Augustine, writing in the in the fifth century, cautioned "Let us not treat the saints as gods; we do not wish to imitate those pagans who adored the dead." Nevertheless by 787 the practice had so accelerated that a church council declared that "If any bishop from this time forward is found consecrating a temple without holy relics, he shall be deposed as a transgressor of ecclesiastical tradition."[24] Guibert of Nogent (d. 1124) was sensitive to the dangers of gullibility and superstition in the quest for relics, but he admitted that where they were carried about, "the gracious Judge who comforts with his pity (in heaven) those whom he reproved (on earth) showed many miracles where relics went."[25] The Crusades especially accelerated the search for relics from the Holy Land; pieces of saints' bodies flooded the West, and magnificent reliquaries fashioned to house them were carried in procession. Authentication in most cases was impossible; nevertheless no less an eminence than King Louis IX of France built Sainte-Chapelle to receive Christ's crown of thorns, and the first crusaders were spurred on to victory through the discovery of the lance which had pierced his side. Relics in themselves were not as significant as the miracles they produced, which were understood as the power of the saint whose relic it was, or the power that God granted to the saint. The zeal for collecting them extended to relics of Christ: the cords that bound him, the sponge at the crucifixion, bread which he had consecrated, and pieces of wood from his cross. This veneration extended especially to the Eucharist in the Feast of Corpus Christi (1264) in which a consecrated host was displayed in a receptable with a glass window (*monstrance*) and carried in procession through the streets or exhibited on an altar for adoration. The collection and veneration of relics, although rooted in antiquity, accelerated in the twelfth century with a growing interest in the humanity of Christ and in his passion.

Pilgrimage was another means of identifying with Christ and the saints in their earthly life. The oldest witness to this activity is the travelogue of a pilgrim from Bordeaux (330), who together with Etheria of Spain (380) popularized trips to the Holy Land. At least eighteen travelogues have been preserved from the mid–fourth to the eighth centuries. A recent commentator explains this interest in "devotional tourism" by suggesting that "The veneration of martyrs (through pilgrimage and relics) thus served to assure the Christians of a local church of its continuity with its own heroic, persecuted past, and the universal Church of its continuity with the age of martyrs."[26] Jerusalem and the

Holy Land was the premier goal of pilgrims, the very place that Jesus and his apostles hallowed by their presence, and from 1100 to 1300 the temporary success of the Crusades made it accessible. But shrines of saints were everywhere, and it was a rare person who had not taken the pilgrim's staff in hand, even for a short distance to a nearby shrine, at least once in a lifetime. After Jerusalem, the most popular attractions were Rome and Compostella in northern Spain. Others included the tomb of Thomas à Becket at Canterbury, the shrine of the Magi at Cologne, the tomb of St. Martin of Tours, and the sanctuary of the archangel at Mont St. Michel—all attracting thousands of visitors each year by the twelfth century. Such an undertaking was a levelling force in society, as serfs jostled with princes, bishops with laymen, craftsmen with laborers. Why did so many people make long, arduous and dangerous journeys? Some went in order to fulfill a penance, but many went voluntarily. The tedium of a rustic existence was undoubtedly relieved by the stimulation that travel brings, and a pilgrim who returned to his German farm after having traveled to Jerusalem was never quite the same again. But such adventures were not without critics. A thirteenth-century German Franciscan friar, Berthold of Regensburg, "warned his congregation not to put trust in almsgiving or pilgrimages, for they are all vain without true contrition. What was the point, he asked, of going all the way to Compostella to honor some bones, for the real St. James was not in Galicia but in heaven, and did they not realize that by going to mass in their parish church they could enter into the presence of God himself, who was greater than all the saints and angels?"[27]

Although pilgrimages and relics were undoubtedly subject to abuse, they were based in part upon the accepted theological belief that the second person of the Holy Trinity had become a true human being, and because God had entered history, geography and artifacts related to him. In the twelfth century such devotion to the human Christ and his sufferings intensified, supported by Anselm's theology of the cross and Bernard's preaching. The Stations of the Cross appeared in churches, a series of fourteen pictures or carvings depicting Christ on the Way of Sorrows (*via dolorossa*), which was a way of bringing Jerusalem into each church. Francis of Assisi is credited with introducing the Christmas creche as evidence of Christ's humanity, and Bernard wrote enduring hymns on the Passion including "O Sacred Head Now Wounded." The focal point of worship since the fifth century was a cross suspended above the altar, but now it included the body of the suffering Christ fixed on it. Such works of literature as *The Dream of the Rood* were an expression in the vernacular of the cult of the cross. "Among the events in the

Gospels, (Christ's) passion and death clearly made the decisive difference. . . . It was the cross that was the instrument of the victory of Christ
over the devil," for which reason Good Friday was observed as the most
solemn day in the church calendar.[28]

Medieval society was permeated with a Christian atmosphere fostered by the liturgical cycle of festivals, fasts and saint days. Both church
and state calculated time according to the church calendar, as when
parliament met in England at Christmas, Easter, and Pentecost.
Dionysius Exiguus, "the Little," in the sixth century first divided the
calendar into years before Christ and after Christ (A.D. = *anno domini* or
year of our Lord), which became the norm in the West at the Council of
Whitby in 664. The cycle began with the four Sundays before Christmas
(Advent), and Christ's nativity was celebrated with a traditional Midnight Mass, feasting, and folk festivities. The twelve days of Christmas
included a cluster of minor festivals leading up to Epiphany on January
6, the "Gentile Christmas," commemorating the Magi, Christ's baptism,
and his first miracle. February 2 saw the blessing of candles (Candle-
mass) and a commemoration of the purification of the Virgin Mary. Ash
Wednesday marked the beginning of the Lenten fast and people received ashes made from the palm branches of the previous year's Palm
Sunday. Lent was an especially solemn season marked by fasting and
other acts of self-denial. Wooden crosses replaced those of precious
metal, statues were covered, and bells did not ring. Palm Sunday was
observed with processions and the blessing of palm branches. On
Maundy Thursday (*maund* = a new commandment) the church received back into communion those who had been excommunicated, and
priests received the holy oils from the bishop for the coming year. Easter
was celebrated with great jubilation, and its festive atmosphere extended for forty days until Ascension The festival cycle ended with
Pentecost, the coming of the Holy Spirit and the birthday of the church.
In the spring the priest led a procession around the fields for the blessing
of seeds and soil.

Other days which were observed include June 24, the day of St. John
the Baptist (also Midsummer's Day), marked with bonfires on the hill-
sides; Holy Cross day on September 14; St. Michael and All Angels
(Michaelmass) on September 29; All Saints' Day on November 1, and
days associated with the life of the Virgin Mary. Work was suspended
on major festivals which tended to increase in number. The observance
of a common Christian way of reckoning time fostered a sense of unity
in Christendom; regardless of where one lived or traveled, from Ireland
to Constantinople, Sicily to Scandinavia, the same worship and rites

prevailed. Agobard, Bishop of Lyons, is undoubtedly speaking in hyperbole when he writes, "All have been made brothers, the serf and the lord, the poor and the rich, the ignorant and the learned, the humble artisan and the great lord address one and the same God and Father. Now no one denigrates another, no one despises himself as inferior to another, no one exalts himself above another."[29] Yet it is useful to be reminded of the medieval ideal and self-understanding, even though it certainly fell short of realization.

How far reality was removed from the ideal can be seen in a parody of a prayer: "O Lord, who hast made the multitude of the rustics for the service of the clerics and soldiers, and hast sown discord between us and them, grant that we may live from their labors . . . and rejoice in their mortifications."[30] Blasphemy was endemic to medieval society, but no one was ever burned for it because it was a form of faith. More incongruous yet realistic were statements of doubt and inability to believe.

The Bible was at the center of medieval religious thought, the supreme textbook of the medieval world, and a teacher of theology was called a Master of the Sacred Page. "Extracts from it were constantly being sung and recited in churches all over Christendom; echoes of biblical texts can be heard in every corner of the Latin literature of the age; stories from the Bible meet us wherever we find painted books and walls and religious sculpture. The Bible was everywhere."[31] The fact remains that most people were illiterate, and their knowledge of the Bible came secondarily through hearing and seeing. It was essentially in the lay religious groups of the twelfth century that reading of the vernacular Bible was revived, and since these groups were considered heretical, such reading became suspect. Ecclesiastical authority was understood as one homogenous and complementary whole, which included the Fathers, church councils, and other traditions. Henry of Ghent (d.1293) wrote: "Concerning the things of the faith the fact is that the church and Holy Scripture agree in everything and testify to the same thing, namely to the truth of the faith, in which it is reasonable to believe both of them: Scripture on account of the authority of Christ; the church on account of what is seen in it by man."[32] The crisis of Scripture, church, and tradition became a central issue of theology from the fourteenth century on.[33]

Superstition, ignorance, coarseness, and abuses existed, yet from birth to death people in the medieval world were surrounded with reminders that their life was tending toward union with God. They were supported in this belief by the ministrations of the church, where in the best of circumstances they could find serenity and stability in a society where life was often brutal, hard, and short.

The Church and Society

The structure of European society from roughly 900 to 1200 has been described as being feudal. It was never planned coherently nor did people living at that time think in terms of feudalism. The word itself first appeared as a noun in the nineteenth century.

There was a late-Roman practice in which an aristocrat surrounded himself with clients who served him while he saw to their needs. A similar tradition was known among the Germans, whose leaders were attended by a circle of warriors. In both cases the bond between leader and follower was expressed through a personal oath of loyalty. These two institutions merged, and the personal bond between a wealthy lord and his retainers became a fixed practice known as *vassalage* which was entered into by a ceremony of *homage*. The church superimposed the oath of *fidelitas* (fealty) in which the vassal swore on the Gospels or relics to observe the terms of the contract.

Another ingredient of feudalism was the economic bond stemming from a late-Roman system whereby small landowners would deed their land to large estate owners who then assumed their debts. The farmer retained the use of his land, but at his death it was absorbed into the estate. The estate owner leased tracts of land to his vassals in return for rents or a supply of warriors. The land was called a *fief*, and the ceremony of conferring a fief was *investiture*. When the economic bond represented by the fief combined with the personal oath of vassalage, Europe was well on its way toward feudalism. Becoming a vassal did not involve loss of prestige or social standing. Most lords were also vassals. Such relationships could become complicated, since a lord could be someone's vassal on one piece of land, but their position could be reversed on another. The King of England, who was also the Duke of Normandy in France, was a vassal of the King of France in Normandy, but in England he was his equal as king. It often happened that one had several lords, and it was difficult to choose who received priority service, especially if two lords were fighting one another. This called for the introduction of a *liege* lord, the one to whom a vassal owed first *allegiance*. Feudalism could function only so long as wealth was reckoned on the basis of land. With the increase of commerce and money beginning in the twelfth century, feudalism began to decline.

Churches and clergy, by holding lands under various forms of tenure, became part of the feudal system. Each land holding carried with it various obligations of rent or service, and in this way the church became involved in the economic and political system. Entire towns, forests, roads, waterways, fairs, and other economic assets could be under the supervision of a church, bishop, or monastery. It was not unusual for a count-bishop to lead an army which included clergy-knights.

At the other end of the social scale was the manor, a tract of land farmed by serfs who may have been "bound" to the land in a semi-servile condition or by free men who had the liberty to move elsewhere. In return for their labor they received housing, such as it was, and their own plot of ground on which to grow their food, although most of their labor was on the lord's land (*demesne*). Manors were self-sufficient, as in the early Middle Ages when there were few if any towns to buy things and no commerce to generate economy. Society was decentralized; there was no concept of a "state" or "nation," central government or uniform laws. Where there were kings they were usually one of the weaker lords. Centralization began in the twelfth century with the emergence of strong kings in England and France, facilitated in large part by the revival of commerce, capitalism, and especially civil law (royal justice). A large number of churches and monasteries were built by lay lords who retained the right to appoint the clergy who served them and the revenues they produced. These were called proprietary churches, and it was the church's struggle to gain freedom from lay control that precipitated the Investiture Controversy. It was under these conditions that the only unifying institution in society to which almost all professed loyalty was the church. Christianity became the "glue" that held things together, and from this was born the concept of Europe as being synonymous with Christendom in the West.

At a time when there was no central justice or government, in a society where princes had complex loyalties, war became a condition of life. The oath of vassalage required military service, and such resources were tempting to be used. It was to this situation that a synod at Charroux in 989 spoke when it decreed that the common people, peasants and the poor, should be spared in time of hostilities, and cattle stealing was condemned. The goal of this protection, known as the Peace of God, was to spare the defenseless from harm, but it did not condemn warfare. In 1027 a council at Toulouges-Rousillon prohibited attack on enemies from the ninth hour on Saturday until the first hour on Monday out of respect for Sunday. It also prohibited attacks on unarmed priests and monks, on anyone going to or coming from church, on anyone in female company, and on church buildings or any other structure within forty-five meters of churches. "This treaty or truce has been agreed on because the law of God and the whole Christian religion has been virtually destroyed, and iniquity abounds and love for neighbor has vanished."[34] The Peace and Truce of God were extended in time to prohibit warfare from Wednesdays to Mondays, and all of Advent and Lent. These attempts to curb the violence of the system failed as often as they succeeded. A modern observer, however, finds that the real consequence of the attempt was that "it gave legal status to a system of justice that answered (violators) with punishment. Thus a penal code developed that provided medieval society with a legal system," at least in those regions where rulers were not at war with each other.[35] The Truce of God did not bring an end to war.

At the beginning of the church, celibacy had not been a requirement for the priesthood. Some of the Fathers of the church, such as Gregory of Nyssa, were married, and his own father had been a priest. In some churches a place of honor was reserved for the priest's wife. At the Council of Nicea (325) an attempt was made to require priestly celibacy, but it was defeated by monks who spoke against it. In the ninth and tenth centuries a large percentage of the clergy were married. At the same time attempts continued to be made to realize the ideal of clerical celibacy, in part from a "monasticization" of the church in which the model of the monks became the ideal for all Christians. By the time of the Gregorian reforms under Hildebrand an economic aspect had entered the picture, and that was the number of clergy sons who were inheriting their father's church, true to the feudal system of *primogeniture* whereby sons inherited their father's property.[36] Opposition to clerical marriage thereby became a facet of the Investiture Controversy because of the alienation of churches from bishops' control through filial inheritance. The success of Hildebrand's program of mandated clerical celibacy clearly had ramifications for the church in society and the role of the priesthood.

An often overlooked aspect of the medieval church and society is its relationship with Judaism. From the beginning of Christianity, tensions existed between the church and Jews, although many early Fathers such as Origen and Jerome expressed themselves positively about Jews and even studied the Hebrew Scripture under them. In a recent essay, Adrian Bredero comments that one cannot find any hatred expressed by Christians for Jews before the twelfth century.[37] One exception is Agobard, Bishop of Lyons (d. 840) who wrote a treatise against them. But an escalation of polemics occurred in the twelfth century, preceded by the persecution of Jews which accompanied the first two Crusades, in 1096 and 1146. Peter, "the Venerable," Abbot of Cluny (d. 1156), reached the depths of vitriol in his diatribe, following an earlier essay in a similar vein by Guibert of Nogent (d. 1124). In 1215 the Fourth Lateran Council ordered Jews to be identified by a symbol on their clothing, and they were not to be seen in public on Christian fast days. Some Christian leaders, notably Gilbert Crispin at the end of the eleventh century, Abelard, Stephen Harding, Abbot of Citeaux, Nicholas of Lyra, among others, took a balanced and positive view, but they were all overwhelmed by the preponderance of antipathy expressed by the majority. Even so, in 1247 Pope Innocent IV vigorously opposed accusations against Jews in a letter to German and French bishops, and in 1338 Clement VI condemned persecution of Jews, saying that cupidity was the driving force behind anti-Jewish activity, since accusers stood to gain if the suspect was condemned. Jews were expelled from England in 1290, from France in 1306, from Spain in 1492, and from Portugal in 1497. Only in Islamic Spain did medieval Jewish culture and thought reach its maturity in the West, of whom Maimonides was a preeminent example. Clear and compelling reasons for such anti-Jewish fanaticism are not yet at hand. Charges of "Christ killers," or the fact that Jews were money-lenders do not adequately explain this melancholy phenonmenon.

One of the most magnificent and inspiring legacies bequeathed to posterity by medieval Christian society is its architecture and art. Models for early church buildings were Roman public buildings known as basilicas—rectangular, with a flat roof and a long central aisle, and a semi-circular dome at the front. The basilica form was adopted by the church after the fall of Rome and the conversion of the Teutonic tribes, resulting in a form known as Romanesque (Roman-like). These buildings were of stone with half-circular ceilings (barrel vault) and, in order to carry the weight of the heavy roof, the walls were thick and not very high, making for a relatively low building. Such churches were cruciform in their ground plan, with transepts or side spaces toward the front at right angles to the nave. At the upper level of the nave a row of windows called the clerestory allowed for more light. Because of the thickness of the walls, windows were usually small, but the large spaces provided by walls and ceiling were covered with gold, tapestries, and pictures, making the interior a true garden of visual delight. Europe's largest church in the twelfth century was the Romanesque cathedral at Cluny (555 feet long). In the Romanesque period, lifesize sculpture was used for the first time since late antiquity, sometimes elongated in order to fit into the space and architectural pattern.

Several innovations transformed Romanesque into Gothic architecture around 1140. The ceiling vaults were thinner and pointed, directing their weight to supporting arches outside the church called flying buttresses. Thick walls were no longer necessary, so it was possible to have large spaces of window, usually with stained glass depicting biblical scenes. Ceiling vaults could be raised higher and higher, giving the church the appearance of soaring into the air. The highest Romanesque ceiling, at Cluny, was 98 feet, but the Gothic vault at Reims is 126 feet, at Amiens, 144 feet, and at Beauvais, 160 feet.

Abbot Suger of St. Denis in Paris is credited with introducing Gothic architecture, and he has left us a detailed account of the construction of his church, from initial plans to its dedication. "The Almighty revealed to us a quarry nearby. The columns were hauled by common folk and noble who alike harnessed themselves as beasts of burden. . . . I penetrated the thickets and found twelve trees which the Lord Jesus had protected from plunderers and reserved for Himself. . . . Summer and winter for three years we labored."[38] King Louis VII of France and his court attended the dedication. "After the consecration of the main altar and twenty others, a solemn mass was celebrated whose melody, ravishing in consonance and congruent harmony, seemed rather a heavenly than an earthly symphony."[39] Four masterpieces of Gothic architecture were completed in the thirteenth century: Paris (1260), Chartres (1260), Amiens (1270), Rheims (1300). The number of cathedrals (or large churches) constructed during the twelfth and thirteenth centuries is amazing. France alone, in a single century from 1170 to 1270, built eighty cathedrals and over five hundred churches of cathedral proportions. Not only was this a display of religious devotion, but there was also an element of local pride in having a cathedral. Many churches were built to accomodate a number of worshipers far in excess of the population of the locality, because the magnificence and grandeur of the church was to reflect the glory of God and not merely to accomodate the faithful.

Churches were built as sacred space for the mass, and as liturgy was drama it gave rise to dramatic art. An extension of the liturgy was the mystery play: a dramatization of an event from the Bible, an incident from the life of Christ, or a missionary journey of St. Paul. From these dramas there developed the morality play in which abstract virtues and vices were personified and made into living characters. The miracle play depicted the life of a saint or other post-biblical character. All of these derived from the Christian liturgy and served to teach virtue in a way easily accessible to the average person.

167

The influence of monasticism on Western society in the medieval period was profound. In terms of the intellect, the internal and external schools and the scriptoria were virtually the sole means of transmitting the culture and learning of Graeco-Roman civilization. When Renaissance thinkers derided medieval culture as inferior because of its alleged preoccupation with religion, they did so by way of the humanistic literature of antiquity that had been saved by the monasteries. The monastic schools gave rise to the cathedral schools, from which emerged a creation unique to Western society, the university. The scriptoria and monastic libraries kept alive the lamp of learning simply by virtue of Benedict's *Rule*, which required several hours each day in reading. It was by way of monastic authors that letters were fostered by such as Gregory, Bede, Alcuin, Anselm, Abelard, and a host of chroniclers, archivists, and historians. Society was also shaped by contributions in law, medicine, art, architecture, and spirituality made by the medieval church through monasticism, a legacy which remains vibrant today.[40]

CHAPTER EIGHT

DECLINE AND VITALITY

Whereas the early Middle Ages were a time of preserving the legacy of the Graeco-Roman civilization, and the High Middle Ages a time of consolidation and self-assurance, the later Middle Ages (1300–1500) were a time of unprecedented challenge. "Basic social structures and values were put to a terrible test. As never before, not even during the century of the Roman Empire's collapse, Western people walked through the valley of the shadow of death."[1]

Economic and Social Disruption

Western Europe witnessed a revival of commerce as early as the twelfth century, and by the mid–thirteenth century trade and merchants were flourishing. Confederations of towns joined together for mercantile activity, such as the Hanseatic League, Rhenish League, and the Flanders Fleet of Venice. Trade routes opened up from the Mediterranean to the Baltic and East to China, resulting in a revival of urban life, merchant princes, guilds, craft guilds, money economy, instruments of credit, banking, and fairs. "Europe was covered with towns from which the activity of the new middle class radiated in all directions."[2] But this situation was arrested and then reversed as a series of calamities came upon society.

A succession of poor harvests brought about appalling famines in 1315–17 throughout northern and eastern Europe as well as the Mediterranean areas in the south. The price of grain rose in England from 5 shillings a quarter in 1313 to 26 shillings in 1315, and in Antwerp the price tripled within seven months.[3] During the summer of 1316 one-tenth of the population, three thousand people, died in Ypres. The decline of population was accelerated by the Black Death, to be discussed below, but plague was endemic throughout the century. These statistics dramatically display the decrease in population of various European cities: Freiburg 9,000 (1385), 6000 (1500); Toulouse 30,000 (1335), 22,500 (1405); Modena 22,000 (1335), 8000 (1405); Florence 110,000 (1350), 70,000 (1385).[4]

Unrelated to these natural calamities were those stemming from the new economy itself; that is, the clash resulting from the transition from an agricultural and domestic economy to a monied and commercial economy. Feudal princes now demanded rents instead of produce, not only from their serfs but from the towns situated on their lands. Money lenders often charged exhorbitant interest, which practice the church attacked in its strictures against usury. Added to this was the steady flow of the rural population to the urban centers, unemployment, the fixing of artisans' and laborers' wages, and the rise of powerful banking families who controlled cities such as the Fuggers in Augsburg, the Medicis, Bardis, and Frescobaldis in Florence, Jacques Coeur in France, Chigi of Siena, and Dick Whittington, and de la Poles in England. Towns became polarized between the rich (*majores*) and the wage-earners (*minores*), with the merchant guilds becoming hereditary and dominant. These tensions finally found expression in nearly one hundred urban insurrections in the fourteenth century. The plutocratic guilds had become oligarchic bodies in which a fortunate few guided, ruled, and restricted the livelihood of the many.

Already in 1251 northern France was stirred by a restless spirit among shepherds and rural laborers who vowed to go on a crusade, but their purpose was soon forgotten, and they became mere brigands openly hostile to church and nobility. In the end they were ruthlessly crushed. In 1282 there was an uprising of Sicilians against the ruling French nobility in which hundreds of the foreign occupiers were killed, a massacre known to history as the Sicilian Vespers. Monasteries and churches were likewise invaded. "It is the unexpected intrusion (of the common people) into the relatively orderly course of events, the unbridled license of their actions, and its overwhelming if temporary success that attract the attention of the historian of the period."[5] The Netherlands were more given to popular insurrection than any other part of Europe. In the Matins of Bruges of 1302 the Flemish rose up against their French overlords, and within a few days all of Flanders was in the hands of the revolutionaries. Later that same year the French king led his forces against the Flemish and was decisively defeated at the battle of Courtrai, where it is said twenty thousand people were left dead on the field. Between 1323 and 1328 another bitter series of battles occured in Flanders between landlords and peasants. Another sudden and brutal uprising was that of the Jacquerie of 1358, which spread to more than two hundred towns before it was put down. Italy experienced the same disorders when Cola do Rienzi forcibly inaugurated a new government for Rome in 1347 which lasted seven months. In 1378 the Ciompi or workmen of Rome rose in rebellion and were defeated after four years. The peasant revolt of 1381 in England was among the most famous, with the battle cry of "When Adam delved and Eve span, who was then the gentleman," a blunt declaration that all people were created equal.

It would be a mistake to interpret such uprisings simply as expressions of democratic aspirations opposed to tyranny. Motivations were complex, and often as not the revolutionaries had no goal other than plunder. But three common denominators appear in many of these uprisings: they burned tax records and court rolls, evidence of their services, rents, and disabilities; they opposed the privileged class of nobles; and they often attacked churches, monasteries, and clergy. Although most of the uprisings were ruthlessly suppressed, urban unrest was a symptom of the emergence of a new economic order which also marked the end of feudalism.

At the middle of the fourteenth century (1347–1351) there occurred one of the most appalling disasters in Western history. By way of trade routes to the East a form of bubonic plague carried by rats entered the West, against which there seemed to be no immunity or medical knowledge. Because the infection was accompanied by black blisters on the afflicted, it became known as the Black Death. Within three years Europe lost over one-fourth of its population, and some communities lost over one-third. The plague recurred several more times before the end of the century. These catastrophes caused a revival of the flagellants who appeared all over Europe, bands of men who scourged themselves in public processions in order to call people to repentance. There was also a renewed interest in the prophecies of Joachim of Fiore, who had predicted the end of the world because of God's displeasure with humankind. Others, however, were not as religious in their response. Boccacio of Florence in *The Decameron*, written between 1350 and 1354, described the horrors of the pestilence: "so many corpses would arrive in front of a church every day and at every hour that the amount of holy ground for burials was insufficient."[6] He continued by relating how four young women and three young men took refuge in a villa away from the city where they spent their time in telling stories, which "are purely pagan; the book contains no element of Christianity excepting a Friday fast."[7]

Clearly the swift loss of a large segment of the population led to social disruption, but more specifically it resulted in economic tension which precipitated urban unrest. Because of a labor shortage after the pestilence was over, workers demanded higher wages. In England the Statute of Laborers (1351) and others like it required that the same wages be offered as before the scourge. Rural peasants also agitated for the commutation of services into cash, which escalated into the demand to abolish all manorial obligations. Since the workers and peasants had no legal means for resolving their disputes, they resorted to force. Although their grievances antedated the Black Death, the shortage of labor which resulted from it intensified their unrest.

To add to the melancholy of this time, England and France were intermittently engaged in a series of hostilities known collectively as the Hundred Years' War, fought almost entirely on French soil. There were several causes for the war. First was the dispute over English lands in France, notably Aquitane, which had been held by the English ever since king Henry II (1154–1189) secured it through marriage to Eleanor of Aquitane. At a time when nationalism was growing stronger, and the French in particular were trying to unite the kingdom geographically, the expulsion of the English seemed a desirable goal. Entangling alliances was another cause of friction. The French supported the Welsh and the Scots in their hostilities against England, and Flanders enjoyed English support against the French. A third issue had to do with claims to the French throne. Charles IV, the last direct male heir to the French throne in the Capetian line, died in 1328. There were two possible claimants to the throne—his cousin, Philip VI of Valois, or his nephew, Edward III, King of England and the grandson of Philip IV of France. The French peers and prelates declared for Philip.

In 1337 Edward III attacked France through Flanders, a military engagement which ended in a truce. In 1340 the English were victorious in a naval battle fought off Sluys in Flanders, but the first major battle was fought at Crecy in 1346 in which the English again prevailed. Philip VI fled the battlefield in disgrace while the Black Prince, Edward's eldest son, won admiration for his courage and chivalry. The English went on to besiege and take Calais. Ten years later (1356) the English, though outnumbered, again decisively defeated the French at Poitiers and captured King John. Four years later by the Treaty of Bretigny, Aquitane, Calais, and Poitiers became English possessions without terms of vassalage.

The war was resumed in 1369, but the death of monarchs on both sides, peasant uprisings, and polarization caused by the Great Schism in the Papacy postponed any decisive military activity until 1415, when the English with a much smaller force again defeated the French at Agincourt. By the Treaty of Troyes in 1420, Henry V, King of England, became heir to the French throne. But most Frenchmen remained loyal to the dauphin, son of the current but ailing Charles VI of France. In 1429 the English siege of Orleans appeared to be successful when a peasant girl from Lorraine, Joan of Arc, claiming to have experienced supernatural visitations, succeeded in lifting the siege. "France, through Joan, had won a great moral victory. The sun began to shine once more."[8] Joan of Arc was also instrumental in having the dauphin crowned King of France at Rheims ten weeks later, a direct challenge to the claims of Henry V of England. Either by war or diplomacy, in the next two decades the French gradually won back territories which the English had claimed. In 1453 the Hundred Years' War ended when the French regained Acquitaine.

The war brought sustained social and economic disruption, primarily to France, not only from the ravages of military engagements but especially from the gangs of freebooting soldiers who wasted the countryside in times of "peace." England lost its possessions in part because of the threat of civil war at home, which erupted in 1455. Where were the peacemakers—specifically the emperor and the pope—while England and France were engaged in these sustained hostilities? Imperial (meaning German) power was involved in succession contests, defense of the eastern frontiers, and intramural squabbling. Also, by the fourteenth century, concepts of royal sovereignty were so well developed that any intervention seemed unlikely. Because this was the time of the "Babylonian Captivity of the Church," in which a succession of (mostly French) popes lived at Avignon, France, followed by the Great Schism—during which one set of popes resided in Avignon, while their rival claimants lived in Rome, with England and France supporting the different parties to the schism—help from this quarter seemed unrealistic. The growth of nationalism in the fourteenth century challenged papal power as it was known in the thirteenth. "By the outbreak of the Hundred Years' War, kings could already tax their clergy without papal sanction. National churches operated independently and under considerable monarchical influence."[9] English kings dispossessed French monasteries on English lands. Discords between the warring parties and the Papacy furthered the development of national churches in France and England.

Despite what has been said, the majority of peace conferences before 1378 (the beginning of the papal schism) were initiated by papal mediation. Clement VI was personally involved in 1344 and papal legates took initiatives in 1352–1354, 1375–1377, and in 1435. "Papally-sponsored negotiations and truces failed not because of papal bias but because of the reluctance of the English and French to come to settlement."[10]

What impact did the economic changes and the peasant revolts have upon the church? As we have seen, church institutions and clergy were often included as targets of the uprisings. This is because the church was also a principal landowner at this time, and as such participated in attempts to resist the changes to a money economy with its threats to the status quo and allegedly to personal morality. "Stadtluft macht frei" (city air makes one free) was a familiar perception which attracted thousands of rural folk to the urban centers in the hope of being free, not only from the authority of rapacious and oppressive landowners, taxes, and demands, but from all authority, including the church and its moral restrictions. In many cases monasteries or churches were the feudal lords who not only controlled large tracts of land which included hundreds of peasant families, but entire cities as well. Although Christianity originated in an urban culture, from the sixth century on the West was rural, and the church with it. It has been said that the church was uneasy with cities, basing its reservation on the fact that Cain, the first fratricide, was also the builder of the first city (Gen. 4:17). Yet the church's positive response to the new phenomena of urban centers was the authorization of the mendicant orders, the Franciscans and Dominicans, who were established primarily to work in the cities. The former worked in the ghettos with the poor, leprous, and needy; the latter with the rising universities and the intellectual class. The church, as with all landed proprietors, felt the need to accumulate fluid capital not tied to the land and, in an age of rapid inflation, found it necessary to design ways of increasing its income. That discussion appears in the following chapter.

What was the effect of the Black Death on the church? Several studies indicate that in England over half of the parish clergy died in 1348 and 1349.[11] In Germany there was "great [clerical] mortality, with consequent enforced ordination of men and youth of inferior qualifications; demoralization of both seculars and regulars; the wiping out of the entire personnel of some monasteries; the closing of many parish churches."[12] Another study indicates that 207 bishops perished and 368 survived.[13] Perhaps of greater interest is how the church responded to the crisis. One commentator has gathered evidence for both England and the continent that many priests initially ran from their parish duties, but a new breed of priests, who were more responsive to the suffering of the people, replaced them, often serving several parishes because of the shortage.[14] Another argues that education suffered a decline, including that of clergy. The intellectual life of Europe lost its optimism and yielded to gloom, anxiety, and mysticism.[15]

The Way of the Mystic

From the beginning of Christianity there was an attempt on the part of many to experience the presence of God in one's life in a direct and personal way. Mysticism is not unique to Christianity, but there is a mysticism that is uniquely Christian. Gregory of Nyssa (d. 395) is said to be the "father of Christian mysticism," although many of the early Christians, with their emphasis on deification as salvation and following the three stages of purgation, illumination, and union with God, were cultivating the interior life through a true inwardness rather than mere conformity to external rites. Dionysius the Pseudo-Areopagite (c. 500) provided a significant stimulus to mysticism through his book, *Mystical Theology*, which was introduced to the West by John Scotus Erigena (d. 877), whose own works provided a further stimulus to mystical theology. Although mystical practices were always present in the church, particularly within the contemplative orders, the twelfth century witnessed the beginning of a flowering of mystical expression which intensified in the late Middle Ages. We have already considered Bernard of Clairvaux's emphasis on devotion to the passion and cross of Christ and to the Virgin Mary. Of equal significance was William of St. Thierry, Bernard's contemporary and biographer, who distinguished between mystical knowledge and love of learning.[16] Theology itself was an act of adoration. He dwells on the ascent of the soul to God until it moves only under the influence of the Holy Spirit. Hugh, Richard, and Walter of St. Victor were also mystics, scholars, and poets of the twelfth century.[17]

Hildegarde of Bingen (d. 1179), founder and abbess of two convents, was gifted in horticulture, music, medicine, politics, and hymnody, but her foremost vocation was that of a contemplative. She recorded her twenty-six visions in a book, *Scivias*, carried on a lively correspondence with kings, prelates, and saints, and was the first great figure in the line of medieval mystics. She also held that the decadence of the church and society was caused chiefly by masculine weakness: women must therefore act where men had failed.[18] Mechthild of Magdeburg (d. 1280) was a German mystic who joined the Beguines (see below) and later moved to a Cistercian convent. In her visions described in *The Fleeting Light of*

God she writes of the journey of the soul, traveling to paradise via hell and purgatory. It may be that Mechthild was the same Matilda who accompanied Dante through Purgatory, leading him to Beatrice.

Communities of women founded in the Netherlands in the twelfth century were known as Beguines. They were loosely organized, without vows, permitted to own private property and even to leave the community to get married. Their male counterparts were known as Beghards. Throughout the thirteenth and fourteenth centuries they fell under suspicion of heresy, which in their case was identified as striving for perfection through union with God; that such deification made all religious acts (sacraments or good works) unnecessary; and that they claimed exemption from church authority. In 1310 Marguerite Porete, a Beguin from Hainault, was burned at the stake for allegedly supporting such ideas in her book, *Mirror of Simple Souls*, and the Council of Vienne two years later condemned eight propositions attributed to them. Further persecutions followed when some Beghards were killed by burning or drowning in 1327.[19]

Foremost among the German mystics was John "Meister" Eckhart (d. 1328), a Dominican who taught at Paris, Strassburg, and Cologne. He spoke of the soul as being a spark of the divine, as one's ground of being. One must withdraw from material things and ideas in order to enter the soul and thus be restored to God. By so doing one actually becomes one with God. The determining factor in his mental formation was his encounter with Neoplatonic philosophy, for which he was in debt to Pseudo-Dionysius. He evidenced some disdain for history, affirming that the most real was the unknowable. Because of Eckhart's sometimes ambiguous expressions, he was accused of pantheism by the Archbishop of Cologne and died while Pope John XXII was reviewing the accusation, but who posthumously condemned twenty-eight of his propositions.

Another Dominican, John Tauler (d. 1361) was Eckhart's leading student, who sought to avoid any hint of pantheism by stating that the soul is distinct from God, and that its progress toward God is only by grace. He is known through one hundred fifty surviving sermons, which show him to be intensely pastoral. All good and humble people should be able to return to their origins, that is, to God. All things in which one cannot find God will seem as a wound, and the truly spiritual soul requires complete detachment from personal desire. He called himself the "secret emperor" of a "secret kingdom" (i.e. the soul). Tauler was critical of the "walled church" (i.e. the institutional church) and encouraged his hearers rather to find solace through inward migrations into the soul. He warned against the possibility of "popes, bishops, and prelates preying upon me like wolves," insisting rather that true religion was in the inward experience of suffering and self-denial.[20] Henry Suso (d. 1360), the third great German Dominican mystic, was a disciple of Eckhart and Tauler. He spent much of his life in preaching and pastoral ministry, writing a devotional book on Christ's suffering, the *Book of Eternal Wisdom*, which achieved great popularity. He describes in almost sensual terms the sweet savour, ardent fires, and heavenly music which visited his soul. He practiced an intense and severe asceticism.

These German mystics had a profound influence in several directions. A new group from the Rhineland and Switzerland came under their influence; they called themselves the "Friends of God," and emphasized the transforming power of uniting their souls to God. Many were recruited from older Beghard groups and were simply attempting to bring spiritual renewal and Bible study to laity outside the existing church structure. The highly influential *Theologia Germanica* came from these circles, which followed the ideas of the German mystics, especially in their emphasis on interior conversion and grace. Luther supervised its first printed edition (1518), and later Pietists admired it. The Friends of God also had an apocalyptic side, revealing their dependence on the German prophetic tradition which began with Hildegard.

John Ruysbroek, a secular priest in Brussels and thereafter an Augustinian canon (d. 1381) was a follower of Tauler and one of the Friends of God. Although he was critical of some Beghards and Beguines, and while his own writings betrayed Eckhart's pantheism, "his place was all important in helping to bridge the gap from the more formal monastic mysticism of the age to a religion increasingly popular in its mystical form."[21] He is ranked among the greatest of those who have written of the contemplative union with God in the light of their own experience, and some consider him the greatest of all the mystics. "Ruysbroeck seems often to use Eckhart's ideas as a means of expressing his own experiences, but the ardor and realism with which he invests them are his own."[22] He understands the spiritual life as one of progress, beginning simply on the human level and proceeding through struggle to a higher plane. Ruysbroeck was a devoted follower of the church, its corporate and sacramental life. The German mystics also exerted influence in their pastoral work with Dominican nuns and Beguines in the Rhineland. Many Beguines were among the disciples of Tauler and Suso, and they continued to exist into the later centuries, either merged with Common Life groups or becoming absorbed within Protestantism.

Gerard Groote (d. 1384) was a professor at Cologne where, as he admitted later, he lived in luxury and self-indulgence. He came under the influence of the Friends of God and then of John Ruysbroek. He was never ordained, although he became a licensed preacher (deacon) centered at Utrecht in 1379. So outspoken were his condemnations of ecclesiastical abuses that his license to preach was revoked. He retired in 1381 to Deventer, where in the company of a few friends he planned the idea for a new community, the Brethren of the Common Life, which had as a primary goal the reform of monastic life. Groote died in 1384 before he could realize his goal, but his friend, Florent Radewyns, continued the work. As with the Beguines, the Sisters and Brothers of the Common Life took no vows and were left free to pursue their ordinary vocations in the world. They flourished especially in the Netherlands—Kempen, Zwolle, and Windesheim—and later in Germany and Switzerland. In 1395 the movement divided into two tracks, one led by the house at Windesheim and the other by that at Deventer, "two streams from one source, which often unite, and usually flow side by side."[23] At Windesheim the residents followed a more conservative communal regimen by adopting the Augustinian Rule for canons. Their influence and example spread rapidly. At one time sixteen "missionaries" were sent out to reform other monasteries, and twelve of them became priors at the reformed houses. By 1464 the Windesheim group included eighty-four houses and by 1500, over one hundred. In addition to these, numerous other monasteries adopted Groote's reforms without affiliating with Windesheim. The principal modern historian of the movement maintains that its popularity was in "practical mysticism, where poverty and manual labor did not seem a hardship. . . . They worked, read, and loved each other as brothers."[24] The reforming spirit exemplified by Groote's foundation and most clearly reflected in the Sisters and Brothers of the Common Life was called *The New Devotion* (*Devotio Moderna*), as contrasted with the *Devotio Antiqua* which was associated with Thomas Aquinas and scholasticism. Perhaps the finest flower of the Windesheim piety and the New Devotion was *The Imitation of Christ* by Thomas à Kempis, who spent his entire life in a monastery of the Windesheim congregation, Mount St. Agnes near Zwolle. The work appeals to people of every age, background, and nationality. In it he recounts the reality of original sin, that is, the human condition as one of frailty, "fallen and corrupted by sin." The reader is encouraged to fight against evil, to examine one's conscience daily, and to ignore the opinions of others. "He enjoys great tranquility of heart who neither cares for the praise or dispraise of men." The reader, who is called both a pilgrim and a prisoner, is to acquire virtue through the imitation of

Christ, but in this effort one has the help of divine grace. Salvation comes only through faith, but faith is defined as assuming good works.[25]

Meanwhile the Deventer group closely paralleled that at Windesheim, devoted to copying books, Bible reading, works of charity, and working among the laity. They were suspected of heresy, perhaps because they read Scripture in the vernacular, did not take vows, and did not mirror traditional monasticism as Windesheim appeared to do. They were investigated by the Inquisition in 1398, but the Masters who conducted the inquiry "upheld the organization and life of the Brethren and also the lay reading of vernacular books of Scripture and devotion."[26] Followers of the New Devotion revered the sacraments and supported the church. The congregation at Deventer eventually included about forty-five houses and close to one hundred affiliated houses.

The Brothers of the Common Life also fostered education. Groote's chief aim had been the reform of the church; the surest and best way toward that end he believed, was the education of young men. The curriculum included classical and Christian literature, grammar, rhetoric, logic, mathematics, and philosophy, as well as the nurture of spiritual life. But most Brethren were not university trained or highly educated, and it was not until the late–fifteenth century that "practically all the larger schools in Western Germany were reorganized and reformed." Among the "vast host of really great teachers and scholars"[27] who went forth from their schools were Thomas à Kempis, Pope Hadrian VI, Gabriel Biel, Nicholas of Cusa, Rudolph Agricola, and Martin Luther.

During the fourteenth century in England there were five major authors of mystical literature who were contemporary and interacted with each other. All were followers of the solitary life, wrote in the vernacular, and were drawn to the Passion of Christ. Richard Rolle (d. 1349) emulated Francis in that he left a promising career to embrace poverty, living the life of a hermit missionary. "He represents for his day almost the extreme of individualism possible to a mystic who remained obedient to the church. He passionately proclaimed liberty of conscience, declaring himself to be directed by the Holy Spirit."[28] He also displays a sense of warmth and joy that is appealing to many readers.

The author of *The Cloud of Unknowing* remains anonymous, although clearly a trained theologian. "We get from this nameless mystic a vigorous and amusing picture of a fourteenth century cloister with its ardent, sanctimonious, hypocritical, fidgety, and variously tired inhabitants."[29] The author is deeply influenced by the negative mysticism of Pseudo-Dionysius in that God is beyond all reason and knowing, but the "cloud" can be pierced "by a sharp dart of longing love, speedily springing unto God as a sparkle from the coal."

Walter Hilton (d. 1396) was an Augustinian canon who is best known for *The Scale of Perfection* by which the defaced image of God in the soul may be restored, first through faith, and then through faith and feeling. The experience includes the "dark night of the soul" in which one becomes completely detached from the material and directed to the spiritual. He is more pastoral than others, and writes for ordinary people in offering such sound insights that not only does behavior need to change, but with it the motivations which cause such behavior. He was critical of ostentatious piety which neglects practical things, referring to it as "tending God's head but neglecting His feet."

Julian of Norwich (d. 1413), an anchoress, received sixteen revelations on Christ's Passion and the Trinity which she recorded in *Revelations of Divine Love*. Like Walter Hilton, she is down to earth, tender-hearted, and generous. "Most people are spiritual babies, and sins are best dealt with from this point of view. . . . All people are lovable."[30] A saint is not a holy recluse but someone whose very real sins have been transcended, citing King David as an example. "Julian's work forms a fitting crown to the golden period of English mysticism."[31] Mention must be made of Margaret Kempe (d. 1433) who wrote the *Book of Margery Kempe,* which is our only source for her life. She was married and had fourteen children, and after having visions at Canterbury she and her husband decided to take vows of chastity. She made a pilgrimage to the Holy Land, and upon her return to England she spent most of her time traveling throughout the land denouncing the ecclesiastical establishment, especially bishops and their entourage, for their luxury, lack of spirituality, and greed.

Among Italian mystics two stand out, Catherine of Siena (b. 1347) and Catherine of Genoa (b. 1407). At age sixteen Catherine of Siena joined the Third Order of St. Dominic, after having a vision of "The Mystical Marriage with Christ." Although she practiced severe asceticism, she displayed extraordinary strength, declaring that her desire was "to know and follow the truth in a more *virile* way." She is especially known for her public career in urging the pope at Avignon, Gregory XI, to return to Rome. She did this through direct and pointed letters: "Answer the summons of God. Possess the place of the glorious Peter, whose vicar you are." When letters were of no avail she went to see the pope in person. Her influence was decisive in convincing the pope to return to Rome.

Catherine of Genoa received a vision ten years after her marriage to a pleasure-loving husband who eventually followed her example of asceticism and became a Franciscan tertiary. Catherine is especially known, apart from her many hours of prayer and austerities, for her work among the sick. Indeed, she is credited with founding the first hospital in Genoa. She is a primary example of a mystic in the world, reaching the heights of contemplation yet going to the depths of human misery to bring healing and compassion.

Bridget of Sweden (d. 1373), born to a wealthy family, was married and became the mother of eight children. After the death of her husband she established the order of the Brigittines in Sweden, and in later life she lived in Rome where she worked with Catherine of Siena to restore the Papacy to Rome. She received a number of visions similar to those of Hildegarde, including apocalyptic prophecies, and she was vocal in her denunciations of abuses in the church.

The Church and the Early Renaissance

Beginning in the fourteenth century and continuing through the sixteenth, there was a marked change in interest and accomplishments within European culture that affected virtually every area of life, including the church. This flowering of culture found its roots already in the High Middle Ages with the revival of Roman law and the discovery of Aristotle in the eleventh century, as well as humanistic interests in literature and art. But from the fourteenth century on, renewed interest in Graeco-Roman civilization, classical literature, and humanism intensified to the point that the civilization of Europe during this period, and particularly that of Italy, has been designated by historians and popular culture as the age of the Renaissance, a term first used in the late–sixteenth century.[32]

Although the Renaissance was many things, it began in Italy with a revival of interest in the spirit of classical antiquity and especially literature. The most important figure in the literary culture of fourteenth-century Italy was Petrarch (1304–1374), considered the founder of humanism, that is, the study of humanity and the products of human endeavor. As used in the fourteenth century it implied the cultivation of Greek and Roman life ignored in the Middle Ages, and by some it was understood in opposition to sacred or religious interests. Petrarch, a Florentine by descent, lived his early life near Avignon, then studied Law, traveled through Europe seeking classical manuscripts, lived for many years at the papal court in Avignon, and finally ended his days in Venice and Padua. He collected hundreds of manuscripts of classical authors, searching monastic and episcopal archives and often copying them in his own precise handwriting. Indeed, he died while copying a manuscript. He had enormous admiration for Quintilian, Livy, Virgil, and Homer, but his favorites were Cicero and Seneca. At the same time he held both Augustine and Plato in high regard; to the former he wrote a series of dialogues called the *Secret,* which forms a type of confession, and Plato he hailed as the greatest of all philosophers.

Besides being a collector, Petrarch was famous as a writer on classical subjects. In an attempt to imitate Vergil's *Aeneid,* he wrote *Africa* about Scipio Africanus, and he produced the *Lives of Illustrious Men,* a collection of thirty-one biographical sketches of famous Romans. He was in the habit of addressing his thoughts to the great writers of antiquity which he collected in the *Familiar Letters.* "Petrarch, thus living and talking with his antique preceptors, heralded a new period of fruitful converse with the past."[33] Petrarch is credited with introducing a new periodization in history by regarding the fall of the Roman empire as a dividing point between 'ancient' and 'modern' history. Other historians of the age, Flavio Biondo and Leonardo Bruni, following the idea of a "fall" of Rome, created the notion of a "middle age" lying between Rome's decline and the Renaissance.[34]

Despite his love of classical literature, Petrarch never learned Greek. His close friend, Giovanni Boccaccio (1313–1375), the author of the *Decameron* mentioned earlier, was more successful in promoting Greek study. He was instrumental in bringing Leontius Pilatus to Florence to lecture on Greek literature, and in 1397, Manuel Chrysolaris from Byzantium began to teach Greek at the university in Florence; Cosimo de Medici, a member of the wealthy banking family, was one of his first students. This same Cosimo conceived the idea of founding a Platonic Academy which took form when Marsilio Ficino (1433–1499) was appointed its first director in 1462. One of the brightest stars of the academy was Giovanni Pico della Mirandola (1463–1494) whose *Oration on the Dignity of Man* epitomized the best of the humanist tradition. He also knew Hebrew, Aramaic, and Arabic, and attempted to find in Jewish mysticism some reflection of the Christian mysteries.

Dante Alighieri (1265–1321) was an older contemporary of Petrarch, also a native of Florence, who was exiled in 1301 for opposing pope Boniface VIII. His *Divine Comedy* is one of the best known and most enduring poems of the Renaissance, a vision in which he describes a journey through hell, purgatory, and heaven. At first he is guided by Virgil, then his love, Beatrice, and finally Bernard of Clairvaux, who presents him to the Virgin Mary. The work exercised a wide influence in English literature as well as much commentary related to the people Dante met on his journey, especially the various popes and churchmen he met in hell.

Interest in antiquity was not limited to the classics, but it also included early Christian literature. Cardinal Bessarion (1403–1472), a Greek prelate who moved to Italy, enthusiastically supported the study of the early Christian fathers as well as pagan authors. The best-known scholar of the early church was Lorenzo Valla (1406–1457), a forerunner of modern historical criticism. By pointing to anachronisms he showed the Donation of Constantine to be a forgery, the works attributed to Dionysius the Areopagite to be spurious, and the Apostles' Creed not to be of apostolic origin. He opposed scholasticism and sharply criticized the ideals of religious orders. He also insisted that the Latin Vulgate of the New Testament was inferior to more ancient Greek texts.

Humanism also found its way north of the Alps, though somewhat later, toward the end of the fifteenth century. One powerful catalyst for the dissemination of the new ideas was the invention of movable type by Johann Gutenberg of Mainz, who printed the first dated book, a Psalter, in 1457. The newly available printed texts were diffused by a new breed of wandering scholars (*ordo vagorum*) who went from city to city and school to school in search of new things. This phenomenon in itself was new, as in earlier times people were far less mobile, indeed the *gyrovagi* or wandering monks were condemned in Benedict's *Rule*, "although the Irish monks were notorious wanderers."[35]

German humanism was represented by Rudolph Agricola (1444–1485), the "educator of Germany," who spent much time in Italy and then traveled in the Netherlands and northern Germany. He wrote on education, opposing the intellectualism of scholasticism, and he produced a biography of Petrarch. Johannes Reuchlin (1455–1522) was another German humanist, the first to master Latin, Greek, and Hebrew. Through study with Jewish teachers he became an excellent Hebraist, and he published a grammar and a dictionary which served scholars for many years in their study of the Hebrew Bible. He became the leading Christian expert on Jewish mysticism and an influential opponent of anti-Semitism which caused him to be condemned for heresy just before he died. His grandnephew was Philip Melanchthon, prominent humanist scholar among the Lutheran reformers. The "prince of humanists," Desiderius Erasmus (1469–1536) whose life falls outside the parameters of this study, was heir to a rich legacy of biblical and historical scholarship that was already two centuries in the making at his birth.

Was the Renaissance pagan or Christian? Asked in such stark terms the question cannot be fairly answered, because essentially the new birth of culture was neutral, and it could be used either to support or oppose religion. Petrarch held Augustine in the same reverence as Plato, and his work *On the Solitary Life* was a defense of monasticism. Marsilio Ficino became ordained as a priest after he gained prominence as a scholar, and Dante considered himself to be a Christian. As to the wealthy patrons of the arts, the banking families of the cities in northern Italy, they lavished as much of their resources on building or refurbishing churches as they did on palaces and portraits. Yet there was not the same uncritical acceptance of the church and its teaching as before. Christianity had become more self-critical and introspective, and the critics increasingly were educated laity from the cities who were not interested in leaving the church but in changing it. "People did not cease to believe, but they were believing in different ways, and while many of them were imitating Christ with the utmost fervor they found ways of doing so which did not always bring them into church."[36] As to the use of pagan mythology by writers such as Dante, it has been suggested that mythology became usable precisely because paganism was dead. "As for out and out skepticism, there was, if anything, less in the Renaissance than in the Middle Ages."[37] There were, however, those who muted the distinctiveness of Christianity. Boccacio believed that Judaism, Islam, and Christianity were equally valid, and Pico della Mirandola, anticipating twentieth-century theologians, believed that Christian truths could be discovered in other religions.

That there was religious fervor there is no doubt, but it was no longer channeled exclusively through ecclesiastical institutions. Many with a deep sense of religious vocation chose to avoid promotion in the hierarchy or even ordination. New attitudes toward monasticism are a case in point. Whereas in earlier times monks tended to leave the world behind to worship God and contemplate in solitude, the new orders exemplified especially by the Sisters and Brothers of the Common Life chose not to separate from society. Gerard Groote wrote that "If devout women separate themselves from the world and try to serve God in the privacy of their homes without taking monastic vows, they are just as religious as nuns in their convents. . . . My desire is that you remain in the world."[38] Jean Gerson (1363–1429), the chancellor of the University of Paris, had six sisters who desired to take religious vows, but he strongly urged them to remain at home rather than join an order. Lorenzo Valla argued the case against monasticism by insisting that lay persons active in the world were equal in virtue to monks. Renaissance

culture was secular, lay, and urban, harboring some anti-clerical sentiments, but it was not irreligious.

The church was not alone in being the focus of criticism, because all
established authorities were under suspicion if not outright attack. As
we have seen, popular uprisings against entrenched urban aristocrats
were common. On the national level we find the growth of representative institutions in opposition to the growing power of monarchs.
The churchly counterpart to this was the rise of conciliarism (see chapter
9). The engine that drove this new-found skepticism of entrenched
authority was in large part the growth of middle-class merchants, lawyers, and entrepreneurs. Cities in northern Italy, especially Venice,
Florence, Milan, and Genoa, had maintained their commercial interests
while northern Europe was reduced to self-sufficiency. This meant that
secular and lay education had been maintained for the children of the
merchant class, and the literacy rate was relatively high. In 1320 the
majority of the male citizens in Florence received some schooling, and
the number of private teachers was large already in the twelfth century.[39]
The curriculum was to prepare students for a mercantile vocation, hence
the *quadrivium* (geometry, astronomy, arithmetic, music) prevailed over
the *trivium* (grammar, logic, rhetoric).

The Renaissance also fostered civic patriotism, especially in Italy.
While nationalistic forces were creating unitary states in England,
France, and Spain, Italy was divided among smaller city-states: the
duchy of Milan, Venice, Genoa, Savoy, Mantua, the Papal States,
Florence, Siena, Naples, and Sicily. Each of these entities was autonomous, with its own political history, coinage, laws, and government.
Civic pride was a powerful force in prompting the wealthy to foster
projects which would enhance their own municipality, not only patronage of the arts but of the arts in the service of the church. Italy's
decentralization into numerous city-states had an effect on later church
history entirely unrelated to the Renaissance. By virtue of being the
political head of the Papal States, the pope was competing as an equal
with the rulers of the other municipal states, which of necessity involved
his entanglements in warfare and inter-city intrigues. Being one of the
players in the secular game considerably compromised his claims to
serve as the spiritual arbiter in the same game. North of the Alps rulers
far more powerful than mere municipal dictators were emerging, not
only kings but churchmen as well. When late medieval popes failed to
recognize this distinction between northern kings and Italian city rulers
they encountered difficulties.

The forces that drove the Renaissance were permeated with a spirit of individualism that characterized the age. Unlike earlier medieval periods, where corporate entities served to give people worth and standing, the Renaissance tended to do away with such distinctions. This can be seen in the paintings of Giotto in which a human personality is depicted with realism, just as sculpture and portraits began to reflect individual qualities of a human person. "Natural man was recovered—the individual in his natural state—it was a period of humanism."[40] In a dispute over immortality with the Italian Aristotelians, Marsilio Ficino strongly defended personal and individual immortality as opposed to the impersonal immortality of the Averroists, because the dignity and worth of the individual must be maintained.[41] Individualism in this context does not have to do with personal assertiveness, idiosyncrasies, or achievement, but with rights. Walter Ullmann observes that such individualism began during the Renaissance with the emergence of the citizen, and he cites with approval this description as applicable to the fourteenth century: "The freedom of a people consists in being governed by laws in which no alteration can be made without their consent."[42] On the ecclesiastical side of the dignity of the individual, Ficino, in the dispute referred to above, supported the concept of individual worth and immortality by appealing to the Sacrament of Baptism.

The Church in the East

Our last notice of the Byzantine church was the great schism between East and West of 1054, in which pope and patriarch mutually excommunicated one another, a schism which persists today.[43] But even after 1054 friendly relations continued between the two churches. Most ordinary Christians were unaware of the schism or did not take it seriously, as the two churches had been in schism a number of times before. What fixed the rupture as permament was the Crusades, specifically the fourth in 1204, in which Constantinople was sacked by Western crusaders and a Latin patriarch controlled the church in the East until 1261. In the one hundred fifty years between the schism and the Crusade, however, significant developments were taking place in the East.

When Emperor Basil II died (1025) the Byzantine empire was wealthy, powerful, and extensive. With the recent conversion of Russia as well as the inclusion of Bulgaria, the Orthodox church appeared to exceed the Latin church by every measurement of superiority. When the churches went into schism in 1054 the East was in a position of power, whereas the West was about to embark on the Investiture Controversy which had ruinous and debilitating consequences. But within a half-century the empire had declined to a mere shadow of its former glory. This was due to a number of factors, one being strife between civil bureacrats and provincial generals, a prolonged struggle marked by the loss of several ethnic groups, insurrections, and social mayhem. "[This] imbalance between sword and pen ranks foremost among the causes which led to the collapse of the Byzantine empire."[44] Another internal crisis was the elimination of the free peasant class by the landed magnates, which resulted in social and economic stagnation as severe as anything in the West under feudalism. At the same time a new threat appeared on the eastern borders from a warlike nomadic people, the Seljuk Turks, who centuries earlier had migrated from Mongolia. In 1071 the Byzantines lost their last possession in Italy, and at the battle of Manzikert the emperor was defeated by the Seljuks, who proceeded to enter into Asia Minor unopposed.[45] The Normans in Sicily were the first to take advantage of the weakened empire by attacking imperial strongholds under the leadership of Robert Guiscard, but they were successfully repulsed under the direction of Emperor Alexius Comnenus (1081–1118). In order to meet the threat of the Seljuk Turks, the emperor had appealed for aid to Pope Gregory VII, who was preoccupied with the Investiture Controversy. But Pope Urban II responded in 1095 by calling for the First Crusade. And so it was that a request from the Byzantine emperor for assistance against the Seljuk Turks ultimately became a vast outpouring of Western adventurers to the Holy Land.

The Crusades were decisive in making the schism permanent. "It is rare for western historians to pay adequate attention to the really disastrous part played by these great expeditions in worsening the relations between East and West, from the viewpoint of church unity."[16] The Fourth Crusade (1204) instead of going to the Holy Land, captured and sacked Constantinople, massacred its citizens, smashed icons, and sent tons of precious booty to the West. Among the best-known prizes that came to Europe were the great bronze horses of St. Mark's Cathedral in Venice. For the next half-century (1204–1261) a Latin kingdom and patriarch governed Byzantium. In 1261 the Byzantine general, Michael Palaeologus (Michael VIII 1259–1282) succeeded in expelling the hated Franks from Constantinople and was crowned emperor, thus founding the longest of all Byzantine imperial dynasties.

About 1243 the Seljuk Turks were overrun by the Mongols, and after several decades of internal fighting a new group emerged as the Ottoman Turks, equally bent on expansion and pillage. The Turkish danger seemed omnipresent and always ominous. Michael Palaeologus took the initiative to secure a reunion with the West in the hope of finding help against them. In 1274 a reunion council was held at Lyons, called by Pope Gregory X, attended by five hundred bishops, sixty abbots, and more than one thousand other prelates. Albert, "the Great," and Bonaventure were in attendance, and Thomas Aquinas died en route to the council. The representatives of Michael accepted papal supremacy as well as the *filioque* in the Nicene Creed (also known as the Double Procession of the Holy Spirit, i.e. from the Father and the Son). But the Byzantine patriarch and church refused to ratify these concessions to the Papacy, made under duress, and the attempt at reunion failed. The fact that the Eastern Christians were unwilling to accept the concessions negotiated by the emperor's representative is a telling example of the relative independence of the church in the East, and serves as a caution not to portray the church as submissive to all imperial directives under the general aegis of Caesaropapism. In any event, even had the Byzantine church agreed to the concessions of Florence, it is highly doubtful that the pope could have produced the promised military aid against the Turks.

During the fourteenth century a controversy arose in the Eastern church over a form of monastic prayer called *hesychasm* (from *hesychia* meaning quiet or spiritual repose). The Hesychasts attached particular importance to the Jesus Prayer—"Lord Jesus Christ, Son of God, have mercy on me"—and they prescribed that while saying the prayer the head should be bowed, eyes fixed on the heart, and the words should be repeated rhythmically as one breathes. The goal of the Hesychasts was to achieve union of mind and heart, which, among those given the gift, will lead to the vision of the Divine Light. The Hesychasts believed that this light was identical with the light of the transfigured Christ on Mt. Tabor that was seen by the disciples. The problem raised by a violent critic of the Hesychasts, Barlaam the Calabrian, was that God is totally transcendent and unknowable, and any who claimed to have an immediate experience of God were mistaken. He charged the monks with falling into gross materialism by claiming to behold God's essence. It was in response to this controversy that Gregory Palamas (1296–1359), Archbishop of Thessalonica, took the side of the Hesychasts by saying that God can indeed be seen, but he distinguished between the divine essence and divine energies. God's essence cannot and never has been seen by any mortal, but God's energies can be apprehended. The source for this distinction goes back to Basil of Caesarea (d. 379) who wrote: "We know our God from his energies, but we do not claim that we can draw near to his essence. For his energies come down to us, but his essence remains unapproachable."[47] Palamas therefore preserved God's transcendence but still allowed for God's immanence. The divine energies manifest God's own self, but they can also be called God's grace, for grace is not merely a gift but the very manifestation of God. In 1351 a council at Constantinople approved the doctrine of the Hesychasts and condemned Barlaam; this council was never ratified by the Latin church. But why, when the empire was in such dire straits, virtually in its death throes, should society be so divided over such an issue? One commentator suggests that "it is difficult not to see in the Hesychast movement, with its concentration on individual perfection, its markedly anti-intellectual tone, and its abjuration of political responsibility, a despairing response to the apparently insoluble problems of a decaying empire, in which the gap between traditional ideology and reality grew ever wider."[48]

The story of the empire following the death of Emperor Michael VIII (1328) is one of disaster on the battlefield, economic chaos, and political ineptitude. In 1347 the Black Death visited Constantinople on its way west. There were internal struggles for power during which time the Serbs made territorial gains at the expense of the empire. The Venetians and Genoese had a stranglehold on commerce and therefore on the economy. Already in 1359 Turkish bands encamped before the walls of Constantinople. In 1363 they cut off the city from the west. In 1369 they captured Adrianople. The relentless advance continued with the fall of Sofia, Thessalonika, and the annexation of Bulgaria, all before 1400. In 1394 the Turks began the blockade of Constantinople, which caused a famine in the city. But then help came unexpectedly from an unlikely source. The Mongols under Tamerlane had built up an empire from Delhi in India to Moscow, and they felt threatened by the rise of Turkish power. In 1402 the Mongols crushed the Turks and almost destroyed their empire, but the Byzantines were too weak to take advantage of it. The Turks revived their strength and again isolated Constantinople.

A second reunion council was held in Florence (1438–1439). Both the emperor, John VIII, and the patriarch attended in person along with a large number of Byzantines. It was a repetition of Lyons in 1274 in that the pope insisted on their acceptance of the *filioque* and papal primacy, which the delegation, in desperate political straits, finally did by signing an act of reunion. Only the metropolitan of Ephesus refused to sign. Predictably, the act of reunion met with widespread disapproval at home, and even those who had signed it repudiated their act. Even though the emperor and the patriarch remained loyal to the Union of Florence, no military help was forthcoming.[49]

By now the fall of Constantinople was inevitable. In 1451 Moham-med II (Mehmed) became the Sultan of the Turks and planned the final assault on the city. On April 7, 1453, the attack began by land and sea. The Turks outnumbered the Byzantines by more than twenty to one, yet the defenders held out for seven weeks. On May 29 the final Christian service was held at the Church of the Holy Wisdom (Hagia Sophia), with the emperor receiving communion before he went to the walls where he died fighting. The next day the city fell, and the Turks entered the church to give thanks to Allah for their great victory. Con-stantinople, the city of the Caesars, now after 1,123 years became the capital of the sultans who renamed it Istanbul, and so it has remained since. From there the Ottoman Turks ruled over all of southeastern Europe.

The sultan was not about to let Constantinople, the Jewel of the Bosphorus, be reduced to insignificance. He permitted the Christians to maintain their worship as long as it did not interfere with imperial policies. The authority of the Church of Constantinople was still recog-nized in the Orthodox world, and the patriarch still maintained his jurisdiction over Greeks, Serbs, Albanians, and Russians. Meanwhile a large number of Byzantine refugees made their way to Italy, the most notable being Bessarion, the later cardinal, who helped to feed the Renaissance appetite for Greek culture and literature. The fall of Con-stantinople did not appear to generate any remorse or sympathy in the West other than the realization that the Turks may now become a threat to Europe. "To Italian humanists the end of the Byzantine world was of little consequence. Their interest in Hellenism was directed to the past, not to the present. Aeneas Sylvius, the future Pope Pious II, did not so much weep for . . . Orthodox Christianity as to lament 'the second death of Homer and Plato.'"[50] The Greek refugees found that it was better to present themselves as the descendents of Pericles and Plato than as homeless Christians. The eminent scholar of Byzantium and the Cru-sades, Steven Runciman, wrote this eulogy on the fateful event: "On May 29, 1453, a civilization was wiped out irrevocably. It had left a glorious legacy in learning and in art; it had raised whole countries from barbarism and had given refinement to others; its strength and its intelligence for centuries had been the protection of Christendom. For eleven centuries Constantinople had been the centre of the world of light. . . . [All of these] were now put to sleep."[51]

CHAPTER NINE

A CONFLICT OF AUTHORITIES

Philip, Boniface, and the Avignon Papacy

By the end of the thirteenth century the kings of France possessed an increasingly large measure of autonomy resulting from the process of centralization which was the constant occupation of the Capetian dynasty. Although their authority was challenged by the presence of the English and frustrated by rebellious nobles, the monarchy controlled the municipalities and laid claim to overlordship in other areas. It was primarily through the judicial system and as a court of final appeal that the king's power asserted itself. Ever since the days of Louis IX the church enjoyed a special relationship with France (her "eldest daughter") and during those times when Rome was inhospitable, the popes found refuge in France. Indeed, since the 1240s residence in Rome had been exceptional. In return, the French monarchs enjoyed some rights of control over the church in France, notably the appointments of church leaders to key offices. It was this reciprocity that precipitated the dramatic confrontation between king and pope at the turn of the century.

Philiip IV, "the Fair" (1285–1314), son of Philip III, was at war with England in a prelude to that series of intermittent hostilities known as the Hundred Years' War. At the same time he was fending off challenges from stubborn nobility who sought greater freedom for themselves. Both in England and France, churches were being taxed to finance the conflict, since both kings had declared theirs a "just war." Meanwhile, Boniface VIII (1294–1303) succeeded Celestine V as pope, replacing the saintly but ineffective hermit who had resigned the Papacy. The pope's enemies accused Boniface of using physical threats to persuade his predecessor to abdicate. One commentator suggests that Boniface was, "convinced of the unlimited prerogative of the Papacy to manage the affairs of Christendom . . . a champion of ecclesiastical privilege."[1] On the other hand, another historian suggests that Boniface had the thankless task of neutralizing the harm produced by those who exploited his predecessor's inexperience.[2] In any case, in 1296 Philip levied a special tax against the clergy in France to help finance his wars, and the pope responded with a bull, *clerici laicos*, in which he declared that any cleric who paid taxes to a secular lord, and any lay lord who levied or received taxes from the church, incurred automatic excommunication. In effect the bull denied absolute authority to a sovereign within his own kingdom. The king had no doubt that he had authority over all his subjects, and he responded by forbidding the exportation of gold and silver from France, thereby cutting off papal revenues. This first quarrel lasted less than a year with the pope capitulating completely to the king's right to tax the clergy. No doubt Philip's negotations with the Colonna family of Rome, which was opposed to the pope, influenced Boniface's decision to back down.

In 1300 Boniface declared a Jubilee Year during which thousands of pilgrims flocked to Rome to gain the special indulgences made available. Its overwhelming success may have given the pope a false idea of the support he commanded among the faithful in Europe. Whether from conviction or confidence, he had occasion to renew the struggle with the king when Philip imprisoned a bishop. Philip had continued his taxation of clergy, appropriation of revenues, and appointments to clerical offices. In addition, he surrounded himself with decidedly antipapal lay advisors—Pierre Flote, the chancellor, William of Nogaret, Pierre Dubois—a group described by David Knowles as "rootless, insecure, and unscrupulous."[3] In a deliberate provocation Philip arrested a bishop for treason, blasphemy, and heresy, and cast him into prison following a trial in the king's court.[4] It was a basic principle of canon law that clergy could be tried only in church courts, especially for heresy. The pope could ill afford to permit this challenge to legitimate papal jurisdiction to go unanswered. He commanded all French bishops to appear in Rome to discuss the ecclesiastical situation in France. In a long personal letter to Philip he began, "Listen, son! God has set us over kings and kingdoms. Let no one persuade you that you have no superior or that you are not subject to the ecclesiastical hierarchy, for he is a fool who so thinks."[5] Philip had the letter burned, and he forged another as having come from Boniface which made extreme claims for the Papacy, hoping thereby to stir up popular resentment. In April 1302 Philip convened an assembly of clergy, nobles, and townspeople at the cathedral of Notre Dame in Paris, an assembly that established a precedent for the Estates-General (not unlike the Model Pariament in England in

1285). The nobility and commons sent a letter to the cardinals in Rome declaring their refusal to recognize Boniface as the lawful pope. The French bishops sent a more irenic reply, but they requested to be excused from a council to which they had been summoned by the pope. The council met in November 1302, with about half the French bishops in attendance. One of the bulls issuing from this council was *Unam sanctam*, perhaps the most famous of all medieval papal bulls.

The two best-known assertions of this document are these: "There is only one Catholic church, and outside this church there is no salvation or remission of sins" and "Therefore we declare, state, define and pronounce that it is altogether necessary to salvation for every human creature to be subject to the Roman pontiff."[6] Extreme as these statements appear to be, they rest on old and accepted traditions. It has often been pointed out that *Unam sanctam* was not innovative or radical.[7] However, to bring heretofore disconnected and theoretical pronouncements into one lean and forceful statement of papal prerogative—and this in the context of an acrimonius feud over power with the French king—gave the document an immediacy and pointedness that could not be mistaken. Philip delayed a response, probably because he was engaged in warfare with the Flemish. In June 1303, the king held a council at the Louvre where charges were brought against the pope, including simony, fornication, demon possession, and illegal election to office. The king also received word that the pope was planning to excommunicate him. One of the king's counselors, William of Nogaret, was sent with three hundred horses and a thousand footmen to the papal residence at Anagni, outside of Rome. They physically abused the aged pontiff, and although he was not captured, he died a month later. This event came to be known as the "outrage of Anagni."

Assessments of the meaning of this altercation between king and pope range widely. Both were imperious and stubborn, the king was brutal and the pope was not in touch with reality. But it was more than a personality conflict. In the century since Innocent III ruled as "Lord of the World," powerful secular princes had arisen to challenge the church's hegemony. Some suggest that Boniface had never met a king before, having known only petty Italian tyrants. At the same time the pope recognized the necessity of permitting religion to be free of royal control, but in securing this freedom he was forced to use the weapons of the world under the cover of religious language, competing as another prince rather than as a spiritual mentor. Nationalism emerged as a powerful factor in the rise of royal power, and its realities complicated church-state relations. Mandell Creighton suggests that "Boniface could not read the signs of the times," that "with Boniface fell the medieval papacy," and that "the drama of Anagni is to be set against the drama of Canossa."[8] A contemporary historian of the Papacy simply concludes that Boniface was "a disaster of the first magnitude for the church."[9]

Boniface's successor excommunicated Nogaret and attempted to negotiate with Philip, but he died within a year. He was followed by Clement V (1305–1314), a Frenchman who lifted the excommunication of Nogaret and commended Philip for the piety and zeal that he had displayed in his relations with Boniface. Clement, who was Bishop of Bordeaux, decided against residing in Rome, partly because of the civil strife there and mostly because of pressure from Philip to remain in France. After being crowned pope in Lyons he established his residence in Avignon on the banks of the Rhone in southern France where the popes continued to live for over seventy years. This period has come to be known as the papal "Babylonian Captivity," a term coined by Petrarch, Italian poet and humanist.

Although the Avignon period in papal history has often been understood as one of decline and even corruption, others see it as "the culmination of the medieval papacy and the greatest extension of its (geographical and institutional) influence."[10] In terms of accessibility to the medieval churches, Avignon was almost an ideal residence. However, the Papacy was seriously compromised with other European powers in its decidedly French tilt. Of 24 cardinals created by Clement V, 23 were from France; of the total of 134 cardinals created by the Avignon popes, over half were French. There were seven Avignon popes altogether, and they varied remarkably in their gifts and interests. Geoffrey Barraclough has demonstrated that every type of pope was tried in order to set the church back on its feet, but none succeeded. The problem was that "in the end, it was not the persons that mattered, but the system was at fault."[11]

Clement V actually was a dependent of the English king, Edward I (1272–1307), and he attempted to move to Rome upon his election. He was thwarted by the threats and the army of Philip IV and by the opposition of Robert of Naples, who did not want to see a strong pope in Italy. After taking up his residence in Avignon, the pope found himself cut off from his usual revenues from Italy, and in order to secure needed funds he introduced the practice of *annates*, which required the recipient of every papal appointment (bishops, abbots, etc.) to give the equivalent of the first year's revenues to the pope. This naturally tended to increase the number of such appointments. Although this method brought in great sums of money, most of it went to Clement's relatives and as gifts to the French king.

John XXII (1316–1334) had the longest rule of any Avignon pope. He was decidedly different from Clement in his simplicity of life, energetic and efficient administration, and shrewd political judgment. One of his goals was to contain the ambitions of Robert of Naples, who sought to become king over all of Italy. The pope supported a Hapsburg (German) ruler to govern northern Italy, which would leave the way open for the pope to return and reclaim central Italy. This strategy resulted in confrontations with Robert of Naples and Louis of Bavaria, the anti-Habsburg claimant to the imperial title. The pope's armies also did battle with the northern Italian states, notably Bologna and Milan. When Louis of Bavaria managed to get himself crowned emperor in Rome in 1328, he also declared John deposed as a heretic and he elected a new pope. Louis henceforth provided a haven for all royalists and critics of the Papacy (see following sections in this chapter). In church polity John opposed the Spiritual Franciscans and their insistence on apostolic poverty (see below), and he limited the number of benefices to two per holder, but recipients of those benefices which were given up were required to pay the annates. As a result of John's talents as organizer and administrator the Papacy became centralized as never before, which in itself may have been a good thing. However, the pope also fostered a relationship with secular powers which put the Papacy at risk, and in his schemes to centralize and fill papal coffers he alienated the clergy and put into place structures that were liable to abuse. "Nonetheless, this old man (he was eighty-nine when he died), said to have been ugly to the point of repulsive, must be classified among the greatest of the popes."[12]

His successor, Benedict XII (1334–1342) was a Cistercian monk, one of whose most important acts was the reform of monastic orders. He lived simply and continued to wear his monastic habit as pope, but his simplicity did not inhibit him from laying the foundations for the great papal palace in Avignon, a visual statement that the Papacy was there to stay. Upon assuming office he sent home all the clergy in Avignon who had no good reason for being there. He failed to make peace with Louis of Bavaria, who then became allied with England against France at the beginning of the Hundred Years' War. On the debit side, he increased the number of reservations under papal control (papal rights of appointments to office), which proved to be a temptation for abuse by his successors to the detriment of the traditional rights of clergy, chapters, bishops, and abbots. Benedict was a devout monk and not an administrator, whereas John had displayed brilliance in organization but was not noted for piety; yet neither of them was able to bring needed reform to the church, because it was not the administration or legal system that required attention, but the church's very reason for being.

Clement VI (1342–1352) came from the French court and maintained a subservience to it. "It was his pontificate which created the common picture of the Papacy of Avignon as an instrument of France."[13] During his reign the Black Death ravaged Europe and thinned the ranks of the clergy, but despite this catastrophe, the prodigality of the pope prompted him to levy more burdensome taxes. He defended his extravagence by saying, "My predecessors did not know how to be pope," and through his lavish gifts he depleted the substantial treasury which had been left by his frugal predecessor. Clement decreed that a Jubilee Year should be held every fifty years instead of every one hundred years, thus reaping the financial rewards of the year 1350. More than anything else it was the pope's dissolute private life that brought on him and the Papacy the scorn of the faithful, moving Catherine of Siena to call him the devil incarnate. Edward III of England (1327–1377) declared in the Statute of Provisors (1351) that henceforth no churchly office in England could be filled through papal appointment, and in the Statute of Praemunire (1353) he forbade any appeals from an English court to be made outside of England (i.e. Avignon). It was during his time that a revived spirituality and a piety devoted to Jesus' sacred heart, passion, and the sacraments took hold of the people as a result of the devastations of plague and warfare. Simple faith such as this, which ordinarily would have been a welcome support to the hierarchy, under the circumstances turned into biting criticism and satire of ecclesiastical pretension. Criticism of the Papacy originated in and was accompanied by a revival of religious fervor among the people.

Clement's three successors were all men of high virtue and reforming zeal. Innocent VI (1352–1362) reformed the papal court, reduced taxes, and appointed competent bishops. He laid the groundwork for a return to Rome by delegating Cardinal Albornez to bring order from chaos in the Papal States. Sentiment for a return to Rome was fostered by the sorry condition of France following the Peace of Bretigny (1360) when mercenaries plundered the countryside and threatened Avignon. This city was again visited by the Black Death in 1361 when over seventeen thousand people died, including nine cardinals and one hundred clergy. Urban V (1362–1370) was a Benedictine abbot, not a cardinal, who actually journeyed to Rome intending to remain there, despite the displeasure of the French king and cardinals. But in Vierbo, a few miles north of Rome, the people rioted, shouting, "Long live the people, death to the Church." He gained entry to Rome only with the help of mercenary troops, and after a short time he was persuaded to return to Avignon. Gregory XI (1370–1378) devoted most of his attention to the return to Rome. In this he was opposed by Florence, Perugia, and Milan, who saw such a return as a threat to their independence. The pope met this resistance by sending ten thousand mercenaries, which further alienated the Italians. Catherine of Siena, who was a severe critic of the Avignon papacy, deserves as much credit as Gregory for restoring the pope to Rome. She wrote to Gregory, "Do not fear [to return to Rome] for any reason. Come in security. Up, father, like a man! Beware lest you be negligent in this."[14] Although Gregory was a Frenchman who knew no other language, he met the formidable obstacles of the French king, cardinals, and Italian troops with determination, and his entrance into Rome on January 17, 1377, marks the end of the "Avignon Captivity."

In summary, this period of the Papacy witnessed several developments that were ominous for the life of the church. One of these was the increased need for revenue and the methods designed to secure it. Not only were taxes increased, but such innovations as *annates* and provisions to benefices and costs of litigation were all designed to make money. Other means for increasing capital were *reservations*, in which the revenues from vacant dioceses reverted to the pope so long as the vacancy existed; *expectancies*, in which, for a fee, a person was promised the right to succeed to an ecclesiastical office; and *commendation*, by which, for a fee, a bishop was permitted to receive the revenues from a vacant diocese. The interval between Years of Jubilee was shortened from 100 to 50 to 33 to 25 years. The remission of sins by way of indulgences, first associated with the Crusades in 1095, now accelerated to include a multiplicity of occasions. In the bull *Unigenitus*, Clement VI in 1343 declared that indulgences owed their efficacy to the pope's dispensation of the accumulated merit of the church. Little wonder that about 1370 Petrarch denounced the Papacy in scathing terms, referring to Avignon as the "Babylon of the West," with its clergy "loaded with gold and clad in purple, who cannot be approached except presents be offered."[15]

Another development was the increased power of the cardinals over against that of the pope. "Secular aristocratic interests determined their actions. Above all, they were concerned to maintain and build up their position."[16] The cardinals shared in the revenues that flowed to Avignon, and the fewer their number the more each received. In 1352 they forced the pope to accede to an electoral principle which stated that the number of cardinals should not exceed twenty, and no new cardinals should be created until the existing number fell to sixteen. When Urban VI proposed a reform of the cardinals he was threatened with open rebellion. At the same time that the cardinals were asserting themselves over against the pope, the popes were diminishing the office of the bishops. Whereas heretofore bishops had been elected by their cathedral chapter, and abbots by the monks, John XXII and Benedict XII reserved all episcopal appointments to the pope, as the edict of 1335 declared: "We reserve to our own ordination, disposition and provision all patriarchal, archepiscopal and episcopal churches, all monasteries, priories, dignities, parsonages, and offices . . . of whatever kind."[17] Furthermore, the power of papal legates throughout Europe took precedence over episcopal rights, and the papal court was both appelate and a court of first instance, both of which undermined the authority of bishops' courts. The exempt religious orders, notably the Dominicans and the Franciscans, were not under episcopal authority but were directly under papal control, further undermining a bishop's effectiveness in his diocese. "The work of a bishop had so successfully been reduced to routine that the permanent staff could do very well without a bishop. The machine, under remote control of the pope and the immediate control of his legate, could do everything."[18] These legacies from the Avignon period would continue to alienate the hierarchy from the faithful and bring on a growing demand for reform.

Popes and Princes

Although the fourteenth-century popes centralized their power within the church, despite the challenges from the cardinals, the secular princes launched a counter-force to get control over the churches in their lands. They sought the rights of revenues and appointments in order to make the church a dependent of the state, resulting in a conflict of authorities. This tendency was marked during the Great Schism (1378–1417), but it began already during the Avignon period. We have already seen the efforts of the French monarchs to control the church and to reduce it to a department of state. Papal insistence on universal authority was more easily ignored by European princes who considered the pontiff a mere chaplain of the French government.

England had always shown some reserve toward the Papacy since William, "the Conqueror," declared himself in 1066 to be the final arbiter in matters of ecclesiastical appointments and appelate jurisdiction. His archbishop, Lanfranc, although loyal to the pope, maintained strict neutrality in the Investiture Controversy. English rulers did not hesitate to oppose archbishops, notably Anselm and Becket. King John engaged in a bitter quarrel with Innocent III over the election of Stephen Langton to the see of Canterbury. Later the pope condemned the Magna Carta and threatened its signers with excommunication. Anti-papal attitudes grew more acute during the Avignon period as France was the natural enemy of England, and the period of French popes coincided with the early years of the Hundred Years' War. It was natural for the English to resent sending taxes to France, which might be used to fight the war against them, as a contemporary complains, "The pope levies taxes and subsidies on the English clergy to pay the ransoms of French-men who are prisoners of war in England, or to carry on the war in Lombardy."[19] When Boniface VIII forbade the taxation of clergy in *clericis laicos* he was supported by Winchelsea, the Archbishop of Canturbury. In retaliation Edward I confiscated Winchelsea's lands and ultimately had him exiled. When Clement V launched his campaign against the Templars (see chapter 10) using all the resources of the Inquisition, English anti-papal sentiment was exacerbated. Under Edward III the most stringent legislation was adopted, which curtailed papal influence in England on the assumption that the power of the Papacy in England "has increased, is increasing, and ought to be diminished."[20] In the Statute of Provisors (1351), "roused by the grievous complaints of all the commons of the realm," emphatically forbade papal nominations to English benefices.[21] The statute expressly charges the pope with filling English vacancies with foreigners so that "a great part of the treasure of the realm is carried away." However, evidence suggests that the statute was never strictly enforced, because Edward III, for a fee, permitted the pope to continue his appointments. Two years later the Statute of Praemunire was passed forbidding court cases to be appealed to the pope. Once again, the statute was evaded to the benefit of both king and pope, but to the detriment of the commoners. This led to several repe-titions of the statute in later years and finally to a "highly dangerous attitude to the Papacy. The unrest of a whole nation cannot be stifled indefinitely. If it is perhaps too much to assert that a national church was already beginning to form, it is at least true that men's minds were ready to listen to Wycliffe's violent attacks on the constitution of the church of Rome, and that England was gradually becoming ripe for schism."[22] Discontent was not limited to the Papacy but to all clergy who abused their position and friars who had forgotten the vow of poverty. In William Langland's *Piers Plowman*, Sloth is personified as a parson who was illiterate and neglected his duties in favor of the hunt. The stage in

England was set for the appearance of John Wycliffe (1320–1384), who grew to maturity during the period of Avignon.

Frederick II, Holy Roman Emperor and last of the Hohenstaufen line, died in 1250. The empire was in fact a loose collection of practically autonomous German states dominated by a few powerful duchies. The Germanies had a long history of anti-papal sentiments reaching back to the Investiture Controversy of the eleventh century and earlier. After an interregnum, the electors chose Rudolph of Hapsburg (1273–1291) to succeed Frederick II, the first of a long line of Hapsburg rulers that ended in 1918. He considerably increased his family holdings, but he died before he could officially be crowned emperor in Rome. His successor, Adolph of Nassau (1292–1298), although chosen by the ecclesiastical electors, pillaged churches and monasteries. With Edward I of England he declared war against Philip IV of France, but nothing came of it. Albert of Hapsburg (1298–1308), the son of Rudolph, followed Adolph, but Boniface VIII refused to acknowledge him as king until Albert relinquished all claims to Italian territories. He was never crowned emperor. Henry VII of Luxemburg (1308–1313) came next, whose reign closely corresponded to that of Pope Clement V. On the surface the two rulers were civil if not congenial toward each other, but there was underlying distrust. The pope wanted to prevent Henry from creating a strong base in Italy, and Henry wished to emulate earlier emperors by a series of Italian campaigns. At this time Italy was divided among a number of claimants. In the north were several autonomous and powerful cities, including Genoa, Pisa, Florence, Milan, Bologna, and Venice. Within these towns domination fluctuated between the Guelphs (papal) and Ghibilline (imperial) factions. One of the most famous Ghibelline exiles of this period was Dante, who among his writings included a strong defense of imperial over ecclesiastical authority. In the center of Italy we find the remnants of the Papal States, and in Rome there was civil war between the Orsini and Colonna families. To the south was the kingdom of Naples, ruled by Robert, brother of Philip IV of France, and a strong Guelph. Henry was determined to travel south to Rome for his coronation, but en route he met stiff resistance by the Lombard towns. When he arrived in Rome he found the city shut against him, and he was unable to battle his way to St. Peter's Basilica, the traditional site of imperial coronations, because it was in the possession of Robert of Naples. He was crowned by the papal legate at St. John Lateran in 1312. He died going south to do battle with Robert. Thus far we have not seen much overt hostility toward the Papacy from these early Hohenstaufen rulers. This will be more than compensated by Louis of Bavaria (1313–1347)

There was now a double election in Germany, Louis of Bavaria and Frederick of Austria, and each was crowned the same day, in Aachen and Bonn. Robert of Naples, hoping to gain control of all Italy, requested the pope, John XXII, to remove Italy entirely from Louis' empire. This he refused to do. Thereupon Louis began the journey to Rome, hoping to be crowned emperor, but it took him fifteen years to arrive at the Holy City. On the way he became involved in the Guelph-Ghibbeline controversies, encountered papal hostility, and finally incurred excommunication. Since papal endorsement for coronation was not forthcoming, Louis appealed to the principle of popular sovereignty so avidly championed by his guests, John of Jandun and Marsiglio of Padua. The Roman populace enthusiastically called for his coronation, and two bishops were found to oblige. The pope deprived Louis of his home duchy of Bavaria and summoned him to Avignon. Furthermore, he declared him to be a heretic and pronounced the coronation null and void. Louis responded by calling for a solemn conclave in the forecourt of St. Peter's in Rome where he declared the pope a heretic and deposed him from office. This act opened the way for Louis to replace John XXII, which he did by appointing Nicolas V as pope (or anti-pope). One writer calls Nicolas V an "egregious hypocrite" and another says, "he spent his short months of power in blustering against the Avignon pope, and at the first sign of danger he fled."[23] Within two years he abdicated, after making abject apologies to John XXII in Avignon, where he died. Meanwhile Louis' attempt to return to Germany was thwarted by a coalition of north Italian cities. The pope insisted that the emperor must resign his imperial title before any reconciliation could take place. In the face of the coalition formed against him, Louis abdicated, but after the pope's death in 1334 he again assumed the imperial title. Benedict XII followed a more conciliary line, but he was also under heavy pressure from the kings of France and Naples to confront Louis. It was in this context that the prince electors of the empire declared at Rense in 1338 that election by them was sufficient for legitimate kingship, and although the pope had a right to crown emperors, such coronation added nothing to the power that the king already had through election. This clearly expanded the conflict between king and pope to one which included the German nobility, or at least the electors, in opposition to the pope. In 1343, Louis again abdicated his title, and he died four years later. One of the factors which contributed to his significance in the religious politics of the age was the hospitality of his court to anti-papal pamphleteers and conciliarists. The most notable of these writers was Marsiglio of Padua, John of Jandun, Michael of Cesena, Minister-General of the Franciscan Order, and William of Occam. All were critical of the Papacy and all were under excommunication, and their writings provided an intellectual and theological foundation for Ghibbeline assumptions.

Louis' successor, Charles IV (1347–1378), gained the election in part by promising Pope Clement VI whatever he asked, but he conveniently ignored these oaths once he became king. It was only under Pope Innocent VI in 1355 that Charles was crowned emperor. Considering the endless conflicts caused by papal intervention in the selection of German kings, the golden bull was issued in 1356 to exclude all outside interference in such elections. "[The Golden Bull of 1356] . . . remained to the end the empire's basic and most important constitution. It provided for election of the emperor by seven electors meeting under the chairmanship of the archbishop of Mainz."[24] The bull also effectively weakened any central authority in the Germanies, which ultimately became a confederation of more than two hundred autonomous states. Its effect was to accelerate the further development of German particularism, postponing German unification until well into the nineteenth century. It also meant abandoning all claims to Italy, which had so distracted German rulers for centuries, but conversely it also excluded the pope's temporal claims in German affairs. What has preceded is an account of papal and princely interaction during the Avignon period. What follows is a description of their relationships during the schism that followed Avignon.

The Great Schism, as it has been called, was not caused by any significant administrative, doctrinal, or liturgical differences, but primarily it was the result of competing nationalities and the vested interests of individuals. After Gregory XI died in 1378 the cardinals gathered to elect his successor. An insistent crowd in St. Peter's Square clamored for a Roman to assure that the pope would remain in the city, and the cardinals offered a reasonable compromise by electing an Italian, the archbishop of Bari (and not a cardinal) as Urban VI. The compromise was also a result of the differences among the sixteen cardinals present at the election.[25] Urban displayed forcefulness and determination (others say lack of tact and diplomacy) by reducing the income and privileges of the cardinals. There is no doubt that he lacked polish when he called one cardinal an imbecile and another a libertine. More significantly, he alienated the French cardinals, who were in the majority, by choosing to stay in Rome. They left Rome and declared Urban VI deposed, pleading that the decision had been made under duress by the

Roman mob; they proceeded to elect one of their own as Clement VII. It seems clear that the rebellious thirteen cardinals who elected Clement were at fault in the schism, as Urban had been legally and canonically elected, and the dissident cardinals were acting for the French crown and for their own privileges. The pope in Rome responded by creating twenty-eight new cardinals loyal to him. The countries of Latin Christendom were about equally divided in their loyalties to the two popes. Roman allegiance was given by England, Germany, Scandinavia, Bohemia, and most of Italy. France supported Clement VII as did Scotland, Naples, Castille, and Aragon.

The situation was untenable and led to confusion and strife. In areas where both popes had a following, there was rivalry between claimants for the same post as bishop, abbot, or even parish clergy. Neither line of popes enjoyed the freedom to act independently of political pressures, and both became pawns of princes. For this reason it soon became clear that the schism could not be healed through papal initiative. Had there been a will to end the impasse, one simple measure would have been to unite in support of the pope who outlived his rival. But upon his death Urban VI was succeeded by Boniface IX (1389–1404), Innocent VII (1404–1404), and Gregory XII (1406–1415). On the French side, Clement VII was followed by Benedict XIII (1394–1422).

More important than the schism itself was the reaction to it. Early in the Avignon period there were thoughtful essays on the proper relationship of king to pope, and these were influenced in part by earlier discussions which had come from the Investiture Controversy two hundred years before. Such literary activities now accelerated in a movement known as conciliarism, or the idea that the supreme authority in the church is a general council. Others became suspicious of all institutional authorities and took refuge in the Bible alone as the church's infallible guide. The schism also gave a stimulus to reform movements, most prominently that of John Wycliffe and John Huss. Others found mysticism more satisfying than following the rites of the institutional church, or at least such practices became a matter of indifference.

Upon the death of Clement VII in France, the king ordered the cardinals not to elect a new pope, a directive they ignored by selecting Benedict XIII. The king responded by the "Withdrawal of Obedience" of 1398–1403, during which time no pope was acknowledged in France. Instead, papal prerogatives were simply taken over by the king and the princes. The French already were leaning toward a national church administered on a national basis, a situation known as Gallicanism. In

1408 the king's ministers set out a list of "liberties of the Gallican church" which denied temporal authority to the Papacy. These "liberties" became a part of the French constitution. Meanwhile, the cardinals of both popes finally agreed to convene a council in Pisa in 1409 to settle the schism. Both popes were deposed, and Alexander V was declared the rightful pontiff. However, there was a serious question about the legitimacy of the council, and since both deposed popes retained their following, there were now three popes. "Christendom was in spiritual chaos. Spiritual loyalty gave way to purely political consideration, for no one could be sure who was the true pope. And Europe was still deeply religious. . . . Some said that no soul entered heaven during the entire period of the Great Schism."[26] It was this shameful situation which brought about a united effort by the princes and theologians to end the schism, but first we must consider the great debate over authority in the church known as conciliarism which was precipitated by Avignon and the schism.

Conciliarism

Conciliarism, or the idea that a church council was the supreme authority in the church taking precedence even over a pope, was a reflection of similar thinking in secular politics. Ever since the days of King John and the Magna Carta in 1215 the nobility claimed more and more prerogatives over against the king. In England a significant precedent was established in 1295 with the Model Parliament in which commoners were included with clergy and nobility in advising the king. A similar milestone was reached in France in 1302 with the Estates-General. The principle of representative government found exponents among the principle university faculties and thinkers throughout Europe. Pressure for action in the church was building long before the Great Schism during the Avignon papacy, and with the schism advocates of conciliarism became more insistent on the need for a church council.

Already at the turn of the century John of Paris, a French Dominican, wrote about the right relationship of the spiritual to the temporal power and the right relationship of rulers to their subjects (*On The Power of King and Pope* 1302). He argued that civil government had its origin in human nature, and not, as Augustine had said, that government was a remedy for sin. Priests were greater in dignity, but could exercise authority only in the spiritual realm, just as the pope's authority was limited to people's souls. All legitimate authority came from God, but God left to human choice the designation of who should wield this authority. The pope was subject to rebuke and in the last resort to deposition by a general council or by the cardinals acting on behalf of all the people. Authority was not "concentrated in the person of the pope but was diffused among other members of the church as well."[27] John advocated the idea that participation in government should be the right of all people through duly chosen representatives. Authority derives from the community: "The lord Pope as head and supreme member of the universal church is the general and universal administrator of all the goods of the churches . . . he is not the owner of them. Rather, the community of the universal church is the only lord and owner of all ecclesiastical goods."[28] John continued by suggesting that a pope "might be deposed provided that, after admonition, he would not mend his ways."

Another prominent writer of this time, Dante (d. 1321), wrote *On the Monarchy*, in which he argued for a universal monarch to promote the general welfare in temporal affairs, with the pope strictly limited to spiritual things and dispossessed of lands and possessions. The work was condemned as heretical.

Marsiglio of Padua (d. 1342) wrote one of the most challenging works of the late Middle Ages in his *The Defender of Peace* in collaboration with John of Jandun. In 1327 Pope John XXII condemned the book and excommunicated the author, who fled to the court of Louis of Bavaria under whose protection he spent the rest of his life. Marsiglio declared that the state is supreme and that it derives its authority from the people; the church is a human institution and should come under state jurisdiction. Among other propositions, he suggested that:

- For the attainment of eternal beatitude it is necessary to believe in the truth of only the divine Scriptures, together with its necessary consequences;
- Doubtful sentences of divine law . . . must be defined only by the general council of the believers;
- Only the whole body of citizens, or the weightiest part of them, is the human legislator;
- An elected ruler, or any other official, is dependent only upon election by the body having authority therefore, and needs no other confirmation; (That is, papal confirmation or coronation is unnecessary. Ed.)
- The bishops collectively can excommunicate the Roman bishop and exercise other authority over him;

- Only the general council of all the faithful has the authority to designate a bishop or any metropolitan church highest of all, and to deprive or depose them from such positions.[29]

Marsiglio further declared that Peter never possessed a primacy transferable to the popes and that all general councils should include laity as well as clergy, and such councils may be called by secular rulers.

The Franciscan, William of Occam (d. 1349), did not go so far as Marsiglio in placing the church under the state, but in a series of anti-papal tracts he advocated a separation of church and state which denied all temporal power to the Papacy. He believed that popes could err and fall into heresy, and he distinguished between the whole church as genus with the Roman church as species. A general council, which should include women, was the supreme authority in the church. When he took the side of the Spiritual Franciscans against the pope in 1328 he was excommunicated, and he fled for protection to Louis of Bavaria. Of Benedict XII he wrote: "Benedict XII has forsaken the paths of both Christ and Peter. For Peter, who was appointed pastor of the sheep by the prince of pastors, not only fed the sheep entrusted to him, but also in no way refused to lay down his life for them."[30] Benedict, on the other hand, kills Christ's sheep, blasphemes the King of Kings, and usurps the property and rights of others. William concludes that "the empire does not depend on the pope, for the true empire has preceded him." These writers flourished during the Avignon period and none lived to see the Great Schism. But under the intolerable conditions of two and then three popes after 1378, advocates of church reform "in head and members" multiplied, drawing heavily on the ideas of John of Paris, Marsiglio, and Occam. The center of the movement was the University of Paris.

The first formal statement of conciliar principles was by the German master at Paris, Conrad of Gelnhausen, in his *Short Letter* of 1379, in which he appealed to the French and German kings to convene a council. Another German, Henry of Langenstein, wrote *Letter on Behalf of A Council of Peace* in which he recalled the rise of the Papacy to prominence in the church and came to this conclusion: "The power of appointing the pope resides primarily with the whole company of the bishops of the faithful. This power should revert to them whenever the cardinals are not able to elect, or do not wish to elect, or have all died."[31] Henry believed that a council was infallible, and that no single method of papal election had divine approval, since the church throughout its history had used many methods.

In 1381 the University of Paris called for a general council, but the king demanded that the university promise obedience to the French pope. The German masters and students, comprising one half of the university, left in protest and began the universities of Vienna and Heidelberg. This also ended temporarily the attempt to find a solution by way of a council (*via concilii*). Now efforts were made to convince both popes to resign (*via cessionis*), but this also failed. Peter d'Ailly, chancellor of the University of Paris, wrote a *Treatise on the Reformation of the Church* in which, following Occam, he believed that bishops and priests received their authority directly from Christ, and that both popes and councils were fallible. Jean Gerson, who followed d'Ailly as chancellor of the university, wrote *On the Manner of Conducting Oneself in the Time of Schism* in which he asserted the superiority of a council over the pope and demanded that doctors of theology have a deliberative voice in church affairs equal to that of bishops. He proposed the principle of equity, which stated that in extraordinary times law must be set aside for the common good if reason and sense clearly required it. His suggestion that councils may remove unworthy popes and elect others formed the agenda for the Council of Pisa in 1409. Dietrich of Niem defended the idea that councils may simply withdraw obedience from a pope, and following Occam he said that the true church is universal with Christ as its head, of which the Roman church is a part. The schism could be ended by the resignation of the popes, by their deposition or expulsion. As a final resort, a general council was superior to any pope and was the final arbiter in disputes.

The schism was finally ended at the Council of Constance (1414–1418) which succeeded in deposing or ignoring all three popes and electing Martin V in 1417. In addition to the question of authority the church faced the issue of reform, but at Constance there was not enough energy remaining to address this complex issue. The new pope promised reform of the abuses which had come to be associated with the late medieval church. The principle of conciliarism reflected at Constance appeared to be a radical departure from tradition, and as if to reassure the church that it was truly orthodox, the council condemned two prominent theologians. Over two hundred propositions of John Wycliffe were declared heretical, and his body was exhumed from consecrated ground. The Bohemian priest, John Huss, after arriving under the promise of safety by the emperor, was declared a heretic and burned at the stake. Although the schism had been healed, failure to effect genuine reform made the turmoil of the next century inevitable.

At Constance provision was made for periodic future councils. The decree *Sacrosancta* (1415) stated that a council was superior to the pope, and *Frequens* (1417) called for regular councils. Such meetings were held at Pavia in 1424 and at Basel from 1431 to 1449. These councils sought to control the pope by controlling his revenues, but Eugenius IV (1431–1447) fought back. He called his own Council of Ferrara-Florence (1438–1439) which briefly reunited the Roman and Eastern Orthodox churches, and he voluntarily relinquished some judicial and financial rights to secular rulers. In the bull *Execrabilis* (1460) Pious II condemned the idea appealing from a pope to a council, and conciliarism was dead. But nationalism and its manifestations was not. In France, Spain, and England the church was severely restricted in the practices of reservation and provision, and in the collection of revenues, which was dramatized in the Pragmatic Sanction of Bourges (1438). This was a statement of Gallican principles which upheld the right of the French church to administer its property independently of the Papacy and disallowing papal appointments to vacancies. Such reform of the church took place where there was a strong ruler. The Germanies, however, which lacked a strong central political power, did not engage in such reform or create a national church. Late medieval abuses of clerical privilege continued unabated there, which is one reason why the reformation movements of the next century began in Germany.

The Challenge to Scholasticism

The thirteenth century witnessed the height of the "Medieval Synthesis," that is, the triumph of the church. Politically and institutionally the pontificate of Innocent III (1198–1216) is usually considered the apex of papal prestige and power. In terms of theology, Thomas Aquinas (d. 1274) represents the summit of medieval thought as the one who completed the synthesis of faith and reason, nature and grace, in scholasticism. During the fourteenth century the church's position and role in society was being challenged from various directions, and so were the assumptions and the authority of the scholastic theologians.

Duns Scotus (d. 1308) was born in the British Isleas, educated at Oxford where he also lectured as well as Paris, and he became a Franciscan. He has been called "the pinnacle of scholasticism," and "the most penetrating critic produced by scholasticism."[32] Whereas Aquinas had placed much value on grace as that which produced virtue in humans, and on the church's sacraments and ministry both as aids and conveyors of grace, Scotus believed that people were saved simply because God willed it, apart from grace or virtue. In this he was influenced by the strong predestinarian views of the later Augustine. "Severe qualifications were theoretically placed on the media of salvation—churches, priests, sacraments, and infused grace—lest they presume upon God's sovereignty."[33] Although God has perfect freedom, He has disposed himself to save those who lead virtuous lives, but only because in His freedom He has chosen to do so. There is nothing intrinsically "good" about virtue which compels God to reward it, because nothing can compel God. Whereas Aquinas held knowledge and reason in first place, Scotus discounted empirical knowledge as contributing in any way to one's understand of God. Scotus began the separation of theology, which was by revelation alone, from philosophy, which was demonstrable from human experience. In fact theology itself, being a product of human intellect and analysis, limits God's freedom by capturing his essence in a system of thought, thus not permitting God to be God. The application of dialectic to matters of faith, even though it was intended to support it, as with the earlier scholastics, was to limit God. Scotus is especially significant as the first theologian to defend the Immaculate Conception of the Virgin Mary, a teaching which had been condemned by Aquinas and Bonaventure. Despite his opposition to some of the propositions of Aquinas and scholasticism, Scotus remained a loyal churchman and a respected doctor, unlike William of Occam who was under excommunication during most of his career. "Duns was not a rebel against church authority. He did not question the legitimacy of the 'ordinances' of God, including the priesthood and the sacramental system. Indeed, by his very stress on the limits of reason, he exalted the authority of the church as the bearer and interpreter of revelation."[34]

William was born at Occam in Surrey, England, and like Scotus, studied at Oxford and became a Franciscan. When he went to Paris he studied under Scotus before he began to offer his own lectures. These caused enough suspicion that he was taken to Avignon and detained for three years under house arrest waiting for "the irrascible octogenarian Pope John XXII" to adjudicate his case.[35] There he made the acquaintance of Michael of Cesena, minister-general of his order who was defending the cause of the Spiritual Franciscans. When their mutual causes were clearly losing favor, both men escaped Avignon on May 26, 1328, and were taken by an imperial boat to Emperor Louis of Bavaria, in whose court they remained the rest of their lives under the ban of excommunication. Occam is said to have told the emperor, "Protect me with your sword, and I will defend you with my pen."[36] At the imperial court they were joined by Marsiglio of Padua and John of Jandun in producing numerous literary works aimed at the abuses in the church in general and at the Papacy in particular. Occam died about 1349, probably as a victim of the plague.

Occam followed Scotus in his strong affirmation of the primacy of the will (God's and ours), in his insistence on the separation of theology from philosophy, and on the contingent character of churches, priests, sacraments, and grace. As to the first, human salvation depends entirely on God's will and initiative, which makes churchly ministrations secondary if not superfluous. As to the separation of theology from philosophy, Occam taught that all knowledge originates outside of man in experience and sensory perception. But God cannot so be perceived, but He is known only through revelation which is accepted by faith. Unlike Anselm or Aquinas, he taught that it is impossible to know God through reason, but only through love and faith. Indeed, a rational faith is a contradiction, as faith is apart and above reason. "The provinces of science and faith are different. Faith's assent is not required for what is known through evidence; science does not depend on faith. Nor does faith or theology depend on science."[37] This led (or was a result of) Occam's insistence on the Bible as the supreme and infallible source of authority in the church. "The only truths that are to be considered Catholic and necessary to salvation are explicitly or implicitly stated in the Bible. . . . All other truths, which neither are inserted in the Bible nor can be inferred formally and necessarily from its contents, are not to be held as Catholic, even if they are stated in the writings of the Fathers or the definitions of the Supreme Pontiff."[38] Assenting to nonbiblical requirements is not necessary to salvation. It is not surprising that Martin Luther found much of Occam congenial to his own thoughts.

But later Reformers would not have agreed with Occam's views on grace, which was offered as a reward to all who made an effort at virtuous behavior. Occam closely associated the credibility of church and sacraments with their custodians, the clergy and the pope. Given this assumption, it is clear why he energetically opposed clerical abuses. Occam was also opposed to the idea of universals, that is, against those who followed the notion that ideas (universals) had a separate existence apart from their manifestations. Such a universal idea related to theology could be the Trinity, which no one has seen or comprehended, but the idea is confessed as a reality apart from its empirical manifestation to the world, either in unity or trinity. Another is the concept of an invisible church, i.e. the idea of church being more real than its manifestation in the world. Such ideas Occam considered merely mental images or vocal sounds and others called them mere names (*nomina*); hence, Occam's entire theological construct came to be called nominalism, which dominated theological discussion for the next century and beyond. This approach to theology was also called the *via moderna* in contrast to that of Aquinas and his followers which was called the *via antiqua*. By withdrawing all theological data from the scrutiny of reason and basing belief solely on arbitrary authority, nominalism undermined theology and paved the way for the disintegration of scholasticism. This in turn encouraged some Christians to turn to mysticism for satisfaction in their religious life, of which there was a great resurgence in the next two centuries. The Great Schism was ended at Constance in 1417, but there was yet no attempt at reform "in head and members." It is to these movements that we turn in the next chapter.

CHAPTER TEN

A TIME OF FERMENT

The late medieval period, beginning toward the end of the thirteenth century and continuing to the Reformation of the sixteenth, was a time of social upheaval and religious tension. We have already discussed the dislocation and hardship brought on by the Black Death, the wars between England and France, and the turmoil in the church occasioned by the Avignon period followed by two and then three rival popes. Although these events were distinctly melancholy and destructive of social order, the late medieval centuries also saw the birth of the Renaissance, an acceleration of lay education, a growth in religious piety and fervor, and the creation of representative institutions in government. Within the church these various forces sometimes found expression by people and in movements whose ideas were eventually declared to be unacceptable, and therefore heretical. Unlike earlier epochs, late medieval society abounded in heresies, all of which arose from within the church. "Heresy was a deviation from accepted beliefs rather than something alien to them: it sprang from believing differently about the same things as opposed to holding a different belief."[1] No heretic began by expounding ideas which were intentionally outside the church's tradition; but by pressing such ideas too far, to the point that they threatened church authority or its accepted interpretations, such dissidents were expelled and punished.

There are several reasons for the proliferation of movements after 1300 which were critical of the church. For heresy to be recognized and defined, there must be an accepted body of orthodox teaching to violate. The growth of the orthodox tradition was centuries in the making, which may account for few heresies in the earlier periods. For example, in the ninth century Ratramnus denied that in the Eucharist the bread and wine were changed to Christ's body and blood, but he defended this view without fear of ecclesiastical censure. By the thirteenth century, however, the doctrine of transubstantiation had been fixed. Even more important than a recognized tradition of orthodox belief is a recognized authority to enforce it. Earlier there was no such authority, as the Papacy was weak or otherwise engaged, and travel was difficult. But under Innocent III the Papacy was at the height of its power. Another factor in late medieval crises was the emergence of nation-states and strong secular rulers who challenged the hegemony of the church. Added to this was the growing need for all rulers, secular and religious, for more revenue, and taxes were regularly demanded from a populace which had less and less money to give. Strategies by the church to increase revenues by means of the court system, the collection of *annates*, and the selling of church offices and indulgences increased the impatience of many of the faithful. This chapter addresses some of these movements which contributed to a time of turmoil.

Issues in Controversy

One of these controversies took place within the Franciscan Order and lasted for over two centuries. The issue was an interpretation of Francis' insistence that his followers observe strict poverty and own nothing, individually or collectively. In the *Regula Bullata* of 1223 he insisted that they not even touch money. It was difficult, however, to reconcile such poverty with the educational and practical needs of their ministry. In 1230 Pope Gregory IX permitted a *nuntio* or spiritual friend to administer property on behalf of the friars. But this solution was not accepted by some, and in time the order split between the Spirituals, who advocated absolute poverty, and the Conventuals, who accepted the need for the order to own property to foster its mission. Some of the Spirituals went to the extreme of insisting that the entire church accept apostolic poverty as an ideal, beginning with the Papacy. The minister-general who followed Francis, Elias of Cortona, did not help matters by living in an ostentatiously sumptuous style for which reason the pope deposed him. An unrelated issue which caused further turmoil was that after 1242 only ordained priests were eligible for office, whereas the order began as a lay movement, and even Francis himself was never ordained a priest. Neither of these issues, poverty or ordination, was strictly a theological question involving heresy. But when the Spirituals adopted the ideas of Joachim of Fiore to buttress their defense of poverty, they courted censure. They understood themselves to be the the spiritual church of Joachim's Age of the Spirit, and their critics, including the pope, to be the carnal church which would be destroyed. "Nothing in the history of the struggle is more striking than this transformation of Joachism . . . to a justification of Franciscan poverty."[2] They claimed the pope was the anti-Christ and the Conventuals were his agents. Under Bonaventure, who was minister-general 1257–1274, there was a measure of peace as he successfully mediated between the factions, condemning extremists of both sides. "He preached sparing use in practice and relative rather than absolute poverty, but in so doing he sowed the seeds for the continued controversy that agitated the order after his death."[3] In the last quarter of the thirteenth century the Conventuals gained control of the order. In 1318 Pope John XXII demanded the submission of the Spirituals and condemned all who refused, and in 1323 he condemned the doctrine of apostolic poverty for the church as a heresy. This led Michael of Cesena, the Franciscan minister-general, to seek shelter at the court of Louis of Bavaria, where he joined his fellow Franciscan, William of Occam, as an excommunicate. What began as a simple desire to follow poverty ended by joining forces with the spiritually radical Joachism and the philosophically radical nominalism. The Spirituals who continued their protest were known as Fraticelli, and they maintained themselves in Italy for another century. They remained strongly opposed to the wealth and privilege of the church, but in a strictly theological sense they were not doctrinal heretics.

Another controversy centered on the Order of the Knights Templar, a military order founded in 1118 during the Crusades to protect pilgrims in the Holy Land. Following the Crusades, the Templars became wealthy financiers and bankers, with their centers in London and Paris. Philip IV of France simply wanted their wealth, and he fabricated charges against them including idolatry, sacrilege, sodomy, and desecrating the cross. In 1307 the king ordered all Templars in France arrested, and he brought pressure on Pope Clement V to suppress the order, which he did at the Council of Vienne in 1312. The Inquisition hunted down many Templars who confessed to the stated crimes only under torture. The grand-master, John de Molay, was burned at the stake in 1314. The persecution and dissolution of the Templars shows the power of the French king over the pope, even to the point of using trumped-up charges of heresy to gain political ends. That the accused were innocent of the charges is now generally acknowledged.

Even the pope found himself accused of heresy in 1331 when John XXII preached a sermon in which he insisted that the souls which are saved will not enjoy a vision of God until following the resurrection of their bodies. Such a "beatific vision" is reserved until after the final judgment of all people, just as souls who were condemned will not experience the punishment of hell until that day. There was a concerted outcry of opposition to these novel thoughts, led by the University of Paris and all the leading theologians of the day. In Germany, William of Occam and Michael of Cesena no doubt relished their unaccustomed role as defenders of orthodoxy as they called for the pope's deposition. The ninety-year-old pontiff made a partial recantation as he lay dying in 1334.

Another theological controversy which was energetically pursued after the twelfth century was the question of the Immaculate Conception of the Virgin Mary; that is, whether she was, at her conception, preserved from the stain of original sin. Although earlier theologians had expressed themselves on the subject, there was no uniformity of thought; indeed, the Latin church did not promulgate the dogma of Mary's Immaculate Conception until *Ineffabilis Deus* in 1854. In the medieval church there were strong proponents on both sides of the issue. Bernard of Clairvaux strongly opposed a local observance of Mary's Immaculate Conception, and in the next century opponents of the idea included Peter Lombard, Alexander of Hales, Bonaventure, Albert, "the Great," and Thomas Aquinas. In ten different passages Aquinas expressed perplexity on how Mary could refer to Jesus as "God, my Savior (Magnificat)," if she was born sinless, but defenders of the doctrine suggested that she still was guilty of her own sins.[4] The controversy was really one of the Dominicans, who opposed the teaching, against the Franciscans, who supported it, despite the fact that Bonaventure, minister-general of the Franciscans, was also a critic of the idea. Duns Scotus was an ardent advocate of the immaculate conception, as was the university of Paris. At the Council of Basel in 1439 the doctrine was declared to be consonant with the Catholic faith. But the Dominicans criticized this decision, "calling it the synagogue of Satan, whose diabolic first-born was the definition of the Immaculate Conception."[5] Although no excommunications resulted from this controversy, it contributed in no small measure to a time of turmoil.

Scripture and Tradition

In addition to the social and political crises of the fourteenth century, and as a result of them, theologians found themselves searching for the ultimate and absolute authority in spiritual matters. This quest brought to prominence an energetic discussion on the relationship between the Scriptures, in the narrow sense understood as the books of the canonical

Bible, and extra-biblical tradition. Another way of stating the issue was to speak of Holy Writ or Holy Church.

At the beginning of Christianity, the message preached by Jesus Christ was initially transmitted orally. The first written documents of the faith came in the sixties with the letters of St. Paul, and the Gospels were written somewhat later. Therefore oral tradition preceded the written words, and for a time both oral and written traditions about Jesus and His message existed as equal in authority. It is to this situation that the writer refers in the exhortation: "Hold to the traditions which you were taught by us, either by word of mouth or by letter (2 Thess. 2:15)." In the course of time the written tradition assumed a normative character simply by virtue of its permanence, and though it was an uneven process which took three centuries to complete, by the end of the fourth century the New Testament canon was accepted virtually as it is today. Oscar Cullman insists that the formation of the canon by its very nature assumes it to be normative for Christian doctrine and practice. He refers to the New Testament as apostolic tradition. There was also extra-biblical tradition in the church, that is ecclesiastical tradition, but it was authoritative only in the sense that it was derived from the apostolic tradition. Such secondary traditions included creeds, hymns, conciliar decrees, and theology. "There is consequently a difference between apostolic tradition and ecclesiastical tradition, the former being the foundation of the latter. They cannot therefore be co-ordinated."[6] This is to say that the Bible alone is the final arbiter in matters of faith (*sola Scriptura*) although ecclesiastical traditions derived from it are also authoritative. George Tavard has written that, "Tradition, then, was the overflow of the Word outside Sacred Scripture. It was neither separate from nor identical with Holy Writ."[7] In later disputes over authority, some theologians would claim that the Bible was created and authenticated by the Church, therefore the Church had precedence over Scripture and was the sole custodian of its interpretation. Others claimed that it was the message (*kerygma*) or tradition which created the Church, and therefore the Bible is supreme.

These questions, however, did not arise until the crises of the late Middle Ages. For almost a millennium the two forms of tradition, apostolic and ecclesiastical, or Scripture and Church, were accepted as authoritative. There was no dichotomy of Scripture and Tradition in the sense of tension between them, but Scripture was the source from which all else flowed. Early in the twelfth century Anselm of Laon wrote, "The Gospel . . . is the source and sum total of all our faith. There flow from it rivers, that is, commentaries."[8] Scripture, Tradition, and Church were together. "This coherence is the result of the understanding that both Scripture and Tradition issue from the same source: the Word of God, Revelation. They find their common basis in the operation of the Holy Spirit."[9] Scripture and Tradition in the early centuries were substantially coextensive.

Although this was the dominant view in the church before the fourteenth century, a different understanding of tradition had some adherents ever since Basil, "the Great," in the fourth century suggested that extra-biblical, oral tradition possessed authority equal to that of the Bible. The canonists, Ivo of Chartres (d. 1115) and Gratian (d. 1159) defended this theory, especially since they included canon law in the category of a second source of authority, equal to that of the Bible. Oberman refers to the single source of Scripture and its interpretation as "Tradition I" and the two-source theory of extra-biblical oral tradition as "Tradition II." Tradition I, "represents the sufficiency of Holy Scripture as understood by the Fathers and doctors of the church. Holy Scripture is the final authority."[10] Thomas Bradwardine at the beginning of the fourteenth century was an outspoken proponent of this view. Tradition II, on the other hand, invested ecclesiastical traditions, especially canon law, with authority equal to Scripture and not necessarily related to it or derived from it. Leading nominalists such as William Occam, Jean Gerson, and Peter d'Ailly supported this point of view.

The earliest hint of a rift between Holy Church and Holy Writ came before 1292, in the writings of Henry of Ghent, who in a perfectly orthodox commentary raised the theoretical question about the possibility of there being disagreement between church and Scripture. "Let us see in which of them we should rather believe as to the things of faith. [If the Church and Scripture] should disagree on some point, we could know to which of them it is safer to adhere."[11] His conclusion was that Scripture should be adhered to even though the entire church except one person should believe other than Scripture. In saying this, Henry also suggested that the true church could be a small remnant of the great church, for what made it "true" was not numbers but fidelity to the Scriptures. This, of course, begs the question of how and by whom such decisions were to be made. Henry's question was asked in a purely theoretical context, but it was not long after his death that the question became an urgent political reality.

This urgency came about during a crisis of two and three popes claiming jurisdiction over the church. Proponents of Tradition II, that there existed a separate authoritative tradition apart from the Bible, looked for a solution in this theory. But there were two factions who were diametrically opposed to each other in their understanding of extra-biblical authority: the curialists or papal supporters suggested their pope was supreme in the church, and the conciliarists insisted that a General Council was the highest arbiter. The first group placed the pope at the apex of authority, even above Scripture. An extreme form of this reasoning was that of the anonymous *Determinatio Compendiosa*: "The Pope is above all Council and all statute; he it is who has no superior on earth. . . . The Pope is the law itself and the living rule, opposition to which is illegitimate."[12] This way of thinking reflected the canonists who flourished in the fourteenth century and exhibited "the most extreme instances of devaluation of Scripture."[13] The other group of Tradition II theorists defended the supremacy of a General Council, but they were not united in their thinking. Peter d'Ailly, Jean Gerson, and Nicholas de Clamanges saw the need for General Councils for the church to pronounce on matters of faith, but they also recognized that the quality and utility of councils varied, and they believed that councils could err.[14] Basically the Conciliarists also tended toward advocating the "sufficiency" of Scripture within the context of a General Council, but they also acknowledged an extra-biblical authority in the doctors of the church.

Thomas Bradwardine (d. 1349) was an outspoken advocate of Tradition I (Scripture alone), to which he appeals in his opposition to the alleged Pelagianism of William of Occam. He insists that nothing can be taught in the church which does not derive from the canonical Scripture. Anticipating future developments, Oberman observes that, "insofar as the Scripture has become a standard to Bradwardine by which to judge the Fathers too, it is clear that the Doctor Profundus has a link with the Reformation view of the authority of Holy Scripture."[15] An older contemporary of Bradwardine, Peter Aureolis (d. 1322), a Franciscan archbishop, wrote, "Theology is a discipline whereby one knows only what is written in the Bible and what the Prophets, the Apostles, and the other writers of the Sacred Books meant. Theology consists in knowing the books of the Canon and their meaning."[16]

Marsiglio of Padua (d. 1342) recognized the authority of extra-biblical tradition, i.e. Fathers and Councils, but only in a derivative sense. Supreme authority is vested in a General Council elected by clergy and laity, but even its pronouncements must be in harmony with Scripture. Although William of Occam at times expressed himself as a strong supporter of a narrow submissiveness to Scripture alone, as a leading conciliarist he also recognized non-biblical authority. "Occam did not understand *sola scriptura* to exclude the possibility of an extra-scriptural tradition. His work marks a turning point in the history of the problem of Scripture and Tradition."[17]

During the fourteenth and fifteenth centuries all of these theories of the proper relationship between Scripture and Tradition, the Church and the Bible, were held by theologians. To confuse matters further, there was no uniform method of interpretation of the Bible. During the Middle Ages it was generally held that there were four principle meanings which could be derived from a text of Scripture. The first and simplest was the literal or historical sense, which accepted a statement at face value. The second was the allegorical, which applied the passage to Christ and the Church; the third was the tropological or moral sense which was applied to the soul and its virtues; the fourth was the anagogical which referred to heaven and the future life. At the same time as the debates over Scripture and Tradition were taking place, there was also a lively discussion over the proper method of reading the Bible. The defenders of the Scripture alone position invariably supported the literal sense of the Bible as the preferred meaning, whereas those who recognized Church or Tradition in some way as authoritative tended to accept allegory more readily.[18] Clearly the tensions which precipitated the upheavals in the church of the sixteenth century had been building for nearly three hundred years.

Wycliffe and Huss

John Wycliffe, born in the 1320s, was an English ecclesiastic who spent most of his career as a scholar at Oxford University. His life spanned the period of the Avignon papacy and the beginning of the Great Schism as well as the first phase of the wars between England and France. His theology was therefore influenced by all the tensions we have come to associate with the fourteenth century. Although he became the most prominent instructor at Oxford in his time, he did not follow the nominalism of his celebrated predecessor, William of Occam, but instead followed Duns Scotus, another Oxford luminary, by adopting a form of moderate Realism which allowed the reality of universals. It was his philosophical assumptions which led him to assertions about the nature of the Church and of God's Word which ultimately brought him to the edge of orthodoxy.

Wycliffe's first assault on clerical abuses came from his doctrine of lordship or dominion, which allowed only those enjoying God's grace to have possession (lordship) of property. Christians, above all clerics, should follow the law of apostolic poverty. "Lordship could be possessed, along with God's other gifts, only by the righteous man, the man in a state of grace."[19] But ecclesiastics—monks, clergy, bishops—ought to divest themselves of all property in order to regain spiritual lordship. A corollary of his doctrine was that when civil rulers were not righteous or morally upright, it was legitimate to divest them of their lordship, in effect offering a theological rationale for rebellion. Wycliffe's ideas were proposed at a time when the English king required funds to support his war with the French, and Wycliffe advised that, "If we are involved in war, then we should seize the clergy's temporal possessions which belong to us and the kingdom as a whole."[20] In advocating this strategy, Wycliffe was placing himself in line with the Spiritual Franciscans as well as offering support to rapacious nobles to enrich themselves at the expense of church property. He was also reflecting the views of many commoners who believed that the clergy for too long had been enriching themselves. But he alienated most of the bishops and clergy who did not forget this attack on their privileges.

At the same time as Wycliffe was advising the disendowment of the church, he proposed a new definition of the church. He believed that only the predestined company of the elect constituted the true church of Christ, and not the pope but Christ was its head. True Christians, therefore, were those who were spiritual, lived in accordance with apostolic poverty, and displayed Christian ideals in their lives. Such thinking was hardly new in the history of the church, but Wycliffe's restriction of church membership only to those who are predestined and known to God made ordained clergy, sacraments, hierarchy, and almsgiving superfluous. Following the teaching of Wycliffe, a Lollard document states that, "pilgrimages, prayers, and offerings made to blind crosses or roods, and to deaf images of wood or stone, are akin to idolatry."[21] Likewise prayers for the dead, confession of sin to a priest, and many devotional practices were unnecessary. Inasmuch as all the predestined have equal status before God, Wycliffe emphasized the priesthood of all believers.

It is not difficult to understand why Pope Gregory XI initiated action against Wycliffe, which he did by ordering that he should be arrested and handed over to the Archbishop of Canterbury, Simon of Sudbury. But the English clergy, and Sudbury in particular, were not eager to comply with an Avignon pope who seemed to be intent on discrediting an eminent English teacher, so nothing happened. "The bishops were content to dismiss with a caution the man who was so powerfully supported (by the king and people) . . . and there was opposition to Papal interference in England."[22] Furthermore, in that year of 1378, the pope died and the Great Schism with two popes began; King Edward III died and he was succeeded by Richard II, eleven years old. This year was also a turning point for Wycliffe, as his speculations on the Eucharist and the Bible led him deeper into confrontation with the accepted traditions of the church.

In his treatise *On the Eucharist*, Wycliffe denied the doctrine of transubstantiation as it had been formulated by the Fourth Lateran Council of 1215. Whereas the church taught that the bread and wine had been changed into Christ's body and blood, Wycliffe insisted that the substance and the accidents of the elements remained, for which reason his suggestion has been called remanence. "I believe, as Christ and his apostles have taught us, that the sacrament of the altar, white and round and like to other bread, is very God's body in form of bread. And therefore St. Paul names it never but when he calls it bread. And right as it is heresy to believe that Christ is spirit and no body, so it is heresy to believe that this sacrament is God's body and no bread; for it is both together."[23] His opposition to transubstantiation carried him further to deny any special sacerdotal powers to effect the sacrament and to decry as idolatry any veneration that was offered to the consecrated host. This time he was protected by neither king or clergy; a synod at Blackfriars in 1382 found him guilty of ten heresies and fourteen errors. No further action was taken, however, perhaps because he was now in retirement at Lutterworth and had been physically disabled by a stroke.

As to Scripture, Wycliffe asserted that "it is the highest authority for every Christian and the standard of faith and of all human perfection."[24] The Bible should be understood primarily in its literal sense, and it should be read by all the faithful. To encourage such reading, Wycliffe began its translation into English, omitting all commentary or ecclesial interpretations. John Purvey, a disciple of Wycliffe, completed a second translation about 1395 which was known as the Lollard Bible. It became immensely popular and paved the way for Tyndale's translation which was a forerunner of the Authorized Version (King James Bible) of 1611.

In 1381 there occurred a massive uprising of the peasants in the city of London and in scattered areas of England. This Peasant Revolt had its roots in the social unrest caused by the Black Death in 1350 with periodic repetitions thereafter. Although the number of workers was severely reduced, the same wage scale was offered as before. To make matters worse, a Statute of Laborers fixed wage scales at an unreasanably low level, and that was followed by a poll tax which fell primarily on the laborers, both urban and agricultural. In 1381, Wat Tyler and John

Ball led thousands of peasants in a revolt which resulted in the death of many of the rebels. At the time Wycliffe was faulted for instigating the riot with his teachings on egalitarianism and on lordship, that property belonged to the righteous. A contemporary chronicler writes that "the perverse doctrines of Wycliffe" caused the insurrection, but there is not sufficient evidence to prove any real bond between the reformer and the rebels.[25] Wycliffe died in 1384.

Wycliffe's followers were given the derisive name of Lollards (= mumblers), though there is no reason to believe that Wycliffe had any direct responsibility for the movement. They were a poorly organized and for the most part uneducated group, some of whom became itinerant preachers. In 1401 Parliament passed *De Haeretico Comburendo* against them, a statute that advocated their suppression under pain of death by fire at the stake. The law described "a false and perverse people of a new sect . . . who usurp the office of preaching . . . wickedly incite and stir people to sedition."[26] Lollardy lost its strength within a generation of Wycliffe's death.

Whereas Wycliffe's reform movement did not gain substantial support in England, his ideas found fertile soil in Bohemia at the eastern extremity of Latin Christendom, especially in the life of John Huss. He was born about 1369 and studied for the priesthood at the University of Prague. Upon being appointed chaplain of the Bethlehem Chapel in Prague, he gained popularity by preaching in the vernacular a message which advocated moderate reforms and opposed corruption in the church. In this he was following a tradition of Czech religious reform which was already a half-century old, one which emphasized preaching, elevating the morals of clergy and people, the Bible as the sole source of religious truth, and frequent communion. These ideas were in place long before Wycliffe came to prominence in England, but when Jerome of Prague, a close friend of Huss, returned from studying at Oxford, he brought Wycliffe's writings with him.[27] The ties between Prague and Oxford had been strengthened by the marriage of Richard II of England to Anne, the daughter of Charles IV, King of Bohemia two decades earlier. In 1403 the cathedral chapter in Prague forbade any to hold, preach, or assert forty-five condemned articles alleged to be Wycliffe's. But the Czech masters, who were in the minority against the immigrant Germans, upheld the orthodoxy of Wycliffe. Following his Czech colleagues, the sermons of Huss showed increasing influence by the Englishman. In 1403 a new archbishop was appointed for Prague, Zbinco of Hasenbeurg, who initially befriended and promoted Huss, appointing him to delicate diplomatic missions and preacher to the annual synods of clergy for three years. In none of these sermons does Huss advocate theories or dogmas contrary to the mind of the church, and before 1408 the only opposition to Huss came from clergy whose dissolute lives he had censured.

In 1409 the Council of Pisa deposed both popes, Gregory XII in Rome and Benedict XIII in Avignon. In Prague, the German element continued to follow the Roman pope, the archbishop followed the newly elected Alexander V, but the Czechs maintained neutrality by following no pope. This situation left open wounds and remembered grievances. In the same year all the German students and masters, who had a conservative influence in Prague, left for the University of Leipzig, leaving Huss and the more reform-minded Bohemians masters of Prague. Now Archbishop Zbinco set out to remove Huss, and he excommunicated him in 1410 on the charge of harboring Wycliffe's false teachings, which Huss denied. The university appealed to the Pisan pope, who upheld the excommunication of Huss and seven others on the grounds of being "rebels and disobedient," but thus far no heresy had been proven. The populace in Prague was in an uproar, and they supported Huss by burning the papal decrees. Huss was cited to appear before John XXIII, but he refused the invitation, fearing "snares" along the way and asked instead that the trial take place in Prague. When that city was placed under the interdict, Huss left and took refuge with friends.

During his self-imposed exile he composed his chief work, *On the Church*, in which he echoed some of Wycliffe's ideas but stopped short of declaring that sinful priests had no sacerdotal power. With Wycliffe, he declared that the true church of Christ was not identical with the Roman church, thus denying the famous bull of Boniface VIII, *Unam Sanctam*. "There is one church of the sheep, another of the goats, one of the saints, another of the reprobate. Just as in the case of the body there are waste materials so also in the church there are those who are not of the church." He continues by referring to the wheat and tares, pointing out that some are in the church who are basically pagans and others who are hypocrites, but the true church consists only of the predestined by Christ. "It remains to be considered whether the Roman church is the holy, apostolic Catholic church, the bride of Christ. This church is not the holy, apostolic church because the pope and the cardinals have often been stained by error and sin."[28] He concluded by appealing his case directly to God and Christ without any conciliar or papal mediation.

King Wenzel of Bohemia and his queen were strong supporters of Huss and the reform movement, and opposed to Archbishop Zbinco. The archbishop turned to the new king of the Romans (Holy Roman

Emperor), Sigismund, for help against his own brother, Wenzel. Meanwhile Huss attacked a new issue of papal indulgences and carried on a lively correspondence with friend and foe. The Council of Constance was called to meet in 1414 to end the papal schism, but the Bohemian situation was also high on the agenda. Sigismund was informed that Huss was counted as a heretic only because he took no steps to remove the excommunication. At the urging of the emperor, Huss agreed to attend the council and to respond to the charges against him, and Sigismund promised him safe conduct. Once in Constance, Huss was imprisoned, and shortly thereafter Wycliffe was condemned posthumously, and his bones were removed from their burial place in consecrated grounds. The renowned Parisian conciliarists, Peter d'Ailly and Jean Gerson, were the judges at Huss' trial. He was found guilty of heresy and burned at the stake on July 6, 1415. His colleague, Jerome of Prague, suffered the same fate.[29]

The reaction in Bohemia was rebellion, where Huss was venerated as a martyr and a symbol of Bohemian nationalism. Sigismund was rejected as king to succeed Wenzel. Two national factions emerged, each claiming to be religious heirs of Huss. The moderates wished to preserve unity with the Catholic church, but they insisted on receiving both the bread and wine in Communion, therefore their name, Calixtines (*calix* = cup), or Utraquists (meaning "both"). The Taborites were more extreme in their desire to break away completely from the Roman church. They held to the Bible as the only source of religious truth, opposed transubstantiation, penance, purgatory, prayer to saints, relics, and veneration of images. Both groups were united in opposing the imperial forces sent by Sigismund, which they did successfully under the leadership of the Taborite generals, Jon Zizka and Procopius, "the Great." In 1420 the two groups produced the Four Articles of Prague: (1) free preaching of the Word of God; (2) communion with bread and wine for both clergy and laity; (3) reform of morals; (4) reduction of power and wealth of clergy. In later years the two Bohemian factions turned on each other; the Taborites were defeated by the Utraquists. Bohemia remained in the hands of Hussite sympathizers known as the *Unitas Fratrum* (Unity of Bohemian Brothers) who were the forerunners of the Moravians.

The Emergence of the Laity

From the beginning of Christianity there were recognized leaders who were given offices of respect, notably bishops, priests, and deacons. The earliest reference to a division of labor between clergy (*kleros* = a portion set aside) and laity (= the people) comes from Clement of Rome in 96 A.D. Thereafter the history of relations between clergy and laity followed an erratic path. In the early and High Middle Ages the laity, represented by kings and princes, were especially prominent and powerful. We need only recall patrons of the church such as Clovis, Charlemagne, or Otto I, who deposed two popes and appointed three others. It was also in earlier times that most churches in Europe were established by lay lords and were under their direction, the so-called proprietary church system. This system was opposed by the pope during the Investiture Controversy, and from the twelfth through the early thirteenth century the church control of society reached its highest point. This was based in part on the idea that Christendom, territorially most of Europe, owed premier allegiance to the pope, with secular and political subdivisions being subservient to him. Also, during the growth of Christianity in Europe, clergy usually comprised the bureaucracy and staff of lay princes, as they were literate and educated, thus further enhancing the role of clergy. But in the late Middle Ages there was a dramatic reversal of lay position, not only with the emergence of powerful rulers such as Philip IV of France and Edward III of England, but especially among the merchants, tradesmen, lesser gentry, and the common people.

One reason for this reversal was nationalism and, with it, the concept of a sovereign state, which undermined the idea of the political unity of Christendom. Nationalism was fostered by the concept of territorial law administered by the king—indeed, it was by means of the extension of royal law that modern states were born—and this process was in the hands of lay lawyers. As a result of the revival of civil law in the thirteenth century, there "developed a theory of the sovereign state which could not be reconciled with the old medieval system, which forced a choice between loyalties (of church or prince)."[30] William of Plaisian, a lawyer under Edward I, echoed the belief of many contemporaries when he wrote, "All those in the realm are ruled by the king's authority; even prelates and clergy, in temporal matters, are bound by the laws, edicts, and constitution of the king."[31] As we have seen above, Philip IV even used the charge of heresy, traditionally the church's prerogative, and he used it against both the pope and the Templars. The laicization of society was therefore partly the result of the growth of sovereign secular states supported by civil law as practiced by lay lawyers.

Another reason for laicization was the growing literacy and professionalism among the laity who challenged the higher status assumed by the clergy. During the invasion of Europe by the Indo-European tribes in the early Middle Ages, and partially as a result of them, literacy had declined almost to the point of extinction. The ability to read and write (primarily Latin) was kept alive by the monasteries, which, following Benedict's *Rule*, required that monks engage in daily reading and, during each Lent, to intensify this effort. By copying manuscripts in the scriptoria, monastic houses preserved not only religious literature but a great deal of Graeco-Roman classical material as well. This activity, together with schools fostered by monasteries and cathedrals, kept literacy alive, but it was also largely limited to churchmen who were the beneficiaries of the authority such knowledge brought with it.

But literacy was not the exclusive preserve of the clergy throughout the medieval period. In his study on *The Literacy of the Laity in the Middle Ages*, J.W. Thompson has demonstrated that a large number of princes and aristocrats, including many women, were well versed in letters, not only in Latin but also in the vernacular.[32] In northern Italy, where commercial interests contributed to a more dominant lay society, literacy was kept alive by merchants and bankers. "By the middle of the twelfth century the municipal councils were busy founding schools for the children of the burghers, which were the first lay schools since the end of antiquity. By means of them, instruction ceased to be furnished exclusively for the benefit of the monasteries and priests."[33] The difference between the literacy of the north European nobility and the Italian merchants was that for the former it was an intellectual luxury whereas for the merchant it was a daily necessity. By the thirteenth century vernacular idioms were replacing Latin, which in itself was a lay development for commercial use by urban administrators and businessmen. Such literacy was not without effect on the church; it was subversive of clerical authority. "The advance of (lay) education was a movement away from the church. . . . Those who could read or had access to the world of books felt more capable of talking to their ecclesiastical superiors as equals, or even from a vantage-point of superiority."[34] The fourteenth century witnessed the acceleration of lay education, and large numbers of children attended schools in the cities of northern Italy as well as in England, France, and the Empire. The establishment of new universities continued, but it is significant that every university in Europe founded after 1300 was at the initiative of a lay prince. In this new lay society, office depended upon merit, and that merit could be judged. This critical analysis was often at the expense of the clergy, to whom educated laity now applied more rigid standards of behavior and competence. Lay literacy was accompanied by elements of anti-clericalism brought on by the church's wealth, the Great Schism, clerical privilege, and higher expectations of those holding the priestly office.

The Avignon popes were especially the object of satire because of their strategies for increasing wealth. Petrarch wrote, "I am astounded, as I recall their predecessors, to see these men loaded with gold and clad in purple, boasting of the spoils of princes and nations."[35] Under the Hussites a large proportion of the property of monks and clergy was taken away and given to lay owners. There was also current the idea that the efficacy of a priest's ministry, including the sacraments, depended upon his virtue, and by this standard many priests were found deficient. As we have seen, Wycliffe's concept of dominion, according to which authority and possessions were legitimately held only by the virtuous, was aimed especially at immoral clergy.

The crisis of ecclesiastical authority in the fourteenth century not only resulted in anti-clericalism but also contributed to the privatization of religion. The doctrine of the priesthood of all believers not only assumed the equality of clergy and people but in some cases led to questioning the need for clergy and hierarchy at all. The Bible and not the pope was the ultimate authority, and it could be read and understood by everyone. Wycliffe believed that laymen could hear confessions, absolve, and even become pope. "The ship of Peter is the church militant . . . nor do I see why the said ship of Peter might not in time consist purely of laymen."[36] The strong belief in predestination as taught by William of Occam fostered the privatization of religion in that it made the church or the community of the faithful unnecessary for salvation. Mysticism was another form of turning away from the institutional church to find God in contemplation and solitude. Although the emergence of the laity was also associated with anti-clericalisam, the late medieval epoch did not see a decline in spirituality. Indeed, it was the resurgence of religious sentiment and piety that prompted the movements for clerical reform and apostolic poverty. The revival of commerce, civil law, and cities brought with it a growing secularity of society, but this in no way undermined personal faith and devotion. Such expressions of lay piety can be seen in the growth of numerous clusters of men and women such as the Beghards, Beguines, and Brethren of the Common Life, who were outside the monastic structures of the established Orders. One result of privatization as a rejection of the corporate church was the discovery of the individual, a phenomenon of the late Middle Ages. This development has been attributed to two sources, a revival of Greek values and literature, and to Christianity, which prized the lost sheep, the lost coin, and the lost soul. But this was a Christianity free from the overlay of institutional preoccupations.[37]

Synonymous with the rediscovery of the individual and the emergence of the laity was the growth of a democratic spirit. Not only is this in evidence with the rise of parliaments in the nation-states, but more vigorously in the literature of conciliarism and in the work of Marsiglio of Padua. Accompanying these movements was an acceleration of social unrest and the literature of social injustice. The scores of peasant revolts recorded in the last two centuries of the Middle Ages were a logical result of an age of criticism of authority and skepticism of tradition. John Ball, the leader of the insurrection in England in 1381, was believed to have made this speech: "Good people, things cannot go well in England, nor will they until all goods shall be in common and when there shall be neither villeins nor gentles, but we shall all be one. Why should he, whom we call lord, be a greater master than us? They have ease and beautiful manors, and we have hardship and work."[38] He continued by reminding his hearers that it was only through the peasants' labor that the wealthy could maintain themselves. The same hostility was raised against church leaders, and in the uprising associated with John Ball the Archbishop of Canterbury was murdered.

Toward the end of the Middle Ages, the mid–fifteenth century, many in the church were disillusioned. Although the Council of Constance had restored the Papacy, its promise of reform in "head and members" was not realized. The Bohemians were at war with the emperor, and then with each other. In England the Lollards soon died out, and the church came increasingly under the king's control, as it did in France. The Germanies were politically fragmented, although in theory they were united as the Holy Roman Empire, and the church in each territory came to some accomodation with the prince. On the positive side, the lay movements represented by the *Devotia Moderna* witnessed a revival of religious life, and Thomas à Kempis's *Imitation of Christ* became the religious handbook of the fifteenth century. Theologically there was an increasing emphasis on the humanity of Christ and of His suffering, which was visually represented in crucifixes, paintings, roodscreens, sculptures, and hymns. The fifteenth century was also a great age for the sermon. "More people must have been delivering, hearing, writing, and reading—as well as advocating—sermons in this age than ever before."[39] Two famous preachers of this time were Vincent Ferrer and Bernardino of Siena. The sermon began to replace the mass as the center of people's attention. Such popularity was another indication that there was no diminution of piety or religious devotion, indeed, there appeared to be an intensification of interest in religion in the fifteenth century. Such interest, however, was manifested in new ways and expressed with less reference to the institutional church than in previous centuries. The sixteenth century would see the culmination of the social, political, and religious ferment of this period.

ABBREVIATIONS

ASOC *Analecta Sacri Ordinis Cisterciensis*

Mansi J. D. Mansi, *Sacrorum Conciliorum Nova et Amplissima Collection* (31 vols., Florence, 1759–1798).

MGH *Monumenta Germaniae Historica*

PL *Patrologia cursus completus, Series Latina,* ed. J. P. Migne (221 vols., Paris, 1844–1864).

NOTES

Chapter 1

1. See Donald Kagan, *Decline and Fall of the Roman Empire: Why Did It Collapse?* Problems in European Civilization Series (London: D.C. Heath, 1962); Edward Gibbon, *Decline and Fall of the Roman Empire*, J. B. Bury edition (London, 1909–1914); J. B. Bury, *A History of the Later Roman Empire 395–565* (London: MacMillan and Co, 1923). Jaroslav Pelikan, *The Excellent Empire: The Fall of Rome and The Triumph of The Church*. The Rauschenbusch Lectures, New Series, I. (San Francisco: Harper, 1987); Robert E. Herzstein, *The Holy Roman Empire in the Middle Ages*. Problems in European Civilization Series (London: D. C. Heath, 1966).

2. Donald Kagan, *Decline and Fall*, vii. The decline of the Roman empire as an ideal never took place. The continuation of the idea of Rome in the Middle Ages is one of the fundamental themes of the age, preserved by the church and especially by the popes who understood themselves to be the successors of the emperors. No less did worthies such as Charlemagne and Otto I, the founder of the Holy Roman Empire, understand themselves to be in the imperial lineage.

3. The "Pirenne thesis" is outlined in Henri Pirenne, *Mohammed and Charlemagne* (New York: Meridian, 4th printing 1960); and *Economic and Social History of Medieval Europe* (New York: Harcourt, Brace, 1937).

4. See Norman Cohn, *Pursuit of the Millennium* (New York: Harper, 1961).

5. Tacitus, *Germaniae*, ll. trans. Alfred J. Church and William J. Brodribbe, *The Complete Works of Tacitus* (New York: Random House, 1942), 710.

6. Cited in Jordanes, *On The Conversion of the Goths and Alaric's Sack of Rome. De Origene actusque Getarum* (c. 551), 28, trans. Robinson. In Ray C. Petry, *A History of Christianity*, (Englewood Cliffs, N.J.: Prentice-Hall, 1962), 197.

7. Ibid., 198.

8. William R. Cannon, *History of Christianity in the Middle Ages*, (Nashville: Abingdon, 1960), 18.

9. Gregory of Tours, *Historia Francorum* 2:31, cited in Petry, *History of Christianity*, 203.

10. Christopher Dawson, *The Making of Europe* (New York: Meridian, 1956), 169.

11. Cited in Dawson, *The Making of Europe, 171.*

12. Bernard S. Bachrach, *The Medieval Church: Success or Failure?* (New York: Holt, Rinehart and Winston, 1972), 11.

13. Benedict, *The Rule*, Prologue l, ed. Timothy Fry, O.S.B. (Collegeville: Liturgical Press, 1982), 15.

14. Ibid., 46.

15. See C. H. Lawrence, *Medieval Monasticism* (London: Longman, 1989), "The Social and Economic Role," 127 f.

16. Tertullian, *Prescription Against Heretics* 7.

17. David Knowles, *The Evolution of Medieval Thought* (London: Longman, 1962), 53.

18. See E. K. Rand, "Boethius, The First of the Scholastics" in *Founders of the Middle Ages* (New York: Dover, 1928), 135–80.

19. On the topic of Christianity and classical culture, see C. N. Cochrane, *Christianity and Classical Culture* (New York: Oxford, 1944); E. G. Weltin, *Athens and Jerusalem* (Atlanta: Scholars Press, 1987); H. O. Taylor, *The Classical Heritage of the Middle Ages* (New York: Frederick Ungar, 1957); R. R. Bolgar, *The Classical Heritage* (New York: Harper, 1954); Jaroslav Pelikan, *Christianity and Classical Culture* (New Haven: Yale University Press, 1993).

20. Knowles, *The Evolution of Medieval Thought*, 57.

21. Deno J. Geanakoplos, *Byzantine East and Latin West* (New York: Harper, 1966), 24.

22. Cited in James A. Corbett, *The Papacy* (New York: Van Nostrand, 1956), 98. See Aloysius K. Ziegler, "Pope Gelasius and His Teaching on the Relations of Church and State," *The Catholic Historical Review* 27 (1942): 412–37.

23. Martin Marty, *A Short History of Christianity* (New York: Meridian, 1960), 144.

24. J. M. Wallace-Hadrill, *The Barbarian West: The Early Middle Ages* (New York: Harper, 1962), 36.

25. Procopius, *Buildings* 1, 1, trans. H. B. Dewing, Loeb Classical Library, cited in Charles T. Davis, ed., *The Eagle, the Crescent, and the Cross* (New York: Appleton-Century-Crofts, 1967), 108.

26. Justinian, *Novellae*, Tit. VI, Sixth New Constitution, First Collection, Preface, in Petry, *History of Christianity*, 75.

27. Procopius, *Buildings* 1:1, trans. H. B. Dewing and G. Downey, in *Procopius*, 7:11–13 (Cambridge: Harvard University Press, 1940), cited in Petry, *History of Christianity*, 217.

Chapter 2

1. Shirley Jackson Case, *The Social Triumph of the Ancient Church* (New York: Harper, 1933).

2. Gregory, PL 76:1009–10. See Petry, *History of Christianity*, (Englewood Cliffs, N.J.: Prentice-Hall, 1962), 193 for Gregory's "Letter to Leander" in which he describes the daunting nature of his pontificate.

3. Margaret Deanesly, *A History of the Medieval Church* (London: Methuen, repr. 1962), 21.

4. Gregory, *Pastoral Care*, ed. and trans. Henry Davis, *Ancient Christian Writers*

11 (New York: Paulist, 1950), 45–88. Cf. Carl Volz, *Pastoral Life and Practice in the Early Church* (Minneapolis: Augsburg, 1990), 174–79. Thomas C. Oden, *Care of Souls in the Classic Tradition* (Philadelphia: Fortress, 1984) examines the pastoral method of Gregory, "the Great," in an attempt to find the way back to pastoral identity by reviewing Gregory's method. He suggests that Gregory in his case studies anticipates many themes of modern psychotherapy.

5. Roland Bainton, *Christendom: A Short History of Christianity* (New York: Harper, 1966), 1:141.

6. Bede, *A History of the English Church and People*, trans. Leo Sherley-Price (Baltimore: Penguin, 1965), 98.

7. Tertullian, *Against the Jews, 7*; Origen, *Sermon 28* on Matthew 24; *Sermon 4* on Ezekiel.

8. Patrick, *Confessions* 1, 2, 27, 36. In R. P. C. Hanson, *St. Patrick* (New York: Oxford University Press, 1968), 118.

9. See ibid, chs. 4 and 5, on the question of Patrick's monasticism.

10. Myles Dillon and Nora Chadwick, *The Celtic Realms* (London: Weidenfeld and Nicholson, 1967), 195. See John T. McNeill, *The Celtic Churches: A History* A.D. *200–1200* (Chicago: The University of Chicago Press, 1974), esp. ch. 8, "Learning, Art, and Worship;" Thomas Cahill, *How the Irish Saved Civilization* (New York: Doubleday, 1995).

11. Bede, *The Ecclesiastical History of the English People*, I, xxvii.

12. The opening lines:

> The High Creator, Ancient of Days and Unbegotten / was without origin of beginning and without end / He is and shall be to infinite ages of ages / with Whom is Christ, the only begotten, and the Holy Spirit / coeternal in the everlasting glory of the Godhead. / We set forth not three gods, but we say there is one God, / saving our faith in three most glorious Persons.

Columba, *Altus Prosater* from *The Irish Liber Hymnorum*, ed. J. H. Bernard and R. A. Atkinson (London: Henry Bradshaw, 1898), 2:150. See also Colman Barry, *Readings in Church History* (Westminster: Newman, 1960), 1:216–19.

13. Or some say Christmas Day 597 together with ten thousand new converts. William R. Cannon, *History of Christianity in the Middle Ages*, (Nashville: Abingdon, 1960), 43.

14. Williston Walker, et al., *A History of the Christian Church*, 4th ed. (New York: Charles Scribner's Sons, 1985), 225.

15. Gregory of Tours, *History of the Franks*, trans. O. M. Dalton (Oxford: Clarendon, 1927), 2, pref. 2.

16. See Alcuin, *The Life of Willibrord*, trans. A. Grieve (London: Westminster, 1923); Boniface, *Letters*, trans. E. Emerton (New York: Octagon Books, 1973); G. F. Browne, *Boniface of Crediton and His Companions* (London: SPCK, 1910); C. H. Talbot, *The Anglo-Saxon Missionaries in Germany* (New York: Sheed and Ward, 1954).

17. Eleanor Shipley Duckett, *Gateway to the Middle Ages*— Monasticism (Ann Arbor: The University of Michigan Press, c. 1938, pb., 1961), 104.

18. Alcuin, *The Life of St. Willibrord*, in Talbot, *The Anglo-Saxon Missionaries in Germany*, 11.

19. Willibald, *The Life of St. Boniface*, in Talbot, *The Anglo-Saxon Missionaries in Germany*, 45.

20. Ibid., 214.

21. Ibid., 76–78. Talbot includes forty-eight letters to and from Boniface in English translation. See also Boniface, *Epistle* 23 (ed. M. Tangl, MGH, Epistolae Selectae, 1:38–41).

22. Rudolph, Monk of Fulda, *The Life of Saint Leoba*, in Talbot, *The Anglo-Saxon Missionaries in Germany*, 213.

23. Ibid., 214.

24. McNeill, *The Celtic Churches*, (Chicago: University of Chicago Press, 1974), 172.

25. Philip Schaff, *History of the Christian Church*, vol. 4 (New York: C. Scribner's Sons, 1910), 98.

26. *Capitulatio de partibus Saxoniae*, cited in Stewart C. Easton and Helen Wieruzowski, eds., *The Era of Charlemagne* (New York: van Nostrand, 1961), 119.

27. Ibid., 122.

28. *Snorris Koenigsbuch* (Jena: Eugene Diederichs, 1922), 1:226–28, trans. Conrad Zimmerman and Gunther Rolfson, cited in Barry, *Readings in Church History*, 1:278.

29. Ibid., 279

30. Ibid., 283.

31. For this summary of mission methods I am in special debt to Richard E. Sullivan's doctoral dissertation in the Department of History at the University of Illinois, reprinted in part as "The Carolingian Missionary and the Pagan," *Speculum*, Published Quarterly by the Medieval Academy of America (Cambridge: Medieval Academy), 28 (1953): 705–40.

32. Alcuin, *Life of Willibrord*, 8.

33. Sullivan, "The Carolingian Missionary and the Pagan," 710.

34. Boniface, *Letters*, 12 and 34, cited in Sullivan, "The Carolingian Missionary and the Pagan," 716.

35. Hucbald, *The Life of Saint Lebuin*, 12 (PL 132:889).

36. Bede, *A History of the English Church and People*, V, 10, cited in Sullivan, "The Carolingian Missionary and the Pagan," 722.

37. Boniface, *Letters*, 73, cited in Sullivan, "The Carolingian Missionary and the Pagan," 735.

38. Boniface, *Letters*, 50, cited in Sullivan, "The Carolingian Missionary and the Pagan," 735.

39. See Bernard Hamilton, *Religion in the Medieval West* (London: Edward Arnold, 1986), especially "The Legacy of Paganism," 96–104; J. G. Frazer, *The Golden Bough*, 12 vols. (London: MacMillan, 1894), 1914–27, for examples of pagan rituals surviving in medieval folklore.

40. Robert Hoyt and Stanley Chodorow, *Europe in the Middle Ages* (New York: Harcourt, Brace, and Jovanovich, 1976), 142ff.

Chapter 3

1. J. M. Wallace-Hadrill, *The Barbarian West: The Early Middle Ages* (New York: Harper, 1962), 87.

2. The transfer of authority from the Merovingians to the Carolingians re-

mains an intriguing question among historians. See Stewart Easton and Helene Wieruszowski, *The Era of Charlemagne* (New York: D. Van Nostrand, 1961), 100ff; Carl Volz, "Coronation of Pepin" in Frank N. McGill and E. G. Weltin, eds., *Great Events from History* (Englewood Cliffs, N. J.: Salem Press, Inc., 1972), 2:1131–32.

3. *Admonitio generalis*, 789, University of Pennsylvania Translations and Reprints Series, VI, no. 5 (New York: Longmans, Green, and Co., 1900), 15.

4. *De litteris colendis*; ibid., 12.

5. Agobard of Lyons, *Liber adversus legem Gundobadi*, in Jeremiah O'Sullivan and John Burns, *Medieval Europe* (New York: Appleton-Century-Crofts, 1943), 482. Cf. PL 104:126.

6. "King Charles to Pope Leo on the Two Powers" (796) in Easton and Wieruszowski, *The Era of Charlemagne*, 168.

7. Ibid., 127.

8. Brian Tierney, *The Crisis of Church and State 1050–1300* (Englewood Cliffs, N.J.: Prentice-Hall, 1964), 23.

9. Ibid., 21–22; Carl Volz, "The Donation of Constantine," McGill and Weltin, eds., *Great Events from History*, 1021–1026.

10. See Pierre Riche, *Education and Culture in the Barbarian West*, trans. John J. Contreni (Columbia, S.C.:University of South Carolina, 1976), 137–303. In *The Crucible of Europe: The Ninth and Tenth Centuries in European History* (Berkeley: University of California Press, 1976), Geoffrey Barraclough writes, "If Merovingian society was (in Lot's famous phrase) an 'alliance of decrepitude and barbarism,' an extraordinary combination of the vices and cruelty and corruption of the under-civilized and over-civilized Carolingian society was primitive without the veneer of decrepit civilization; compared with Merovingian society, which was a sort of sterile hybrid, it had fewer pretensions but perhaps fewer of the ills of a pretentious civilization." (22)

11. Ibid., 27.

12. Einhard, *Life of Charlemagne*, trans. E. E. Turner (New York: American Book Co., 1880) in Charles T. Davis, ed., *The Eagle, The Crescent, and The Cross* (New York: Appleton-Century-Crofts, 1967), 210.

13. Ibid., 206.

14. John McManners, ed., *The Oxford Illustrated History of Christianity* (New York: Oxford University Press, 1990), 101.

15. Joseph H. Lynch, *The Medieval Church: A Brief History* (New York: Longman, 1992), 101.

16. Barraclough, *The Crucible of Europe*, 78.

17. O'Sullivan and Burns, *Medieval Europe*, 427.

18. Tierney, *The Crisis of Church and State*, 27.

19. Nicholas I, *Epistle* 86 (PL 119:960).

20. Lowrie Daly, *Benedictine Monasticism* (New York: Sheed and Ward, 1965), 157.

21. The works of both Radbertus and Ratramnus are available in English translation in the *Library of Christian Classics* Vol. IX, ed. G. McCracken and A. Catanius (Philadelphia: Westminster Press, 1957), *Early Medieval Theology*.

22. Jaroslav Pelikan, *The Growth of Medieval Theology* (Chicago: The University of Chicago Press, 1978), 80–81.

23. John of Damascus, *On Holy Images*, in Barry Coleman, *Readings in Church History*, 1:309ff. John of Damascus continues, "We have passed the stage of infancy

and reached the perfection of our manhood. . . . When He who is a pure spirit, without form or limit. . . existing as God, takes the form of a servant in substance and stature, then you may draw His likeness, and show it to anyone willing to contemplate it. The worship of *latreia* is one thing, and the worship given to merit is another."

24. Photius, *Encyclical Letter* (866), in Barry Coleman, *Readings in Church History*, 1:316–18. See Francis Dvornik, *The Photian Schism* (Cambridge: University Press, 1948).

25. The Second Vatican Council (1963–65) addressed itself to the schism in the decree on Eastern Catholic Churches. The decree is positive and irenic, and it has been received by the Orthodox community with rejoicing. Yet some obstacles still remain, including the presence of Uniate churches. As a gesture of good faith, Pope Paul VI and Patriarch Athanagoras on Dec. 7, 1965, in solemn ceremonies at St. Peter's in Rome and at Hagia Sophia in Istanbul, nullified the actions of their predecessors in 1054, thus opening the way for free discussions.

26. See ch. 1, pp. 21ff.

27. Leo VI, *Epanagoge*, in Deno J. Geanakoplos, *Byzantine East and Latin West* (New York: Harper, 1966), 56.

28. Leo III, *Ecloga*, pref. in J. M. Hussey, *The Byzantine World* (New York: Harper, 1961), 86.

29. John of Damascus, *The Orthodox Faith* III, 4, in Hugh T. Kerr, ed., *Readings in Christian Thought* (Nashville: Abingdon, 1966), 71–72.

30. Steven Runciman, *Byzantine Civilization* (London: Edward Arnold, 1933), 134–35.

Chapter 4

1. Norman F. Cantor, *Medieval History—The Life and Death of A Civilization* (New York: MacMillan, 1969), 271. "The period from 1050 to 1130 was dominated by an attempt at world revolution which influenced in highly effective ways the other aspects of social change. It seems, in retrospect, that it was almost necessary for a revolutionary onslaught to shake to its foundations the order of the early middle ages" (272). For more nuanced assessments see Schafer Williams, *The Gregorian Epoch*, in *Problems in European Civilization* (Boston: C. D. Heath, 1964).

2. Geoffrey Barraclough, *The Medieval Papacy* (London: Thames and Hudson, 1969), 73.

3. Ibid., 74.

4. Orderic Vitalis, *The Ecclesiastical History*, book 2, ch. 162, ed. and trans. Marjorie Chibnall, cited in Joseph H. Lynch, *The Medieval Church: A Brief History* (New York: Longman, 1992), 139. See also Ann Llewellyn Barstow, *Married Priests and the Reforming Papacy: The Eleventh Century Debates, Texts and Studies in Religion* 12 (New York: E. Mellon Press, 1982); Charles Frazee, "The Origins of Clerical Celibacy in the Western Church," *Church History*, (Chicago: American Society of Church History, 1972), 149-67, vol. 36.

5. "Decree of Pope Nicholas II on Papal Elections," in James A. Corbett, *The Papacy* (New York: D. Van Nostrand, 1956), 101.

6. Barraclough,*The Medieval Papacy*, 77.

7. T. M. Parker, *Christianity and the State in the Light of History* (New York: Harper, 1955), cited in Williams, *The Gregorian Epoch*, 89.

8. See G. Tellenbach, *Church, State, and Christian Society at the Time of the Investiture Contest* (Oxford: Basil Blackwell, 1940); Norman F. Cantor, "The Crisis of Western Monasticism, 1050–1130," *American Historical Review*, vol. 66, 1960, pp. 47–64; Schafer Williams, *The Gregorian Epoch*; Karl F. Morrison, *The Investiture Controversy* (New York: Holt, Rinehart, and Winston, 1971).

9. Mansi XX, 442, cited in William R. Cannon, *History of Christianity in the Middle Ages*, (Nashville: Abingdon, 1960), 162.

10. In Brian Tierney, *The Crisis of Church and State* (Englewood Cliffs, N.J.: Prentice Hall, 1964), 51.

11. The entire list of declarations is in Lynch,*The Medieval Church*, 147–48; also see Knowles and Obolensky, *The Middle Ages* (New York: McGraw-Hill, 1968), 175 note 2.

12. David Knowles, *The Evolution of Medieval Thought* (London: Longmans, 1963), 175.

13. Tierney, *The Crisis of Church and State*, 59.

14. Ibid.

15. J. W. Thompson and E. N. Johnson, *An Introduction to Medieval Europe* (New York: Norton, 1964), 386

16. Tierney, *The Crisis of Church and State 1050–1300*, 74.

17. Ibid., 77.

18. Ibid., 80.

19. "Urban II's Call To The First Crusade, 1095," in Barry, *Readings in Church History*, 1:328.

20. Margaret Deanesly, *A History of The Medieval Church* (London: Methuen, 1962), 105.

21. Robert S. Hoyt and Stanley Chodorow, *Europe In The Middle Ages* (New York: Harcourt, Brace, and Jovanovich, 1976), 316.

22. Peter Charanis, "A Greek Source on the Origin of the First Crusade," *Speculum* 24 (1949): 93, "Considering it impossible to defeat the Turks alone, Alexius saw that he would have to call in the Italians as allies, which he did with cunning, adroitness, and deep-laid planning. Realizing that westerners found unbearable the domination of Jerusalem by the Turks, he managed by dispatching ambassadors to the bishop of Old Rome and to kings and rulers of the western parts, by the use of appropriate arguments, to prevail over not a few of them to leave their own countries, and he succeeded in directing them to the task which he had in mind."

23. Cannon, *History of Christianity in the Middle Ages*, 169.

24. Anna Comnena, "A Greek View of the Crusades," in J. B. Ross and M. M. McLaughlin, eds., *The Portable Medieval Reader* (New York: Viking, c. 1949, 11th printing, 1960), 444–46.

25. Archbp. Daimbert, Duke Godfrey, Count Raymon, *Letter to Paschal II* (1099), in Barry, *Readings in Church History*, 1:330.

26. Fulcher of Chartres, cited in Anne Fremantle, ed., *Age of Faith* (New York: Time-Life, 1965), 58.

27. Steven Runciman, *Byzantine Civilization* (London: Edward Arnold, 1933), 54–55.

28. Henry Treece, *The Crusades* (New York: Mentor Books, 1962), 113, writes that, "the crusades hastened many changes . . . smaller estates were broken up and made into larger units," in part because some crusaders failed to return home. "Often the fiefs passed into the hands of remaining daughters, and so by marriage passed to other families." Treece also suggests that "a more liberal frame of mind," in the sense of a greater toleration for new ideas took over in the West as a result of the experiences which the crusaders had in the East. In recent years historians have understood the legacy of the Crusades far more negatively than before. See Williston Walker, et al., *A History of The Christian Church*, 290, for a discussion of the totally negative results of the Crusades.

29. See Ernst Sackur, "The Influence of the Cluniac Movement," (13–18) ("Cluny needed the temporal power too much to develop ideas which aimed at complete emancipation from it.") and David Knowles, "The Cluniacs in England," (37–42) in Schafer Williams, *The Gregorian Epoch,*

30. Peter the Venerable, *De Miraculis* II, 28 (PL 189:943), cited in Herbert B. Workman, *The Evolution of the Monastic Ideal* (Boston: Beacon, 1913), 251.

31. Ailred of Rivaulz, *Speculum Caritatis,* II, 17 (PL 195:562f.), cited in O'Sullivan and Burns, *Medieval Europe,* 288.

32. C. H. Lawrence, *Medieval Monasticism,* 180; ch. 9, 174–205, is an excellent introduction to the Cistercian Order. See also L. J. Lekai, *The White Monks* (Okauchea, Wis.: Our Lady of Spring Brook, 1953); David Knowles, *The Monastic Order in England* (Cambridge: Cambridge University Press, 1963), 209–26; Daly, *Benedictine Monasticism,* 173–93; Archdale King, *Citeaux And Her Elder Daughters* (London: Burns and Oats, 1954).

33. Knowles, *The Monastic Order in England,* 212. "The *Carta Charitatis* is a masterpiece, which created in a few pregnant pages all the machinery of a great order. It is one of the small group of documents that have influenced, in the course of the church's history, the constitutional history of all religious bodies subsequent to their composition."

34. Conrad of Eberbach, *Magnum Exordium,* cited in Lawrence, *Medieval Monasticism,* p. 182.

35. For these statistics Lawrence, ibid., cites F. Vongrey and F. Hervay, "Notes critiques sur l'Atlas de l'Ordre Cistercien" in ASOC 23 (1967): 115–52.

36. Bernard of Clairvaux, *On Grace and Free Will* 12, cited in Jaroslav Pelikan, *The Growth of Medieval Theology 600–1300,* 156.On Bernard and grace see also Franz Posset, "The Elder Luther on Bernard," *The American Benedictine Review* 42:1 and 2 (March and June, 1991). Cf. Carl Volz, "Martin Luther's Attitude Toward Bernard of Clairvaux," in Joseph O'Callahan, ed., *Studies in Medieval Cistercian History* (Spencer: Cistercian Publications, 1971), 186–204.

37. Bernard, *PL* 183:995, cited in Gordon Leff, *Medieval Thought: Saint Augustine to Ockham* (Baltimore: Penguin, 1958), 96.

38. M. D. Knowles, *Cistercians and Cluniacs* (Oxford: Oxford University Press, 1955), 5.

Chapter 5

1. Geoffrey Barraclough, *The Medieval Papacy* (London: Thames and Hudson, 1968), 99.

2. R. W. Southern, *Western Society and the Church in the Middle Ages* (Baltimore: Penguin, 1970), 109.

3. On the role of law in medieval society see Walter Ullmann, *Law and Politics in the Middle Ages* (Ithaca: Cornell University Press, 1975). By the same author, *The Growth of Papal Government in the Middle Ages*, (London: Methuen, 1955), and *A Short History of the Papacy in the Middle Ages* (London: Methuen, 1972).

4. R. W. Southern, *Western Society and the Church in the Middle Ages*, 117, "It is remarkable how little business the popes initiated in the great days of growth. They had no need to initiate. The business rushed upon them; they had only to invent the rules and reach the decisions."

5. *De Consideratione*, I, i-ii (PL 182:727–31).

6. *Epistolae Cantiarienses*, cited in Southern, *Western Society and the Church in the Middle Ages*, 118, 119.

7. *Venerabilem* (1202), (Decretales 1.6.34), cited in Tierney, *The Crisis of the Church and State*, 134.

8. *Novit* (1204; Decretales 2.1.13), cited in Tierney, *The Crisis of the Church and State*, 135.

9. See C. H. McIlwain, "To Determine a Matter of Sin," in James M. Powell, ed., *Innocent III: Vicar of Christ or Lord of the World?* (Boston: D. C. Heath and Co., 1963), 27–29.

10. "Letter to the prefect Acerbus and the nobles of Tuscany," (1198; PL 214:377).

11. L. Elliot-Binns, *Innocent III* (London: Methuen, 1931), 164. On church councils see also 150–51.

12. All citations from the Fourth Lateran Council are in Barry, *Readings in Church History*, 1:439–46. On the doctrinal work of the council see Hamilton Thompson, "Medieval Doctrine to the Lateran Council of 1215," *Cambridge Medieval History*, 2nd ed., 6:634ff. Elliot-Binns comments, "[At Lateran IV] it is definitely laid down that the bread becomes the body and the wine the blood of the Lord. This seems to be inconsistent with the later view that the bread and the wine contained each the complete Christ. 'The entire Christ is received under either species,' as St. Thomas states it" (*Innocent III*, 164).

13. See James Powell, *Innocent III: Vicar of Christ or Lord of the World?* (Boston: D. C. Heath, 1963), which contains articles by ten medieval scholars, each with a different interpretation of Innocent's pontificate. See also Colin Morris, *The Papal Monarchy: The Western Church from 1050–1250* (Oxford: Oxford University Press 1989); Christopher R. Cheney, *Pope Innocent III and England* (Oxford: Clarendon Press, 1976).

14. Barraclough, *The Medieval Papacy*, 114–17.

15. Gelasius, "Letter to the Byzantine Emperor, Anastasius I," (494), in Barry, *Readings in Church History*, 1:147.

16. Gelasius, "Letter to the Byzantine Emperor, Anastasius I," in Tierney, *The Crisis of Church and State*, 15.

17. Thietmar of Merseburg, in G. Tellenbach, *Church, State, and Christian Society at the Time of the Investiture Contest* (Oxford: Basil Blackwood, 1966), 59.

18. Hugh of Fleury, in ibid., 149.

19. "The Anonymous of York," in Tierney,*The Crisis of Church and State*, 78.

20. Joseph H. Lynch, *The Medieval Church: A Brief History* (New York: Longman, 1992), 143.

21. Margaret Gibson discusses this possibility in *Lanfranc of Bec* (Oxford: The Clarendon Press, 1978), 133–35.

22. *The Anglo-Saxon Chronicle*, in W. O. Hassell, ed. and trans., *Medieval England as Viewed by Contemporaries* (New York: Harper, 1965), 49.

23. Gibson, *Lanfranc of Bec*, 137.

24. "The Constitutions of Clarendon" (1164), in Barry, *Readings in Church History*, 1:425.

25. Ibid., 428.

26. Brian Tierney, *The Crisis of Church and State 1050-1350* (Englewood Cliffs, N.J.: Prentice Hall, 1964), 114.

27. David Knowles, *Thomas Becket* (London: Adam and Charles Black, 1970), 103.

28. Ibid., 155. On Becket, see Beryl Smalley, *The Becket Controversy and the Schools* (Oxford: Blackwells, 1973).

29. Walter Ullman, *A Short History of the Papacy in the Middle Ages*, 214.

30. The text of the Magna Carta is in Norton Downs, *Basic Documents in Medieval History* (New York: D. Van Nostrand, 1959), 121–31.

31. Ullmann, *A Short History of the Papacy in the Middle Ages*, 271. "In withering tones the English parliament and Edward I rejected the papal claim that Scotland was a papal fief: the claim was 'unheard of,' 'strange,' and 'prejudicial,' to royal interests."

32. Knowles and Obolensky, *The Middle Ages*, 204.

33. Arthur Tilley, *Medieval France* (New York: Hafner, 1964), 56.

34. Joinville, *Chronicle*, trans. in James Bruce Ross and Mary Martin McLaughlin, *The Portable Medieval Reader* (New York: Viking, c. 1949), 372–73.

35. Tilley,*Medieval France*, 63. O'Sullivan and Burns write, "The clergy in France, just as in England and Germany, were not spared royal compulsions. Yet France escaped the bitterness of the struggle between Empire and Papacy which engulfed Germany. There were remonstrances from time to time . . . [but] the timeliness of Louis IX's reign, mildly coercive and religious in character dissipated many antagonistic feelings," *Medieval Europe*, 474

36. *The Digest of Justinian* (533), cited in Tierney, The Crisis of Church and State, 102.

37. J. W. Thompson and E. N. Johnson, *An Introduction to Medieval Europe* (New York: Norton, 1937), 386.

38. Ibid., 400–401.

39. Ibid., 423–24.

40. Ibid., 424.

41. "Letter of Frederick to the kings of Christendom," (1246), in J. Guillard-Briholles, ed., *Historia Diplomatica Friderici Secundi*, VI, I (Paris: np, 1860), 391–93, cited in Tierney, *The Crisis of Church and State*, 146.

42. Robert S. Hoyt and Stanley Chodorow, *Europe in the Middle Ages*, 474–75.

43. The seven German "electors" whose power to elect the emperor stemmed

from the collapse of the Hohenstaufen dynasty were the Archbishops of Mainz, Trier, and Cologne, the King of Bohemia, the count Palatine of the Rhine, the duke of Saxony, and the margrave of Brandenburg, all four lay electors being officers of the imperial household. These electors played a crucial role in the sixteenth century Reformation struggles in Germany.

44. Ullman, *The Growth of Papal Government in the Middle Ages* (London: Methuen and Co., 1962), 455.

45. Thomas Aquinas, "On Kingship," (1260–1265), cited in Tierney, *The Crisis of Church and State*, 168.

Chapter 6

1. For the Renaissance of the twelfth century, see: Charles Homer Haskins, *The Renaissance of the Twelfth Century* (Cambridge: Harvard University Press, 1927); Charles R. Young, ed., *The Twelfth-Century Renaissance* (New York: Holt, Rinehart, and Winston, 1969); Richard W. Southern, *The Making of the Middle Ages* (New Haven, Conn.: Yale University Press, 1961), 193–215; Eva Matthews Sanford, "The Twelfth Century: Renaissance or Proto-Renaissance?" *Speculum*, 26 (1951): 635–41; Peter Dronke, ed., *A History of Twelfth-Century Western Philosophy* (Cambridge: Cambridge University Press, 1988).

2. Williston Walker, et al., *A History of the Christian Church*, 325.

3. Peter Damian, in Gordon Leff, *Medieval Thought: St. Augustine to Ockham* (Baltimore: Penguin, 1958), 96.

4. Anselm, *Proslogion* I, in Barry, *Readings in Church History* 1:358.

5. Ibid., 359.

6. On Anselm, see R. W. Southern, *Saint Anselm and His Biographer: A Study of Monastic Life and Thought 1059–1130* (Cambridge: The University Press, 1963); John McIntyre, *St. Anselm and His Critics: A Reinterpretation of the Cur Deus Homo* (Edinburgh: Olive and Boyd, 1954); Charles Hartshorne, *Anselm's Discovery: A Re-Examination of the Ontological Proof for God's Existence* (LaSalle: Open Court, 1965).

7. Lowrie J. Daly, "Abelard Writes *Sic et Non*," in Frank N. Magill, ed., *Great Events From History* (Englewood Cliffs, N.J.: Salem, 1972), 3:1313.

8. Abelard, *Sic et Non*, (PL 178:1350), in Roland Bainton, *The Medieval Church* (New York: D. Van Nostrand, 1962), 130.

9. Leff, *Medieval Thought*, 112.

10. A. V. Murray, *Abelard and St. Bernard* (Manchester: Manchester University Press, 1967), is sympathetic to Abelard, who remains honest in the face of Bernard's "unscrupulous efforts." In Magill, *Great Events from History* 3:1316. Cf. Peter Sikes, *Peter Abelard* (New York: Russell and Russell, 1965).

11. Abelard, *Letter to Heloise* 17 (PL 178:375), in Knowles, *The Evolution of Medieval Thought*, 123.

12. Knowles, *The Evolution of Medieval Thought*, 129–30.

13. See bibliography in Peter Dronke, *Twelfth-Century Western Philosophy*, 443–86; Etienne Gilson, *Reason and Revelation in the Middle Ages* (New York: Scribner's, 1938).

14. Hugh of St. Victor, PL 176:330, in Knowles, *The Evolution of Medieval Thought*, 144.

15. Knowles, *The Evolution of Medieval Thought*, 146.

16. Leff, *Medieval Thought*, 212.

17. Thomas Aquinas, *Summa Contra Gentiles*, in Hugh T. Kerr, *Readings in Christian Thought* (Nashville: Abingdon, 1966), 109.

18. Thomas Aquinas, *Summa Theologica*, I, Quest. 2, A. 3. in Kerr, *Readings in Christian Thought*, 113.

19. Thomas Aquinas, *Summa Contra Gentiles*, I, 3, 5, in Robert Ferm, trans., *Readings in the History of Christian Thought* (New York: Holt, Rinehart, and Winston, 1964), 466–67.

20. Joseph M. Victor, "Condemnation of Christian Averroism," in Frank N. Magill, *Great Events from History* 3:1565.

21. Ibid.

22. Etienne Gilson, *Reason and Revelation in the Middle Ages*, sees the condemnations of 1277 as justified and beneficial; P. Vignaux, *Philosophy in the Middle Ages* (New York: World, 1959), understands the condemnations as the culmination of a professional dispute between two legitimate systems of thought.

23. See ch. 1, p. 19.

24. Helene Wieruszowski, *The Medieval University* (New York: D. Van Nostrand, 1966), 123.

25. In addition to Wieruszowski, see C. H. Haskins, *The Rise of Universities* (Ithaca, N.Y.: Great Seals Books, 1957–1962); Hastings Rashdall, *The Universities of Europe in the Middle Ages*, 3 vols. (Oxford: Clarendon Press, 1936); Helen Waddell, *The Wandering Scholars* (London: Constable and Co., 1934; Garden City, N.Y.: Doubleday and Co., 1961); "The Rise of the Universities," in B. Tierney, D. Kagan, L. Pearce Williams, eds. *Great Issues in Western Civilization* (New York: Random House, 1967), 1:352–65; Lowrie Daly, *The Medieval University* (New York: Sheed and Ward, 1961).

26. "King Henry III of England Confirms Privileges" in Wieruszowski, *The Medieval University*, 157.

27. Wieruszowski, *The Medieval University*, 63.

28. Ibid., 109.

29. Jacques de Vitry, in Wieruszowski, *The Medieval University*, 114.

30. Celano, *Vita Prima*, p. 19, in C. H. Lawrence, *Medieval Monasticism*, 2nd Ed. (London: Longman, 1990), 246.

31. R. W. Southern, *Western Society and the Church in the Middle Ages*, 282.

32. "St. Francis of Assisi: Second Rule of the Friars Minor Approved Pope Honorius III, 29 November 1223," in Barry, *Readings in Church History* 1:418–19.

33. On Francis, in addition to C. H. Lawrence, see R. H. Moorman, *A History of the Franciscan Order from its Origins to the Year 1517* (Oxford:Clarendon Press, 1968); Marion A. Habig, ed., *St. Francis of Assisi: Writings and Early Biographies* (Chicago: Franciscan Herald Press, 1978), 1–176.

34. Lawrence, *Medieval Monasticism*, 254–55. Walker, *et al.*, *History of the Christian Church*, 312: "It was the most highly developed constitutional system known in the thirteenth century."

35. Southern, *Western Society and the Church in the Middle Ages*, 298–99.

36. In Daniel-Rops, *Cathedral and Crusade* I (Garden City, N.Y.: Image, 1957), 204.

On conflict between mendicants and parish clergy see Lawrence, *Medieval Monasticism*, 261–63.

37. Arthur Tilley, *Medieval France* (New York: Hafner, 1964), 56.

38. On the Albigensian Crusade see Gordon Leff, *Heresy in the Later Middle Ages*, Vol. 2 (New York: Russell & Russell, 1928); Joseph R. Strayer, *The Albigensian Crusade* (New York:Dial Press, 1971); Jonathan Sumption, *The Albigensian Crusade* (London: Faber and Faber, 1978).

39. On the Waldensians see Malcolm Lambert, *Medieval Heresy: Popular Movements from Bogomil to Hus* (London, 1977), 3–178.

40. Bernard Hamilton, *Religion in the Medieval West* (London: Edward Arnold, 1986), 174.

41. See Norman Cohn, *The Pursuit of the Millenium: Revolutionary Messianism in Medieval and Reformation Europe and its Bearing on Modern Totalitarian Movements* (London: Mercury, 1962).

42. On the Inquisition see Bernard Hamilton, *The Medieval Inquisition* (New York: Holmes and Meier, 1981); Arthur Turberville, *Medieval Heresy and The Inquisition* (London: Archon Books, 1964); G. G. Coulton, *Inquisition and Liberty* (Boston: Beacon, 1959).

43. Hamilton, *Religion in the Medieval West*, 177.

Chapter 7

1. See Denys Hay, *Europe: The Emergence of an Idea* (Edinburgh: University of Edinburgh Press, 1957); Southern, *The Making of the Middle Ages*; Christopher Dawson, *The Making of Europe*.

2. Eudes of Rouen, "Episcopal Visitations," in James Ross and Mary McLaughlin, eds., *The Portable Medieval Reader* (New York: Viking, 1960), 79. See also Jeremiah F. O'Sullivan, ed., *The Register of Eudes of Rouen* (New York: Columbia University Press, 1964).

3. Eudes, "Episcopal Visitations," 81.

4. O'Sullivan, ed., *The Register of Eudes of Rouen*.

5. "Decree of Pope Nicolas II," in Donald White, ed., *Medieval History: A Source Book* (Homewood: Dorsey, 1965), 309: "When the Pontiff of the Universal Roman Church dies, the Cardinal-Bishops shall first take counsel together with most diligent consideration, thereupon call into themselves the Cardinal-Clerics and then, in the same manner, the remaining clergy and people shall approach to express their consent to the new election."

6. "Decree of the Lateran Council of 1179 Concerning Papal Elections," in Ernest Henderson, ed., *Select Historical Documents of the Middle Ages* (London: G. Bell and Sons, 1916), 337.

7. Adam of Usk, "The Election and Coronation of a Pope," in Ross and McLaughlin, *The Portable Medieval Reader*, 236.

8. Knowles and Oblensky, *The Middle Ages*, 230.

9. Theodosian Code I, 27, cited in O'Sullivan and Burns, *Medieval Europe*, 192.

10. See ch. 5, p. 95.

11. This description follows that of Theodor Klauser, *A Short History of the Western Liturgy* (Oxford: Oxford University Press, 1979).

12. Rosalind and Christopher Brooke, *Popular Religion in the Middle Ages* (London: Thames and Hudson, 1984), 116.

13. Klauser, *A Short History of the Western Liturgy*, 75.

14. Ibid., 77. Cf. Knowles and Oblensky, *The Middle Ages*, 148: "Thus it may be said that whereas from the fifth to the end of the seventh century Rome was a center of creative liturgical composition, the initiative thereafter was taken by the Gallic church, and the resulting amalgam was in large part adopted by the Roman curia and then once more transmitted to the western church."

15. Yngve Torg Brilioth, *A Short History of Preaching* (Philadelphia: Fortress, 1965), 75. Cf. H. Leith Spencer, *English Preaching in the Late Middle Ages* (Oxford: Clarendon, 1993); William Skudlarek, "Assertion Without Knowledge: The Lay Preaching Crisis of the High Middle Ages," Ph.D. Thesis, Princeton Theological Seminary, 1976.

16. H. Daniel-Rops, *Cathedral and Crusade* II (Garden City, N.Y.: Image, 1963), 65–66.

17. Honorius of Autun, *Speculium ecclesia* (PL 172:830). See also Carl Volz, "Honorius Augustodunensis: Twelfth Century Enigma" (Ph.D. diss., Fordham University, 1966), 137–41; Henry Osborne Taylor (Cambridge: Harvard University Press, 1951), 2:76–85.

18. For medieval hymnody see James Mearns, *Early Latin Hymnaries, An Index of Hymns before 1100* (Cambridge: University Press, 1913); *Latin Hymns of the Middle Ages* (New York: Hymn Society of America, 1948); *Hymni Latini medii aevi* (3 vols.) ed. J. Mone (Freiburg im Breisgau: Herder, 1853–1855).

19. Rosalind and Christopher Brooke, *Popular Religion in the Middle Ages*, 109.

20. *The Martrdom of Polycarp*, ch. 18, in Cyril C. Richardson, ed., *Early Christian Fathers* (New York: MacMillan, 1970), 156: "Afterwards we took up his bones, more precious than the most exquisite jewels and more pure than gold, and deposited them in a fitting place, where with joy and rejoicing we celebrate the birthday of his martyrdom."

21. Canon XV (PL 84:212), cited by Adriaan Bredero, *Christendom and Christianity in the Middle Ages* trans. Reinder Bruinsma (Grand Rapids: Eerdmans, 1994), 160.

22. Ibid., 181.

23. Hubert Cunliffe-Jones, *A History of Christian Doctrine* (Philadelphia: Fortress, 1978), 254–56.

24. Gerald Simons, et al., eds., *Barbarian Europe* (New York: Time-Life Books, 1968), 90.

25. Guibert of Nogent, *Vita sua*, 3.12 (PL 156:938), cited by Pelikan, *The Growth of Medieval Theology*, 181.

26. R. A. Markus, "How on Earth Could Places Become Holy? Origins of the Christian Idea of Holy Places," *Journal of Early Christian Studies* 2:3 (1993): 270. See also Robert Wilken, *The Land Called Holy* (New Haven: Yale University Press, 1992); P. W. L. Walker, *Holy City, Holy Places? Christian Attitudes to Jerusalem and the Holy Land in the Fourth Century*, Oxford Early Christian Studies (Oxford: Clarendon, 1990).

27. Rosalind and Christopher Brooke, *Popular Religion in the Middle Ages*, 26–27.

28. Jaroslav Pelikan, *The Growth of Medieval Theology*, 133.

29. Agobard of Lyons, *Liber adverusus legem Gundovalde* (PL 104:114).

30. Roland Bainton, *The Medieval Church* (New York: Van Nostrand, 1962), 62.

31. Rosalind and Christopher Brooke, *Popular Religion in the Middle Ages*, 130.

32. Henry of Ghent, *Commentary on the Sentences*, 4.

33. See Beryl Smalley, *The Study of the Bible in the Middle Ages* (Notre Dame: Notre Dame University Press, 1964). See pp. 215 ff. for a discussion of this crisis.

34. "The Council of Toulouges-Rousillon in 1027" (Mansi 19:483), cited in Bredero, *Christendom and Christianity in the Middle Ages*, 109.

35. Bredero, *Christendom and Christianity in the Middle Ages*, 129.

36. See Henry C. Lea, *The History of Sacerdotal Celibacy in the Christian Church* (New York: Russell and Russell, 1957); Charles A. Frazee, "The Origins of Clerical Celibacy in the Western Church," *Church History*, (June 1972): "A list of the canons of St. Paul's in London shows that in the eleventh century one-fourth were married, and sons were inheriting the positions of their fathers."

37. Bredero, *Christendom and Christianity in the Middle Ages*, 286. Friedrich Heer, *The Medieval World* (New York: The New American Library, 1962), 310, writes "Until [the Crusades] outbursts of anti-Semitism in western Europe had been rare and sporadic. But now the omens were unmistakable."

38. Abbot Suger of St. Denis, "The Construction of the Church at St. Denis," in Bainton, *The Medieval Church*, 134. The spirit of the Middle Ages is revealed through a study of Gothic cathedrals in Henry Adams, *Mont-Saint-Michel and Chartres* (New York: Mentor, 1961).

39. Ibid.

40. On monastic influences, see Daly, *Benedictine Monasticism*, 245–320.

Chapter 8

1. Steven Ozment, *The Age of Reform 1250–1550* (New Haven: Yale University Press, 1980), 8.

2. Henri Pirenne, *Economic and Social History of Medieval Europe* (New York: Harcourt, Brace, 1938), 193.

3. Daniel Waley, *Later Medieval Europe* (New York: Barnes and Noble, 1964), 99.

4. M. Postan and E. E. Rich, eds., *Cambridge Economic History of Europe* (Cambridge: Cambridge University Press, 1952), 2:339.

5. Edward P. Cheyney, *The Dawn of a New Era 1250–1453* (New York: Harper, 1936), 116–17.

6. Giovani Boccaccio, *The Decameron*, trans. Mark Musa and Peter Bondanella (New York: W. W. Norton, 1982), 11.

7. Cheyney, *The Dawn of a New Era*, 263.

8. Christopher Allmand, *The Hundred Years' War* (Cambridge: Cambridge University Press, 1988), 33.

9. Anne Curry, *The Hundred Years' War* (New York: St. Martin's, 1993), 135. Curry provides an excellent summary of the results of the Hundred Years' War on pp. 122–55.

10. Ibid., 136.

11. Anna Montgomery Campbell, *The Black Death and Men of Learning* (New York: Columbia University, 1931), 133, citing F. Seebohm, "The Black Death and Its place in English History," *Fortnightly Review*, Sept. 1865, 149–60.

12. Campbell, *The Black Death*, 134.

13. Conrad Eubel, *Hierarchia catholica Medii Aevi* (Muenster: np, 1913), 1:15–19, cited in Campbell, *The Black Death*, 135.

14. George G. Coulton, *The Black Death*, (New York: Robert M. McBride, nd. c. 1930).

15. Campbell, *The Black Death*, especially ch. 6, 146–80.

16. William of S. Thierry's suggestions anticipate the magesterial study of Jean LeClercq, *The Love of Learning and the Desire for God: A Study of Monastic Culture*, trans. Catharine Misrah (New York: Fordham University Press, 1961).

17. See pp. 124–25.

18. Friedrich Heer, *The Medieval World*, trans. Janet Sondheimer (New York: New American Library, 1961), 320.

19. For a fuller treatment of these persecutions see Ernest W. McDonnell, *The Beguines and Beghards in Medieval Culture* (New Brunswick: Rutgers University Press, 1954). On Marguerite Porete see *The Mirror of Simple Souls*, trans. by Ellen Babinsky (New York: Paulist, 1993).

20. Friedrich Heer, *The Medieval World*, 375. Steven Ozment, "Homo Viator: Luther and the Late Medieval Theology," in Steven Ozment, ed., *The Reformation in Medieval Perspective* (Chicago: Quadrangle, 1971), 147: "The parallel [of Tauler] with Luther is remarkable. In place of Luther's *Christus incarnatus* we find the simplicity of God, and in place of Luther's *fides* we find the *unio mystica* . . . . The result is identical with Luther's Reformation discovery."

21. G. H. W. Parker, *The Morning Star: Wycliffe and the Dawn of The Reformation* (Grand Rapids: Eerdmans, 1965), 142.

22. Evelyn Underhill, *The Mystics of the Church* (New York: Schocken, 1964), 136–37.

23. Albert Hyma, *The Christian Renaissance: A History of the Devotio Moderna* (New York: The Century Company, 1924), 320.

24. Hyma, *The Christian Renaissance*, 141. On the "New Devotion" also see E. F. Jacob, "Gerard Groote and the Beginnings of the 'New Devotion' in the Low Countries," *Journal of Ecclesiastical History* III (1952), 40–57; Regnerus Richardus Post, *The Modern Devotion: Confrontation with Reformation and Humanism* (Leidan: Brill, 1968).

25. Hyma, *The Christian Renaissance*, 158–70.

26. Parker, *The Morning Star*, 144.

27. Hyma, *The Christian Renaissance*, 134.

28. Evelyn Underhill, *The Mystics of The Church*, 119. For background on the English mystics we are in debt to this study and to David Knowles, *The English Mystic Tradition* (New York: Harper, 1961).

29. Ibid., 120.

30. Ibid., 130.

31. Ibid., 131.

32. Much material is available on the origins of the term "Renaissance." Henry S. Lucas, *The Renaissance and the Reformation* (New York: Harper, 1934), 207–9: "[The term] has varied from time to time. At the close of the sixteenth century it meant the revival of Latin and Greek letters . . . [It] also connoted dislike of the culture of the Middle Ages and even hostility to it." Waley, *Later Medieval Europe*, 167, points

out that "the concept of an age of the Renaissance was the product of the age itself—indeed it states the period's estimate of itself." Margaret Aston, *The Fifteenth Century* (London: Harcourt, Brace and World, 1968), 178 says the term itself and its German counterpart, *Wiedererwachsung*, were first used in the sixteenth century.

33. Margaret Aston, *The Fifteenth Century*, 177.

34. Ibid., 182–83.

35. C. H. Lawrence, *Medieval Monasticism* (London: Longman, 1989), 27. See Helen Wadell, *The Wandering Scholars* (Ann Arbor: University of Michigan Press, 1989)

36. Aston, *The Fifteenth Century*, 173. Wolfhart Pannenberg, "Christianity and the West: Ambiguous Past, Uncertain Future," *First Things* (December 1994), 18, comments on the dependence of the Renaissance on Christianity. "Throughout the medieval period, classical literature and philosophy were transmitted by monks and Christian schools. It is doubtful whether much of the classical culture would have survived had it not been appropriated by Christianity. . . . The classical legacy was disseminated throughout the world along with the faith of the Church."

37. Roland H. Bainton, *The Medieval Church* (New York: D. Van Nostrand Co., Inc., 1962), 76.

38. Cited by Aston, *The Fifteenth Century*, 157.

39. James Westfall Thompson, *The Literacy of the Laity in the Middle Ages* (New York: Burt Franklin, 1960), 54.

40. Walter Ullmann., *The Individual and Society in the Middle Ages* (Baltimore: Johns Hopkins, 1966), 116. See also Ernst Cassirer, *The Individual and the Cosmos in Renaissance Philosophy* (Philadelphia: University of Pennsylvania Press, 1963).

41. Ernst Cassirer, Paul Kristeller, and John Randall, eds., *The Renaissance Philosophy of Man* (Chicago: University of Chicago Press, 1948), 17.

42. Ullmann, *The Individual and Society*, 150.

43. See pp. 68ff.

44. Speros Vryonis, *Byzantium and Europe* (London: Thames and Hudson, 1967), 126.

45. Vryonis, *Byzantium and Europe*, 132, "This process (of settlement in Anatolia) which was to last four hundred years, marks one of the great turning points of world history, since it was the basic factor in the transition from the Byzantine to the Ottoman Empire."

46. John Meyendorff, *The Orthodox Church* (Crestwood, N.Y.: St. Vladimir Seminary Press, 1981), 56. Timothy Ware, *The Orthodox Church* (Baltimore: Penguin, 1964), 71, "The Fourth Crusade inflicted a blow (on Constantinople) which proved mortal in the end."

47. Basil of Caesarea, *Letter 234:1*.

48. Robert Browning, *The Byzantine Empire* (Washington, DC: Catholic University of America Press, 1980), 238.

49. On the Council of Florence (1438–1439) see Deno Geanakoplos, "The Council of Florence (1438–1439) and the Problem of Union Between the Byzantine and Latin Churches," in *Byzantine East and Latin West*, 85–111.

50. Donald Nicol, *Church and Society in the Last Centuries of Byzantium* (Cambridge: Cambridge University Press, 1979), 115.

51. Steven Runciman, *Byzantine Civilization* (London: Edward Arnold and Co., 1948), 299.

Chapter 9

1. Shepard B. Clough, Nina Garsoian, David L. Hicks, *A History of the Western World: Ancient and Medieval*, 2nd. ed. (Lexington: D. C. Heath, 1969), 360.

2. Philip Hughes, "Benedict Gaetani: The Church's Salvation," in Charles T. Wood, ed., *Philip the Fair and Boniface VIII*, European Problem Studies (New York: Holt, Rinehart and Winston, 1967), 24. For other studies see Thomas S. Boase, *Boniface VIII* (London: Constable, 1933); Geoffrey Barraclough, *The Medieval Papacy* (London: Thames and Hudson, 1968); Mildred Curley, *The Conflict Between Boniface VIII and Philip IV, the Fair* (Washington, D.C.: Catholic University of America Press, 1927); Brian Tierney, *The Crisis of Church and State*; and various studies by Walter Ullmann, including *The Growth of Papal Government in the Middle Ages* (London:Methuen and Co., 1955).

3. David Knowles with Dimitri Obolensky, *The Middle Ages*, the Christian Centuries series, Vol. II (New York: McGraw-Hill, 1968), 336.

4. Philip Hughes, "There is no doubt that this was a deliberately engineered *cause celebre*, whose success would mark a new era for the expanding royal jurisdiction, and greatly discredit the ecclesiastical world before the nation," in Wood, *Philip the Fair and Boniface VIII*, 55. Thomas Boase, "(The imprisonment of the bishop) is the hand of Nogaret, and can be no other . . . The spiritual powers will lie after this very much at the king's mercy," *Boniface VIII*, 300.

5. Tierney, *The Crisis of Church and State*, 185–86.

6. Ibid., 188–89.

7. Jean Riviere, "Boniface's Theological Conservatism," in Wood, *Philip the Fair and Boniface VIII*, 70.

8. Mandell Creighton, "Halfway House From Gregory VII to Luther," in ibid., 97–99.

9. Barraclough, *The Medieval Papacy*, 142.

10. George Holmes, *Europe: Hierarchy and Revolt 1320–1450* (New York: Harper, 1975), 84.

11. Barraclough, *The Medieval Papacy*, 142.

12. Cannon, *History of Christianity in the Middle Ages*, 294.

13. Barraclough, *The Medieval Papacy*, 153.

14. Catherine of Siena, "Letters," in Barry, *Readings in Church History*, 1:472–73.

15. Petrarch, "On the Papal Court at Avignon," in Barry, *Readings in Church History*, 1:470–71.

16. Barraclough, *The Medieval Papacy*, 158.

17. *Extravagantes Communes*, III, ii, 13, in Southern, *Western Society and the Church in the Middle Ages*, 158.

18. Southern, *Western Society and the Church in the Middle Ages*, 201.

19. G. Mollat, *The Popes at Avignon* (New York: Harper, 1963), 267.

20. John R. Moorman, *A History of the Church in England*, 2nd. ed. (London: Adam and Charles Black, 1967), 116. A monk of Malmesbury is cited as saying, "Lord Jesus! either take away the pope from our midst or lessen the power which he presumes to have over our people," 116.

21. "Statute of Provisors 1351," in Theodore F. T. Plucknett, *Taswell-Langmead's English Constitutional History*, 11th ed. (London: Sweet and Maxwell, 1960), 259.

22. Mollat, *Popes at Avignon*, 268.

23. Ibid., 213. "He made a show of asceticism while he secretly amassed ill-gotten gains, tirelessly frequented women of doubtful reputation and ran after honors." Mary I. M. Bell, *A Short History of the Papacy* (London: Methuen and Co., 1921), 212: "He showed from the first a complete ineptitude for the part of anti-pope."

24. Friedrich Heer, *The Holy Roman Empire*, trans. Janet Sondheimer (New York: Frederick Praeger, 1968), 117.

25. On the schism see Walter Ullmann, *The Origins of the Great Schism* (London: Burns, Oates, and Wallbourne, 1948), and Clinton Locke, *The Age of the Great Western Schism* (Edinburgh: T & T Clark 1897).

26. Clough, et al., *A History of the Western World*, 364.

27. Brian Tierney, *Foundations of the Conciliar Movement* (Cambridge: Cambridge University Press, 1969), 169. On conciliarism see also C. M. D. Crowder, *Unity, Heresy, and Reform 1378–1460*, Documents of Medieval History 3 (London: Edward Arnold, 1977); Matthew Spinka, ed., *Advocates of Reform*, Vol. 14 in *The Library of Christian Classics* (Philadelphia: Westminster, 1958); Brian Tierney, *Church Law and Constitutional Thought in the Middle Ages* (London: Variorum Reprints, 1979); Antony Black, *Monarchy and Community: Political Ideas in the Later Conciliar Controversy 1430–1450* (Cambridge: Cambridge University Press, 1970); Thomas Bisson, *Medieval Representative Institutions* (Hinsdale: Dreyden, 1973).

28. John of Paris, *Treatise on the Power of the King and Pope*, in Tierney, *The Crisis of Church and State*, 206–7.

29. Marsiglio of Padua, *The Defender of Peace*, in Barry, 487–89.

30. William of Occam, *Tract Against Pope Benedict XII*, in Barry, 1:496.

31. Henry of Langenstein, *A Letter on Behalf of a Council of Peace*, ch. 14, in Matthew Spinka, ed. *Advocates of Reform* (Philadelphia: Westminster, 1953), 123.

32. Henry Osborne Taylor, *The Medieval Mind* (Cambridge: Harvard University Press, 1951), 2:543.

33. Steven Ozment, *The Age of Reform 1250–1550*, 34.

34. Walker, et al., *A History of the Christian Church*, 352. On the question of reason and revelation see Etienne Gilson, *Reason and Revelation in the Middle Ages* (New York: Scribner's, 1938).

35. David Knowles, *The Evolution of Medieval Thought* (London: Longmans, 1963), 320.

36. Ibid.

37. Henry Osborne Taylor, *The Medieval Mind*, 549.

38. William of Occam, *Dialogue Against Heretics* 2:2, quoted in George Tavard, "Holy Church or Holy Writ: A Dilemma of the Fourteenth Century," *Church History* XXIII (September 1954), 203.

Chapter 10

1. Gordon Leff, *Heresy in the Later Middle Ages* (New York: Barnes and Noble, 1967), 1:2. See also Heiko Oberman, *Forerunners of the Reformation* (Philadelphia: Fortress, 1981); Ozment, *The Age of Reform 1250–1550*; Gordon Leff, *The Dissolution of the Medieval Outlook—An Essay on the Intellectual and Spiritual Change in the Four-*

teenth Century (New York: Harper, 1976); Edward Peters, *Heresy and Authority in Medieval Europe* (London: Scholar, 1980).

2. Leff, 52. For a full analysis of the Spiritual Franciscans see Leff, *The Dissolution of the Medieval Outlook*, 51–255.

3. David Knowles, *The Middle Ages* (New York: McGraw Hill, 1968), 347.

4. For a fuller analysis of Marian theology in the late Middle Ages see Heiko Oberman, *Harvest of Medieval Theology* (Cambridge: Harvard University Press, 1963), 281–322.

5. Ibid., 285.

6. Oscar Cullmann, *The Early Church* (Philadelphia: Westminster, 1956), 79–80. See also R. P. C. Hanson, *Tradition in the Early Church* (Philadelphia: Westminster, 1962.

7. George Tavard, *Holy Writ or Holy Church* (New York: Harper, 1959), 8.

8. Anselm of Laon, *Ennarationes in Apocalypsim*, ch. 8 (PL 162:1531), cited in Tavard, *Holy Writ or Holy Church*, 17.

9. Oberman, *Harvest*, 366–67.

10. Ibid., 372ff.

11. George Tavard, "Holy Church or Holy Writ," 197. "Yet Henry of Ghent was no forerunner of the Reformation. He firmly believed that the cleavage he spoke about was a feat of imagination, although he did not deem it absolutely impossible to happen. He moreover held a notion of Scripture which was germane to the general idea of the Middle Ages on what may be called the extension of Holy Writ outside the Canon," 198.

12. Richard Scholz, *Unbekannte Kirchen-politisce Streitschriften* (1914), 2:544, cited in Tavard, *Holy Writ or Holy Church*, 39.

13. Tavard, *Holy Writ or Holy Church*, 38.

14. John Brevicoxa (d. 1423) wrote, "I do not recall having read in all of Holy Scripture—nor has anyone shown me—a place therein from which it is clear that a general council cannot err," cited in Oberman, *Forerunners of the Reformation*, 61.

15. Heiko Oberman, *Archbishop Thomas Bradwardine: A Fourteenth Century Augustinian* (Utrecht: Drukkerij En Uitgevers-Maatschappij, 1957), 26–27.

16. Eligius M. Buytaert, *Peter Aureolis, Scriptum super 1 Sententiarum*, 1952, 136–37, n. 15–16, cited in Tavard, *Holy Writ or Holy Church*, 28.

17. Oberman, *Harvest of the Reformation*, 363.

18. On the study of the Bible in the Middle Ages see Beryl Smalley, *The Study of the Bible in the Middle Ages* (Notre Dame: University of Notre Dame Press, 1964); Robert M. Grant, *A Short History of the Interpretation of the Bible* (New York: Macmillan, 1972).

19. Parker, *The Morning Star*, 25.

20. Ibid., 27.

21. *The Lollard Conclusions* of 1394 no. 8, cited in Henry Bettenson, ed., *Documents of the Christian Church* (New York: Oxford University Press, 1980), 177.

22. Kenneth H. Vickers, *England in the Later Middle Ages* (New York: Barnes and Noble, 1961), 246.

23. Wycliffe, *On the Eucharist* cited in Bainton, *The Medieval Church*, 164–65.

24. Walker, et al., *A History of the Christian Church*, 379.

25. Vickers, 263.

26. *De Haeretico Comburendo* (1401), in Bettenson, *Documents of the Christian Church*, 180. See John A. F. Thomson, *The Later Lollards 1414–1520* (Oxford: Oxford University Press, 1965).

27. There are divergent opinions as to the person responsible for introducing Wycliffe's ideas to Bohemia. Aenius Sylvius writing a century after Huss' death claimed that one Faulfisch brought the first copy of Wycliffe's writings to Prague; another says it was Peter Payne, a traveler to Bohemia in 1410. It is certain that Jerome of Prague, the friend of Huss who followed him to the stake, brought copies of Wycliffe from Oxford to Bohemia.

28. John Huss, *Treatise on the Church*, in Bainton, *The Medieval Church*, 165–66.

29. For an extensive analysis of the Council of Constance, see C. M. D. Crowder, *Unity, Heresy, and Reform 1378–1460: The Conciliar Response to the Great Schism* (London: Edward Arnold, 1977), 65–138.

30. J. R. Strayer, "The Laicization of French and English Society in the Thirteenth Century," in Sylvia L. Thrupp, ed., *Change in Medieval Society* (New York: Appleton-Century-Crofts, 1964), 109.

31. Strayer, in Thrupp, *Change in Medieval Society*, 110.

32. James Wrestfall Thompson, *The Literacy of the Laity in the Middle Ages* (New York: Burt Franklin, 1960).

33. Henri Pirenne, *Medieval Cities* (New York: Doubleday Anchor, 1925).

34. Margaret Aston, *The Fifteenth Century*, History of European Civilization Library (London: Thames and Hudson, 1968), 122.

35. Petrarch, "On the Papal Court at Avignon, in Barry, *Readings in Church History*, 1:442.

36. Aston, *The Fifteenth Century*, 128.

37. See Colin Morris, *The Discovery of the Individual 1050–1200* (New York: Harper, 1972), "The mingling of Christian and classical traditions is to be found in an extreme form in the work of Boethius (d. 525," 17; "Christianity and classicism has assigned to the individual a high value," 37. See Walter Ullmann, *The Individual and Society in the Middle Ages* (Baltimore: John Hopkins Press, 1966).

38. Aston,*The Fifteenth Century*, 144.

39. Ibid., 168.

INDEX